American Musicological Society-Music Library Association Reprint Series

The American Musicological Society and the Music Library Association have undertaken to sponsor the republication of a series of scholarly works now out of print, translations of important studies, essays, etc. An editorial committee representing both organizations has been appointed to plan and supervise the series, in cooperation with Dover Publications, Inc., of New York.

Sir John Hawkins, *A General History of the Science and Practice of Music*
W. H., A. F., and A. E. Hill, *Antonio Stradivari, His Life and Work*
Curt Sachs, *Real-Lexikon der Musikinstrumente,* new revised, enlarged edition
The Complete Works of Franz Schubert (19 volumes), the Breitkopf & Härtel
    Critical Edition of 1884-1897 *(Franz Schubert's Werke. Kritisch*
    durchgesehene Gesammtausgabe.)
Charles Read Baskervill, *The Elizabethan Jig and Related Song Drama*
George Ashdown Audsley, *The Art of Organ-Building,* corrected edition
Emanuel Winternitz, *Musical Autographs from Monteverdi to Hindemith,*
    corrected edition
William Chappell, *Popular Music of the Olden Time,* 1859 edition
The Breitkopf Thematic Catalogue
Otto Kinkeldey, *The Organ and Clavier in the Music of the 16th Century*
Andreas Ornithoparcus, *Musice active micrologus,* together with
    John Dowland's translation, *A. O. his Micrologus, or Introduction,*
    Containing the Art of Singing
O. G. T. Sonneck, *Early Concert-life in America (1731-1800)*
Giambattista Mancini, *Practical Reflections on the Figurative Art of Singing*
    (translation by Pietro Buzzi)

MUSICAL AUTOGRAPHS

from Monteverdi to Hindemith

". . . O, learn to read what silent love hath writ!
To hear with eyes belongs to love's fine wit."

Shakespeare, *Sonnet XXIII*

MUSICAL AUTOGRAPHS

FROM MONTEVERDI TO HINDEMITH

VOLUME I

BY EMANUEL WINTERNITZ

DOVER PUBLICATIONS, INC.
NEW YORK

Published in the United Kingdom by Constable and Company, Limited, 10 Orange Street, London W.C.2.

This Dover edition, first published in 1965, is an enlarged and corrected republication of the work first published by Princeton University Press, Princeton, N. J., in 1955. A new Preface has been written for this edition by the author.

Library of Congress Catalog Card Number 65-12261

Manufactured in the United States of America

Dover Publications, Inc.
180 Varick Street
New York 14, N.Y.

PREFACE TO THE DOVER EDITION

In recent years, an ever growing interest has been shown in the way in which composers confided their ideas to paper, and increasing attention has been given to musical script not only as a highly personal graphic embodiment of musical imagination, but also as a precious document of working methods and writing habits. Witness of this interest is the increasing number of facsimiles and anthologies which have appeared throughout the last generation. But while these anthologies have included more and more material, they have not contained the principles for a systematic and comparative study and investigation of the autographs. My book tries to fulfill this need.

I am grateful to Dover Publications for bringing *Musical Autographs* back into print and thus making it available to students. I have made a number of corrections and amendments which seemed to me advisable, and have also added some illustrations to the introductory chapters in the first volume dealing with the "Written Sign" and the "Writing Act." However, I have left unchanged the choice of plates in the second volume. There is hardly a student of music, of course, who would not like to find among the illustrations some greater or better known works by his favorite composers. Yet the history of style and of writing habits, or an anthology such as this, should not be a mountain range of summits. The lesser works are often of as much interest as the greater, with respect to the writing and working habits of their authors. I hope that the methodical approach to the phenomenon of musical script as I conceived it in the systematic chapters will be found sufficiently supported by the examples as they stand.

I should like especially to thank Mr. Stanley Appelbaum of Dover Publications for the meticulous care with which he helped to prepare this new edition.

New York, 1964   EMANUEL WINTERNITZ

ACKNOWLEDGMENTS

Numerous owners of manuscripts have kindly permitted me to use autographs from their collections: The Library of Congress, Washington, D.C.; The Library of the Yale University School of Music, New Haven, Connecticut; The New York Public Library and The Morgan Library, both in New York City; The Boston Public Library and The New England Conservatory of Music, both in Boston, Massachusetts; Harvard College Library, Cambridge, Massachusetts; The Newberry Library, Chicago; Stanford University Library; The Foster Hall Collection of The University of Pittsburgh; Accademia Filarmonica and Biblioteca del Conservatorio di Musica G. B. Martini, both in Bologna; G. Ricordi & Co., Milan; Biblioteca del Conservatorio San Pietro a Majella, Naples; Biblioteca Nazionale, Torino; Biblioteca Nazionale di San Marco, Venice; The British Museum, London; Bibliothèque du Conservatoire National de Musique and Bibliothèque Musicale de l'Opéra, both in Paris; Österreichische Nationalbibliothek, Vienna; Sächsisches Hauptstaatsarchiv, Dresden; Kungl. Universitetsbibliotek, Uppsala; Mr. and Mrs. Rudolf Floersheim; Mr. and Mrs. D. N. Heinemann; Mr. Paul Hindemith; the late Mr. Charles Ives; Mr. Rudolph Kallir; Mme. Rachmaninoff. The largest number of plates, 66 in all from 54 autographs, came from The Library of Congress, chiefly from The Gertrude Clarke Whittall Foundation Collection and The Elizabeth Sprague Coolidge Foundation Collection. To The Library of Congress I am indebted not only for cooperation in having photographs made but also for gracious hospitality whenever I consulted the originals. Mr. Edward N. Waters, especially, was most generous in giving me his time and valuable advice whenever data concerning the many plates from The Library of Congress had to be checked with the information available there.

My grateful thanks are due The John Simon Guggenheim Foundation, for the fellowship that enabled me to begin my work on this book in 1947, and the Secretary General of this Foundation, Henry Allen Moe, for his continued interest in the progress of the book. I should also like to thank The Metropolitan Museum of Art and its director, Francis Henry Taylor, for granting me time to work in Europe.

Above all I must acknowledge my debt to my good friend, Alfred Schuetz; in countless conversations his clear and critical mind has helped me to clarify the ideas presented in this book. Even this seems an understatement when I recall how intensely we have shared an interest in music and its graphic representation since our early student days.

Maestro Arturo Toscanini and Mr. Raffaele Tenaglia, Librarian of G. Ricordi & Co., provided me with material and advice relating to certain peculiarities of Rossini's script; Mr. Joseph Szigeti offered helpful suggestions about the changes in the violin part of Beethoven's Sonata, Op. 96.

Among the friends who generously helped me to fill *lacunae*, I should like to make grateful mention of: the late Adolph Busch; Paul Hindemith; Mieczyslaw Horszowski; and Ralph Kirkpatrick, my colleague at Yale University. Arthur Mendel read the manuscript and made many valuable suggestions for improving it. Another special debt of gratitude is due William M. Ivins, Jr., that expert penman—to mention only one facet of his many-sided knowledge—who, quill in hand, discussed many tricks of penmanship with me. The Library of The Yale School of Music, with its rich resources, proved of great help during the years devoted to this book, and I am especially indebted to the Librarians, Miss O'Meara and Mr. Brooks Shepard, who kindly supplied or verified information about particular plates.

My sincere thanks go to Miss Sofula Novikova, my former assistant at The Metropolitan Museum of Art, who, with untiring devotion and initiative, helped me to collect material and to prepare my manuscript. I am also indebted to Miss Lillian Green, who patiently and mercilessly pruned out exotic flowers from my English.

Finally, I must express my appreciation to Mrs. Catharine Miller, who read the manuscript and the galley proofs and made many valuable corrections, and to Mrs. Ann Weissmann, who helped me in making the index.

June 1, 1954   EMANUEL WINTERNITZ

CONTENTS

I. THE WRITTEN SIGN

1. CHOICE OF MATERIAL

THIS BOOK is an anthology, with all the shortcomings and advantages which that implies. My intention has been to illustrate by typical examples the evolution of writing conventions and the general history of notation since 1600, and to present against this general background some characteristic working and writing habits of particular masters. Some examples show compositions in various stages of completion, while others illustrate solutions of special problems of graphic expression.

As 196 is a pitifully small number of specimens with which to represent the last three centuries of music, their selection was necessarily influenced by personal taste. There are, however, some unavoidable lacunae. Of some important composers no unquestioned musical autographs are known to exist. Moreover, the war and the postwar situation have made it impossible to procure copies of manuscripts of some compositions which I would have liked to include.

As the number of musical autographs in the United States has greatly increased in recent years, I have selected, wherever possible, pages from manuscripts in public and private collections in this country. From the outstanding collection of musical autographs in the Library of Congress alone I have been privileged to choose no less than 66 pages. In most cases I have tried to present examples from works which have not appeared in facsimile editions.

There is still a word to be said about the comments for the single plates. The reader will find them quite unequal in length. Often the score pages reproduced have had to be related to pages preceding or following them in the original which are not reproduced; or an autograph compared with other written or printed versions; or less familiar symbols of notation, unusual scoring methods and the like, have had to be explained. But in many cases such explanations were not necessary and here the plates will tell their story by themselves. Montaigne said of Tacitus that he abridged everything because he saw everything. My case is different. I abridged where the reader can see everything.

2. THE PHYSIOGNOMY OF SCRIPT

ANYONE who wanders through the plates of this book with open and unprejudiced eyes, surrendering himself to his visual impressions naively and without historic or musical reminiscences, will at once notice their astonishing variety. Like some human faces and some landscapes, they will impress themselves upon his eye and mind as unique configurations, unforgettable and immediately recognizable. There are pages by Handel in which hordes of fat black ants seem to be speedily and busily pressing ahead of one another. Debussy's neat and minute clusters of noteheads make each of his pages look like a bed of tender young grape hyacinths. The dense, chaotic jungles of Beethoven's sketches contrast sharply with the gigantic and intricate clockworks and the architectural blueprints of the scores of Stravinsky and Bartók.

Like all objects having personality, manuscripts are difficult to describe. One can point to them and name them, but it is impossible to define them in words. For words, those worn coins of everyday communication, while useful for describing similarities, are ill-suited to define the unique, the incomparable. Everyone has found himself in the difficult position of trying to describe to a friend someone to be met at a railroad station. A photograph would tell in a second what a verbal description could not convey in an hour, provided the person expected had no "distinguishing marks." The same is true of individual musical scripts; they are personalities. This explains why, in most of the descriptions of the plates, which are the important part of this book, no attempt has been made to translate the living features of the individual scripts into words.

Perhaps it would be wise to begin with the warning that any naively emotional interpretation of a script in terms of the feelings which its contemplation evokes, is bound to remain illfounded and superficial. Unfortunately, this intuitional approach is all too familiar in the pseudo-graphological treatises. They speak of a serious or exuberant, noble or sly, contemplative or passionate, tender or brutal hand, depending simply on the emotional associations of the uncritical beholder. This is not the way—however amusing it may be as a parlor game —to relate script to character and to interpret the former as an imprint of the latter. A simple glance at the personalities and the writing habits of the composers, as they are known to us from sources other than their musical scripts, should expose the fallacy. When we broaden the range of analysis of an individual master by considering the known facts of his life as well as his script, we may easily arrive at a puzzling conclusion. If we choose as examples the scripts of Haydn, Mozart and Beethoven—all of them contemporaries or nearly so, and all belonging to the same tradition—we find a seeming contradiction between their types of writing and their characters, as we know them from other sources.

The vigorous and humorous Haydn has a thin, "hesitating," and somewhat "effeminate" hand. The fabulously fast-working Mozart writes a well-organized, even and transparent script. The rational, over-planning, ever-revising Beethoven has an impetuous, impulsive and irrational hand, irregular in the extreme. And Schubert—to add him to the circle—though a daring innovator in many ways, uses a neat, regular, schoolteacher's hand, almost bordering on the pedantic.

These random examples show how inconclusive must be any attempt to relate script to personality or to read it as a direct manifestation of the character or emotions of its writer.

If the comparison of musical manuscripts of the same period leads us to such paradoxes, the situation becomes even more bewildering when we attempt to compare scripts of different epochs. The writing, for instance, that most nearly resembles that of Mozart in its even flow and unpretentious clarity, is that of Brahms. In both their scripts we find a similar sureness of graphic expression and economy in the use of symbols. Yet it would be hard to find more disparate extremes of temperament and working habits than those of these two men.

One cannot compare an eighteenth century hand with one of the nineteenth century— even if each were typical of its time—without taking into consideration the fact that the writers used different tools and had learned different hands. The script of an individual composer can be measured only against the background of the general writing conventions prevalent in his time.

How then are we to disentangle the maze? We shall try to do so by taking systematic account of the basic factors that influenced individual scripts. For this purpose we must first distinguish between two fundamentally different aspects: the script as an embodiment of musical thought and its communication to the performer, and the script as a manifestation of the personality and a testimony of the working habits of its writer. Musical notation is first of all intended for the communication of operational directions to the performer. Script, however, is also the product of the act of writing which, like other forms of expression, may reflect traits of personality inherent in the writer.

3. PRINTED AND WRITTEN MUSIC

Nec factas solum vestes spectare juvabat,
tum quoque dum fierent; tantus decor adfuit arti.

OVID

PRINTED scores are the stock-in-trade of musical activity today. Their obvious advantages are wide distribution, low cost and easy legibility. But their very standardization of symbols has its disadvantages also. Print is a very coarse web; through its wide meshes many things escape which are important to living music. By its mechanical nature it glosses over individual characteristics. One has only to compare autographs by Bach or Mozart with their printed versions to see how many delicate shadings are suppressed by print.

In the fine lacework of script the relative sizes and shadings of the notes vary, sometimes suggesting hidden accents and dynamics. Subtle and variable groupings of notes clarify the articulation. Dynamic marks and other expression marks can be placed precisely at the proper places where they should begin and end, and with those single strands of the polyphonic texture to which they refer. Part writing often appears clearer and more translucent in script; there the single parts in the fabric of keyboard polyphony are often distinguished by slight variations in shading and in the size of notes.

Of course, we can never hope to find out how much of the delicate and sensitive grouping in musical script was due to the conscious effort of the writer, in direct relation to his musical ideas, and how much took shape automatically as an unplanned by-product, while the quill hastened along the staves. It is, however, tempting to assume that the space-sensitive composers at least—the "visual" type as William James would have called them—generally knew what their quills were doing, and that their individual types of script must have had the closest connection with their musical ideas.

But it is not only the visual aspect of the handwritten score, with all its flavor and fine grain, that suffers by being translated into print. Print frequently suppresses subtleties of script which could easily have been retained by the printer. The distinction between parts within keyboard polyphony is often blurred by connecting the simultaneous tones of various melodic lines to the same stem. Expression marks and pedaling marks are shifted out of their places. Fortunately, more and more facsimile editions are appearing, and the *Urtext* editions have also helped a great deal, but even in good editions the clear intention of the composer can be distorted through what seems to be only a simplification, as may be seen from a comparison of a page by C. P. E. Bach (plate 46) with the best printed edition available. The articulation suggested by A in the autograph is inadequately rendered in print by B.

A   B

Even when good printed editions are available, the autographs are still indispensable. Methods of notation change with time and the evolution of musical style. Each period has its own practices of performance, intimately linked with the occasions for which music was written and the social environment in which it was produced. Almost up to modern times these factors were reflected much more clearly in autographs than in printed music. Printed editions existed, of course, but their number was incomparably smaller than that of the works produced. Cases in which the composer himself supervised the printing and protected his score against distortion are the exception.

The printed version embodies the finished work after all throes of labor are over. Autographs, even of compositions that have advanced beyond the stage of a sketch, frequently show traces of the process of creation. Here we can hope to catch glimpses into the workshop of the individual master, to study changes, cancellations and other records of his afterthoughts, in short, to follow the fascinating spectacle of the growth of the work.

The phenomenon of inspiration, the origin of the creative idea, its development and its intertwining with other ideas, all these evolve in a region which even the modern psychology of personality cannot penetrate. The realm of genius is still closed to the curious eye. But if we remain in due awe and reverence outside the walls which surround the sanctum, is it not a blissful feeling to stand at least on the steps of the temple? Pious souls have always collected locks of hair, penholders and other relics that have been touched by the great. Beethoven's laundry lists bring a fortune at auction. How much more significant is a sheet which has received directly from the hand of the artist the fresh embodiment of his creation! When Verdi saw the manuscript of the *Eroica* in Vienna, he silently lifted his hat.[1]

4. DIMENSIONS OF MUSIC ON PAPER

SCRIPT is the communication of meaning through a system of standardized visual symbols. Musical notation is a special kind of script designed to embody musical thought and to communicate it to the performer. But music flows in time, while the symbols of notation, written or printed, are confined to two-dimensional space. What are the methods and the degree of precision by which the flux of music can be translated into two-dimensional patterns on a page? Though it may seem that the same problem applies also to the written word, that is to say, to the notation of speech, there are important differences. For most people, music does not exist until it comes to them through their ears, while words, in literature at least, come through their eyes. Moreover, when language is committed to paper, it makes fewer demands upon its graphic record than music does upon its notation. The sounds of language in their time sequence are translated into letters. All the other properties of the spoken word, such as the precise duration of syllables, their pitch, timbre and their sound volume, remain unwritten. Quite the contrary is true of music: here the rendering of these very properties is essential to meaning. Thus duration, pitch, timbre, volume—to enumerate only the most important dimensions of musical sound—require adequate graphic expression. How is this achieved in modern notation?

Ingrained conventions are usually taken for granted and there is certainly no need for the practical musician to subject the current system of notation to a systematic analysis. But if a learned visitor from Mars were to become interested in our music and if he were commissioned to devise an easy and consistent system of musical notation, he would probably

---

[1] In 1875; Theodor Helm, "Fünfzig Jahre Wiener Musikleben," *Der Merker*, February 1916.

arrive at something quite different from the one we use today.[2] Our system is the result of a long historical evolution and has been shaped in many ways by the requirements of musical styles which are different from those of our time.

Our present system of notation is a complex, inconsistent amalgam of symbols. Its frame is provided by the two dimensions of the page or the system of staves. Within this frame the progress of time is graphically expressed by the sequence of the notes from left to right. Those at the right are later than those at the left. Pitch is expressed by the position of notes within or in relation to the staff lines; higher or lower in space stands for higher or lower in pitch. It is for this reason that a score has been compared to a system of co-ordinates with the pitch represented by the ordinate and time by the abscissa. The precise meaning of the staff lines is defined by clefs and accidentals. The time elapsing between one bar line and the next is defined by the initial tempo mark. Into this frame of co-ordinates there are fitted notes and rests, indicating by their shapes the relative time value of the tones, and a multitude of signs expressing the other dimensions of music, such as dynamic and other expression marks, and indications of phrasing and articulation. Thus it appears that of the dimensions of music only two—pitch and tempo—are represented by spatial relations, the vertical and horizontal on the page.

Pitch, as we have seen, is represented in terms of the vertical, but this symbolism is not consistently carried out, for two notes indicating a third may mean a major as well as a minor third and only the presence or absence of accidentals makes the meaning clear. In this the spatial intervals G-B and B-D are equal, while the musical intervals they represent are unequal.

Still more complex are the indications of tempo, or in other words, of the absolute duration of the single notes. The shape of notes and rests actually represents with sufficient precision their duration, and for long periods of musical history these were the only indications of time values. But since the establishment of the modern score toward the end of the sixteenth century, score writing has come to employ in addition a more or less approximate representation of time lengths in terms of space lengths. Whenever corresponding bars in the different staves have notes of unequal time values, an arrangement is inevitable in which, say, the span covered by a half-note is twice the width of two quarter-notes and four times that of four eighth-notes.

If this combination of space symbolism with other signs seems inconsistent from a logical point of view, it has its advantages; for the score, besides being a precise record of a composition, is an operational direction for the performer which he must be able to grasp easily and immediately.

We have dwelt on this issue of spatial symbolism at length because we shall later see how various composers differ in this respect with the result that individual types of score-writing can be related to various degrees of spatial sensitivity.

5. CHANGING METHODS OF NOTATION

To EVALUATE the scripts of individual composers one must consider them against the background of general methods of notation and writing fashions of their time. Following the evolution of notation in printed scores alone is bound to give a distorted picture. Up to

---

[2] There is no lack of attempts at reforming, that is, improving semantically our traditional system of notation.

Beethoven's time relatively few composers prepared or supervised the printing of their works, and later editions often alter the original features of their compositions, though sometimes for good practical reasons. Thus it seems advisable to follow the evolution of notation devices in autographs. This will also afford frequent glimpses into working habits characteristic of a period or of a composer and will offer occasion to point out several minor details of writing habits, peculiarities which, though they have no bearing on the history of notation, may be of interest to the present-day performer and enable him to distinguish them from other musical symbols which they sometimes resemble.

In the examples reproduced in our plates, changes in methods of notation may be followed step by step. At the beginning of the seventeenth century two main methods of notation were employed: the modern notation customary today, and vocal and instrumental tablatures which even at that time were already going rapidly out of fashion. J. S. Bach still made occasional use of tablature notation, especially where lack of space compelled him to resort to this space- and paper-saving shorthand as, for instance, in his "Orgelbüchlein." To show survivals of an ancient tradition and to permit a comparison of the writing of the same composer in tablature and in ordinary staff notation, two examples of tablatures are included among our plates. Both of these specimens (Buxtehude, plate 7, and Froberger, plate 10), are written in the so-called new German keyboard tablature; but Buxtehude uses it for a vocal setting.

Elements of the Modern Score

Modern notation, as we find it firmly established by the beginning of the seventeenth century, is the product of a long and slow evolution. Its basic elements, the five-line staff, the bar lines, and the superposition of staves in the manner of the modern score have their roots far back in musical history.

The use of staves has been traced back to the early Middle Ages. The number of lines varies. Gregorian chant even today employs the time-honored four-line staff. The sixteenth century favored six or more lines for the solo instruments that were capable of polyphony, that is, for the lute and for all keyboard instruments. Bar lines can be found occasionally in keyboard tablatures as early as the middle of the fifteenth century.

Notation of polyphonic music in a superposition of single parts was already known in the twelfth century. Simultaneous tones were written in roughly vertical alignment. But all this changed in the early thirteenth century with the advent of the motet. Then we find handwritten choir books which showed the parts for the soprano, alto, tenor and bass in separate sections of a page or on facing pages. Later, during the sixteenth century, each section of the choir had its separate part book, comparable to those used by the four members of a string quartet today. It is still a controversial question whether full scores were used in addition to the choir book and the part book.[3] At any rate, it is hard to believe that the writers of music as rhythmically complex as Renaissance polyphony would not have resorted to a superposition of all the parts for their sketches and the embodiments of their musical ideas.

[3] See Otto Kinkeldey, *Orgel und Klavier in der Musik des 16. Jahrhunderts*, Leipzig, 1910, pp. 98, 99, 136, 190, 191; R. Schwartz, "Zur Partitur im 16. Jahrhundert," *Archiv für Musikwissenschaft*, Jahrgang 2, Heft 1, 1920, pp. 73-78; Willi Apel, *The Notation of Polyphonic Music 900-1600*, Cambridge, Mass., 1944, p. xx; Robert Haas, *Aufführungspraxis der Musik*, 1931, pp. 107, 126, 127; Edward E. Lowinsky, "On the use of scores by sixteenth-century musicians," *American Musicological Society Journal*, spring 1948, pp. 17-23.

Through the rise of orchestral music since Giovanni Gabrieli and its gradual emancipation from the model of vocal polyphony the union of these three essential devices—the five-line staff, bar lines, and superposition of the parts—was definitely established.

Even after 1600, however, we find remnants of the earlier usage. Older writing customs were only gradually superseded. Our plates afford, as it were, a slow-motion view of this laggard development.

BAR LINES. In Froberger's *Toccata* (plate 11), for example, the upper staff still has six lines, the lower seven, recalling sixteenth century usage. Soon afterwards the five-line staff became the rule.

We can trace also the gradual infiltration of bar lines in the following: Praetorius (plates 4, 5, 6) still inclines toward the sixteenth century method of writing; he does not yet make use of bar lines. Buxtehude (plate 8) employs them in the instrumental introduction (*sinfonia*), but not in the vocal sections. Froberger (plates 11, 12, 13) uses them sporadically. With Purcell (plate 14) they have become the rule. Handel, who frequently leaned toward archaisms, presents an exception (plates 37-43). His use of bar lines is somewhat irregular. In his larger scores he employs unified bar lines, that is, cutting through all staves, from time to time but not at regular intervals. In between he usually writes separate bar lines for single staves, but in many passages these are omitted.

Even in much later compositions we find occasionally longer or shorter sections where bar lines for one reason or another were omitted. In most cases these are sections in free rhapsodic or toccata style, or quasi-recitativos in instrumental compositions. Examples, to mention just a few, are found in C. P. E. Bach's *Phantasien für Kenner und Liebhaber*, in the piano part of the introduction to the first movement of Beethoven's *Emperor Concerto*, and in the *Adagio* of Mendelssohn's *Sonata for the pianoforte* in E major, Op. 6.

For a long time after bar lines had been generally adopted they were not written as unbroken verticals cutting through all staves of the score, but separately for each staff (see Rameau, plate 44; Padre Martini, plate 45; C. P. E. Bach, plate 46; J. C. Bach, plates 51, 52). This was still Joseph Haydn's practice (plates 53-57) even in a score as large as the sketch for the *Creation*. Only slowly did the unified bar line extending across all the staves assert itself. In Scarlatti's score (plate 15) the bar lines occasionally run through two staves. In that of Porpora (plate 25) they extend through six staves. J. S. Bach's *Clavierbüchlein vor Wilhelm Friedemann Bach* (plates 26-29) is not consistent in the use of either type.

With the increase of parts in polyphonic ensembles the unified bar line which provides a clearer spatial organization grew more frequent and finally became prevalent. Yet neither Gluck's nor Haydn's use of it was entirely consistent. Haydn preferred separate bar lines for his string quartets and keyboard works (plates 53-56) and longer ones embracing three or four staves in his symphonies. Similarly inconsistent is Mozart. Separate bar lines prevail in his larger works, but there is no established usage, and it is curious that even in pages that are for the most part blank (plates 77, 79 from the *Coronation Concerto*), he took the trouble to draw the lines neatly for the many empty staves. In his *Quintet K. 515* (plate 64) he used unified bar lines.

Beethoven, for all his rugged, irregular writing, was thoroughly systematic in his method; from his early works on he employed the unified bar line. Yet Schubert reverted to the separate lines which on occasion caused confusion (see plate 98, fourth system).

SUPERPOSITION OF PARTS. Baroque polyphony, vocal as well as instrumental, is intimately linked to the adoption of the thoroughbass. With this new emphasis on "vertical" harmonic thought together with the increasing employment of more complex instrumental ensembles, the superposition of the single parts appeared more practical and therefore soon became universal. Thus only a few examples of part-book arrangement appear among our plates. They are from Praetorius' *Euphemia Harmonica* (plates 4, 5, 6) and from a Buxtehude motet (plates 8, 9), the latter furnished with a figured bass.

The multiplication of staves does not necessarily reflect an increased number of instruments, for we know that flutes or oboes often doubled the violins, or bassoons the string basses, though this was not indicated in the score. Therefore an increase in staves often means only refinement of orchestral technique together with a more discriminating feeling for instrumental timbre.

SCORING. With this phase in the development of the orchestra, a new problem comes into focus: the order of scoring.

A great deal of "Aufführungspraxis" is reflected in the way in which the score is organized on the page; but before we attempt to trace, however sketchily, the gradual change in scoring methods, we must mention some factors which often blur or disturb the clarity of the visual organization, or even leave the score in an apparently incomplete or mutilated form. Haste in writing and even the size of a sheet or page, which proves too short or too narrow in the course of writing the music, tend to confuse the logic of the layout as it would appear in print or in calligraphic dedication copies such as the *Brandenburg Concerti*. The copyist would understand and write out the parts as the composer intended. Among our illustrations we find several typical examples: Gluck (plates 48-49) frequently makes his solo instruments change staves in midstream; Mozart often combines within his oblong score page several different vocal parts into one staff (plates 70-71), or has no space left for horns (plate 70), or other instruments.[4] Time and space saving marks, such as Mozart's "colB" (col Basso) (plate 62) are routine in eighteenth century scores.

Baroque scores were not arranged on the principle of timbre groups (woodwinds, brass, strings). Rather they followed the functional tripartition of the baroque orchestra into instruments that carried the melody, those that provided the fundamental bass, and those which supplied the background harmony. The actual order of instrumental parts on the score page was not standardized. There were a number of different local formulas. Among them, however, two main systems stand out. One was the Italian method, with the strings, except for their basses, at the top of the score, followed by the flutes and oboes, then by the horns and trumpets together with the drums, and ending with the thoroughbass provided by the string basses and the keyboard instruments with or without the bassoons. The second, the German method, began with the brass parts and drums, followed by the woodwinds, then the strings, and finished at the bottom of the score with the thoroughbass. In both systems the vocal parts were written immediately above the thoroughbass.[5] In our illustrations the German formula

[4] Mozart's letter to his father, July 20th, 1782 (on the *Entführung*): ". . . es fehlen hie und da die trompetten und Paucken, flauten, clarinett, türkischen Musick—weil ich kein Papier von so viel linien bekommen konnte.—die sind auf ein Extrapapier geschrieben—der Copist wird sie vermuthlich verloren haben, denn er konnte sie nicht finden."

[5] An exhaustive discussion of scoring methods of the late Baroque will be found in A. Carse, *The Orchestra in the XVIIIth Century*, p. 114ff.

is represented by J. S. Bach (plates 31, 32) and also, with some modifications, by Handel (plates 40ff.). The page from Gluck's *Armide* (plate 50) follows in the main the Italian system, which was largely adopted by French composers.

Haydn's score arrangements are clearly the transition to the standardization of the classical orchestra. The "timbre-groups" begin to separate; the strings are written at the foot of the score, arranged according to pitch, but the woodwind section in the sketch for the *Creation* (plate 57) shows flute and bassoon as neighbors below clarinet and oboe. In Haydn's symphonies the trumpets, drums and horns are usually placed above the woodwinds.

In Mozart's *Gran Partita* (plate 62) the thirteen wind instruments are precisely arranged according to pitch. When he employs mixed ensembles, Mozart, unlike Haydn, follows the Italian custom with the high and middle strings at the top of the page, winds following, and the string basses, in continuo fashion, invariably forming the base of the score. The horn parts in his scores are written underneath the woodwinds (plate 75), or inserted wherever there is free space in the score (plate 71), or in staves added at the top or bottom of the score (plate 70), or even added to the score in separate parts. The same general treatment is also applied to the trumpets, which even down to Beethoven's scores,[6] were called by their old name "clarini," and to their traditional brothers in arms, the kettledrums (plate 75). In Mozart's violin concertos, the *violino concertante* appears at the top of the score, immediately above the accompanying violins (plates 60, 61). In his piano concertos the solo instrument appears lower down, just above the basses, and is marked by a separate brace with a little loop in the middle of it (plates 75-80).

The modern standardized subdivision into the three "timbre" sections of woodwinds, brass, and strings appears to be definitely established in Beethoven's works (plate 91) and it became the principal model for later composers. Some interesting exceptions, nevertheless, show the persistence of ingrained conventions. Meyerbeer (plate 118) places the strings between the woodwinds and the brasses, with the string basses still written in continuo fashion at the bottom of the page, separate from the other strings. Schumann (plate 112), often groping in matters of orchestration, changes his method of scoring repeatedly throughout his oeuvre. And a score as late as Verdi's *Otello* still shows the old Italian-French arrangement that we find in Gluck's *Armide* (plate 50) and Rossini's *Barbiere* (plate 100): high strings, winds, string basses.

Of special interest is the position of the horns in the score. They had gradually advanced from a mere "filling up" function to a more versatile and often more prominent role; they lead the brass choir in Beethoven's orchestra (plate 91) with their parts written above the trumpets. They form, as it were, the transition from the woodwinds, which they supplement in color and harmony, to the brass section. It is in this position that we still find them in later scores, by Liszt (plate 117), Brahms (plate 148), Dvořák (plate 155), Leoncavallo (plate 169).

This relation between horns and woodwinds is still more pronounced in Verdi's and Wagner's scores, where the horns appear not in the brass choir but in the woodwind group between the clarinets and the bassoons (plates 125, 126, 127, 129, 130). The invention of valves had endowed the horn with a complete chromatic scale and thus enormously expanded its functions. The valve horn became, in Berlioz' beautiful words, the veritable Proteus of the orchestra. This

---

[6] See, for instance, the first page of the Fifth Symphony and the beginning of the Menuet from the Eighth Symphony, both reproduced in Georg Schünemann, *Musikerhandschriften*, 1936.

is especially true of Wagner's orchestral polyphony, where it sometimes assumes the melodic line, or furnishes the bass for the woodwinds, or merely supplies color or background harmony. It may appear there in two, three, or even four pairs. This very versatility, based mainly on the acquisition of the unbroken chromatic scale, made the horn into a quasi-woodwind. It was Berlioz, moreover, who, as one of the first to use valve horns in his orchestra, had incorporated their parts into the woodwind section (plate 119).

By the end of the nineteenth century the increasing complexity of the orchestral apparatus had resulted in an international standardization of score arrangement. The stereotyped order is that of woodwinds, brasses, strings, with the single members of each group placed according to pitch. Examples of this method are plates 171, 172 (Puccini) and plate 164 (Richard Strauss).

As a conclusion to this chapter on score arrangement we must consider the place assigned to the vocal parts. This is the only convention which has survived virtually unchanged for centuries. A neighborly relation in the score between the vocal parts and the strings, or at least the string bass had, of course, been the obvious thing while thoroughbass was the practice. Reading these parts together was extremely practical for coaching and accompanying singers as long as the conductor himself played the continuo on the organ or harpsichord and provided the accompaniment for the recitatives. This arrangement was still advantageous after the continuo had died out and the whole string body was transferred to the bottom of the score just beneath the vocal parts. If a vocal score was lacking, the accompanist at the rehearsal could simply condense the easily readable string parts, and many of the rehearsals could be held with strings only.

Shape of Notes

The modern shape of notes themselves appears to have been generally established about 1600. Yet survivals of earlier systems of notation, such as tablatures, extend into the seventeenth century. In ordinary measured notation we still find occasionally up to the end of the seventeenth century the old lozenge shape (A) which had been universally employed in the "white mensural notation" used by Ockeghem and his school. In our examples by Praetorius (plates 4-6) we can clearly observe the transition from the old lozenge form to the more rounded modern form of the note-head. And in Buxtehude's scores (plates 8, 9) only the upper point of the lozenge (B) is retained.

Another transition which can be observed in our plates concerns the manner of writing sixteenth notes:

c) is used by Monteverdi (plate 2); D) is employed by Purcell (plate 14) and A. Scarlatti (plates 16, 17); E) shows more modern shapes used by A. Scarlatti (plates 15, 16, often side by side with the older shape as in group c); F) shows the shapes customary in the South German school and which still occur fairly frequently in Mozart's scripts together with the more modern forms (plates 63, 69). For regular notes as well as for grace notes these forms are employed also in Rossini's scores (plates 100, 103).

Increase of Directions

The score page of the early seventeenth century contained hardly more than the notes proper.

Tempo marks were rare; the tempo was still suggested to some degree by the time signatures —a last rudiment from earlier periods when the various shapes of the notes themselves indicated the exact duration of those notes. Tone volume was very rarely prescribed, phrasing never. This is not surprising, for even more important things were delegated to the performer: free improvisatory elaboration of the melody, the execution of the graces, and the realization, in more or less individual style, of the thoroughbass. However, the performer, while not guided by written signs, was by no means left entirely to his own devices. Composer and performer belonged to the very same orbit of style; music, as a rule, was written for special occasions or on local demand, and therefore for performers whose capacities and temperaments were well known to the composer. More often than not the composer participated in the performance as virtuoso or conducted it from the keyboard. Under such circumstances problems of interpretation could hardly arise. Moreover, at that time, and even well into the eighteenth century, only a small part of the music composed was printed and the writing of copies was too slow and expensive a procedure to carry a work to a large number of performers outside the local circle of the composer.

Since then operational directions have increased ad infinitum. Scores which contain more expression marks and other directions than notes do not surprise us (plates 180, 181, 185).[7] Signs have even been invented to help performers to discriminate between melodic lines of primary and secondary importance, not only in large orchestral compositions but even in string quartets (plate 180). Traffic lights shine at every corner; musical travel depends more on regulation than on the instincts and intelligence of the driver. Improvisations have become the cardinal sin; even cadenzas in concertos, those last loopholes of free improvisation, are now mostly performed from published models available in any music store. The only choice for many performers is the alternative between the "Joachim" or the "Kreisler" cadenza. In short, the composer, in his desire to guarantee an "authentic performance," takes no chances with the performer. Musical historians of the future may wonder what befell the musical genius of our time if its creators expected so little understanding of their style from performers.

The evolution of expression marks from the utmost scarcity to the greatest profusion during three hundred and fifty years can readily be followed in our plates. In them we find a gradual multiplication and elaboration of tempo indications and other agogic signs—dynamic marks, articulation marks such as phrasing slurs, accents, directions for touch, fingering, pedaling, bowing and breathing, in ever-increasing gradations.

There persisted one exception, however, one sphere of liberty for the performer. Soloists in vocal compositions and instrumental concertos resisted serfdom for a long time. Whether we examine Mozart's concertos and operas (plates 60, 76, 77, 72-74), the operas of Verdi and Wagner (plates 125, 126) or songs by Brahms (plate 150), we find the protagonists still unfettered while the accompanying orchestra and chorus are strictly bound by dynamic and other directions. Not only is the liberty of the diva and the instrumental virtuoso respected; through their artistic personality they were required to impress their own sense of style upon the other performers. With parts written to fit the gifts of a particular soloist—and this was still the

---

[7] Lovers of Spenglerian parallels may recall similar situations in art and even in mathematical logic: in pre-baroque architecture the stonecutters received only the sketchiest instructions, and Desargues in his mathematical proofs contents himself with a hint to the initiated while Hilbert employs forty axioms.

case in Verdi's operas—it would have been foolish to hang a millstone of directions around his neck.

Expression Marks

The increasing controls of the performer outlined above were not accepted without occasional doubts and opposition, especially in cases where mechanical methods were introduced to measure and control features of performance. A good example of this is furnished by the history of the tempo marks and especially of metronomic indications.

TEMPO INDICATIONS. By the middle of the seventeenth century simple tempo marks such as *largo*[8] or *presto* had been recognized as helpful and practical. Before that time in the last stage of mensural notation there had been no need for them since the shapes of the single notes in combination with "proportion" signs implied their exact duration and so determined the tempo of the music (see description of plate 1a, b). Already in Buxtehude's motet, *Aperite* (plates 8, 9) we find *presto, adagio, allegro*, and in the scores of Alessandro Scarlatti (plates 15-17) *grave, andante, lento* have become quite frequent.[9]

It was, however, the invention of the metronome in Beethoven's time that immediately provoked and continued to raise opposition. Beethoven was at first enthusiastic, in 1826 he wrote to Schott: "Die Metronomisierung folgt nächstens. Warten Sie darauf. In unserem Jahrhundert ist dergleichen sicher nötig—The metronomic marks follow. Wait for them. In our century we certainly do need them." Yet he wrote at the top of his song *Nord und Süd*: "100 nach Mälzel, doch kann dies nur von den ersten Takten gelten, denn die Empfindung hat auch ihren Takt, dies ist aber doch nicht ganz in diesem Grade (100 nämlich) auszudrücken —100 according to Mälzel, but this applies only to the first measures, as feeling has its own tempo and this cannot very well be expressed by this rate (i.e., 100)."[10]

Carl Maria von Weber, discussing the value of tempo marks expressed similar doubts: "For all this" (meaning tempo) he wrote, "we have no correct measurements in music. They only exist in the feeling heart and if they cannot be found there, the metronome will not help, which anyhow serves only to prevent gross errors, nor the very vague tempo marks."

Brahms was obviously of the same opinion. When Henschel asked him, on the occasion of the performance of the *Deutsches Requiem* in London, precisely how the tempo marks should be interpreted, Brahms declared himself against the metronome: "As far as my experience goes," he wrote, "everybody who has given metronomic numbers has renounced them later. The numbers found in my compositions have been talked into me by friends, for I myself never believed that my blood and an instrument can agree so well. The so-called

---

[8] *Largo*, however, like *allegro, grave, andante* and similar marks often indicated the character of expression or performance rather than the tempo alone. Among the treatises which take these signs chiefly as tempo indications is Georg Muffat's *Auserlesene Instrumentalmusik* (Passau, 1701): ". . . In directing the measure or beat, one should for the most part follow the Italians, who are accustomed to proceed much more slowly than we do at the directions *Adagio, Grave, Largo*, etc., so slowly sometimes that one can scarcely wait for them, but, at the directions *Allegro, Vivace, Presto, Più presto*, and *Prestissimo* much more rapidly and in a more lively manner . . ." (in the translation of Oliver Strunk, *Source Readings in Music History*, 1950, p. 451).

[9] Of course, it can be misleading if some of these marks were not written in by the composer himself but added at a later time. If written by a contemporary hand, they may, however, be quite significant.

[10] *Beethoven's Collected Letters*, ed. by E. Kastner, p. 466.

'*elastische Tempo*' is certainly no recent invention. '*Con discrezione*' should be added to this and to how many other things. . . ." It was evidently in this sense that Brahms favored indications like the "tempo giusto" (plate 144). The most precise formulation of this problem was given by Debussy in a letter written to his publisher Jacques Durand on October 9, 1915. "You want my opinion about the metronomic indications: they are true for just one measure."

In addition to tempo marks, that is, indications of the initial tempo of movements or sections, there has been since the seventeenth century an ever-increasing number of directions for variations of tempo, such as *accelerando, ritardando, ritenuto, allargando*, etc.

DYNAMIC MARKS. Directions indicating dynamic shadings gradually came into use during the seventeenth century. Baroque music, with its predilection for contrasting vocal or instrumental bodies, favored echo effects, and the concerto grosso was based upon the contrast between the *tutti* and the *soli*; this dynamic contrast as a rule was understood, and there was no need to indicate it by special directions. An early case of explicit indications of dynamics occurs in the famous *Sonata pian e forte* by Giovanni Gabrieli where changes in tone volume are consistently noted. Praetorius (*Syntagma* III, new German edition, pp. 87, 156) mentions the indications *forte* and *piano* as customary. In England directions, such as *Lowd, Soft, Lowder, Softer by degrees*, were customary and they were often indicated by abbreviations such as *Lo, So.*

Caccini, in the famous preface to his *Nuove Musiche* (1602), mentions a comprehensive terminology for dynamic shadings for the voice, including swells like the *esclamazione viva* and *esclamazione languida*, the *messa di voce*, and combinations of these which in modern symbols would look like these. $\prec \succ < \quad <\!\!\succ\!\!\prec$
These, however, were applied to the vocal parts only. Probably the first composers to use special graphic symbols for gradual dynamic shadings in instrumental performances were Veracini and Geminiani. Veracini, in the preface to his *12 Sonate Accademiche a violino e basso* (1744), used upright signs which indicated the increase or decrease of sound volume by swelling and tapering, short wedged-shaped signs, to be read from bottom to top as follows: A for crescendo, B for decrescendo, C for crescendo-decrescendo. In Geminiani's Treatise of Good Taste in the Art of Music (London, 1749), these signs took on a slanting position: D, swelling, E, diminishing; and it is more than likely that we have here the origin of the modern wedge-shaped crescendo and decrescendo signs. This would be corroborated by the appearance of closed wedges (F or G) in Gluck's scores and later in those of Rossini (plate 102).

In our plates the indications *soli-tutti*,[11] *piano* and *pia:* are already to be found in Scarlatti's manuscripts (plate 17), *Pian* in Lotti's (plate 20), and short abbreviations such as *p.o* and *F.* in Vivaldi's (plate 19). J. S. Bach uses extremely few dynamic marks: mainly, *forte, piano, pianissimo, sotto voce, poco forte*, and *più piano*. Handel used only *forte, piano*, and *pianissimo* in the *Messiah*. Neither of these composers ever employed *crescendo* or *descrescendo* or the corresponding wedge-shaped signs. However, Handel sometimes resorts to a sequence of signs such as *f - senza ripieno - p - pp*,[12] as for instance at the end of the chorus "Glory to God in the highest" from the first part of the *Messiah*.

Even C. P. E. Bach still has a very limited array of dynamic signs but he uses them profusely.

---

[11] "*Tutti*" is found in Buxtehude (plate 8).   [12] J. S. Bach uses similar markings in Cantata 105.

In plate 46 there appear *p.f.* (poco forte) and *m.f.* (mezzo forte). In J. C. Bach the indication *sforzo* appears (plate 51). The great impetus towards multiplication and refinement of dynamic marks occurs in the circle of Jommelli and Stamitz. Haydn is conservative. He uses dynamic marks with great economy, yet his dynamic palette already includes *ff* (plate 56), *pp* (plate 54), *fz* (plate 53) and he employs *crescendo* (plates 53, 56) as well as open wedges (plates 55, 56). Mozart's dynamic vocabulary is incomparably more subtle and specialized than that of Haydn. He includes *ppp*, uses modifications such as *mf* and *mp*, but usually indicates the swell and diminution of volume by words like *crescendo, più crescendo, sempre crescendo* or their opposites. In his scores *calando* also occurs (plate 66). He seldom uses wedge-shaped signs.[13] Of special importance are Mozart's signs indicating sudden dynamic changes, such as *fp, ffp, sf, sfp, sfpp*. They are quite characteristic of his dramatic style and occur more and more often throughout his work until the single letters become intertwined into compound signs of great graphic beauty, usually written with a single stroke of the pen (see, for instance, the *fp* in plates 63, 68, 73, 74; and the *sfp* in plate 67). In his operas we find many pages studded with dynamic marks, so that virtually every bar has one or more of them.

Beethoven's dynamic indications, as a rule, do not exceed those used by Mozart either in number or in kind, although he favors more *ff* and *pp*. In one regard, however, his dynamic directions differ radically from those of Mozart. This is his frequent use of A and B which increases noticeably in his late works.

A   B   C

These wedges often extend through several bars. In his last piano sonatas and string quartets we find these crescendo and decrescendo wedges combined into a single diamond-shaped sign, (c), which suggests with unsurpassed accuracy the peak of the swell. These striking rhomboids sometimes appear in the form of long lozenges (plates 88, 91) occasionally contracted into squares which lend these pages a unique and dramatic fascination (plate 94).

The later history of dynamic marks presents nothing radically new. The reader will easily be able to follow it in the plates. Only a few interesting points need to be noted. Chopin's compositions often show the entire flow of music accompanied by an almost uninterrupted chain of dynamic wedges, all most accurately placed and sensitively proportioned; minute corrections shifting the beginning or end of the wedges reveal the painstaking consideration he gave to the dynamic structure (plate 111). Brahms is economical and precise, as always. Notice, for instance, the care he bestowed upon pages such as plate 145, *Schicksalslied*. In the works of Reger (plate 179) and Schoenberg (plate 180) the profusion of dynamic directions has reached its peak.[14] The music of the twentieth century is split into too many divergent styles to permit a simple summing up, by a contemporary at least; but a decrease in dynamic directions is noticeable, and sometimes changeless volume is explicitly required; Hindemith, Stravinsky and others occasionally prescribe *little expression* or *no expression*.[15]

[13] For instance, in the score of *Idomeneo*.

[14] Extreme cases are also the *pppppp* in the aria of the Princess of Eboli in the fourth act of Verdi's *Don Carlos*, and similar marks in the symphonies of Mahler.

[15] Pfitzner held that superabundance of expression marks degraded the conductor into a *Klang-Polizist* (sound-policeman) and said that it was the fear of being disregarded which led composers to place undue emphasis upon expression marks.

Articulation

PHRASING MARKS. The origin of phrasing slurs seems to have been strongly influenced by early Italian violin practice. It is noticeable at any rate how frequent phrasing slurs are in J. S. Bach's parts for solo strings, while they occur much less often in his keyboard compositions. A typical example of detailed bowing marks for the violoncello and the solo violin is to be found in a page from his cantata *In allen meinen Thaten* (plate 33). Works by A. Scarlatti, Marcello and Porpora do not yet exhibit any phrasing slurs. In the autographs of J. C. Bach short ones occur (plates 51, 52). In the illustration from C. P. E. Bach (plate 46), they are of central importance. A page from Gluck's *Armide* (plate 50) already shows an elaborate system of alternating staccato dots and legato slurs, and in J. Haydn's and Mozart's scores (plates 53, 55, 56, 60ff.), their use has become general.

FINGERING MARKS. In instrumental music articulation is prescribed not only by phrasing slurs but by fingering marks. But as fingering is largely ruled by the tradition of each school, particularly in keyboard music, we usually find explicit fingering marks wherever a master is breaking with the tradition and entering new paths. Thus Couperin gives precise fingering marks. J. S. Bach's fingering method has come down to us through the "Clavierbüchlein für Wilhelm Friedemann Bach" which includes a piece provided throughout with precise fingering marks.[16] Neither Joseph Haydn nor Mozart indicated fingering, as far as I have been able to find out. Beethoven, however, employed fingering marks from his early piano sonatas to his last one. Liszt bestowed much care on fingering. An example of his precise directions is found in a page from the *Soirées de Vienne* (plate 116). Brahms, much interested in piano technique and himself the composer of systematic and intricate finger exercises, uses fingering marks with great economy, and only when necessary to clarify the articulation.

PEDAL MARKS. As far as I know, the first pedal marks occur in J. Haydn's later pianoforte sonatas. He writes them: open pedal 〰〰〰〰

A pedal for lifting the dampers was patented in England in 1783, but knee levers for the same purpose existed earlier, in the piano built in Augsburg by Johann Andreas Stein, for example. It is curious that Mozart, who praised these pianos enthusiastically, never explicitly prescribed the use of the pedal.

Beethoven's pedal marks, however, sometimes covering such long spans that their scrupulous execution on the modern sonorous pianoforte is nearly unbearable,[17] are an intrinsic part of his keyboard style. By a little circle he indicates the precise point for lifting the pedal. Plate 88 from his *Op. 109* shows a correction where one of these circles has been crossed out and transferred to fit the harmony more precisely.

[16] Alessandro Scarlatti, in a *Toccata* for the harpsichord, indicates fingering marks, probably of his own invention, for every note. They are explained at the top of the first page where both hands are drawn, with fingering marks placed above each finger:

　＊ thumb,　❙ index finger,　4 middle finger,　⌒ fourth finger,　△ little finger.

The manuscript of this *Toccata* is reproduced in J. S. Shedlock, "The harpsichord music of A. Scarlatti," *Internationale Musik-Gesellschaft, Sammelbände*, Jahrg. 6, 1904-1905, p. 164. Innovations though these symbols seem to be, they are supposed to help conventional practicing rather than to establish a new system of fingering itself.

[17] One case in point is the largo recitative (*Con espressione e semplice*) in the first movement of *Op. 31, No. 2*. As far as I know, in recent times only Artur Schnabel dared to keep the dampers lifted for the whole length of the recitative. On Beethoven's instruments the blurring thus produced was considerably slighter.

✦ Chopin indicates the lifting of the pedal by this sign. An examination of plates 109 and 111 will show what conscientious and loving care he devoted to pedaling. Brahms indicates pedaling with the utmost economy, merely suggesting it, and usually he marks only its beginning (plate 151). Hugo Wolf and Reger leave pedaling to the discretion of the player.

Abbreviation and Shorthand

Under abbreviations we include all signs, graphic devices and practices invented to save writing labor or paper. There are a multitude of abbreviations of many kinds in musical notation. Among them are the repeat signs and ^{8va} · · · · · · signs, both of which are also used in print. Abbreviations in a narrower sense are those labor- or paper-saving devices which, as a rule, have to be expanded for printed scores or for the fair copies used for performance. Here we find general methods of abbreviation as well as personal shorthand. Simile-signs are frequent, for instance, in the shape of // (see Mozart's *Rondo K. 485*, plate 65, and plate 78 from the *Coronation Concerto*). Beethoven employs them often or writes *siml* (simile). Just as common is the condensation of repeated notes or groups of notes into a sort of skeleton script (see, for instance, J. C. Bach, plate 51, and Beethoven, plates 85, 88).

Chords to be performed in the highly elaborate arpeggio technique of the Baroque, up to C. P. E. Bach, are simply indicated by the chord itself in whole or half notes, sometimes explained by a notation in full of the intended execution (see, for instance, in J. S. Bach's *Clavier-büchlein*, plate 26). Of special interest is Handel's shorthand; plate 40 from the *Messiah* is a typical example of his ingenious methods of graphic simplification. Of course, he could afford to go to the extreme, being sure that his intentions would be well understood by his amanuensis who made the fair copies.

THOROUGHBASS. An especially ingenious form of musical shorthand is the thoroughbass. Condensing the course of background harmony into one single bass line, with or without figures added, meant an enormous reduction of writing labor. This was possible, however, only when the composer could rely sufficiently upon the style of the continuo player to entrust a creative role to him.

Changes in the method of writing thoroughbass can be followed in their main stages in our plates. Monteverdi (plates 1, 2) and Vivaldi (plates 18, 19) employ an unfigured bass with accidentals above, calling for the major or minor third. Alessandro Scarlatti (plates 15, 16, 17), Porpora (plate 25) and Padre Martini (plate 45) use the fully developed code of numbers and accidentals.

During Joseph Haydn's lifetime the continuo gradually went out of fashion.[18] Its function of supplying the background harmony for the orchestra was taken over by the various members of the orchestral ensemble themselves, but Haydn in his sketches for the *Creation* (plate 57), still uses thoroughbass notation as an expedient and practical device, and Mozart in his piano concertos retains one function of the continuo instrument when he directs the pianoforte, where it does not perform solo, to double the basses in continuo fashion (plates 75, 78).

ORNAMENTS. In the category of shorthand symbols belong also the signs for graces,[19] and

---

[18] A good example of the diminishing role of the continuo fashion is found in Haydn's *Nelson Mass*, 1798; there a large part of the autograph score gives the organ merely a figured bass; in other places, however, the organ part is not only written out in full harmony, but even carries prominent melodic passages not assigned to other instruments.

[19] Modern critical accounts of ornaments and their execution can be found in E. Dannreuther, *Musical*

especially the notation of appoggiaturas. Here we find a whole code of short signs that express formalized ornaments. Many composers, like D'Anglebert, Couperin, Kuhnau, and J. S. Bach, explained the ornaments used in their works by tabulations. They are also exhaustively dealt with in treatises, such as those by Türk, Agricola, C. P. E. Bach, Marpurg, Quantz, J. J. Rousseau, and Leopold Mozart. Here we must confine ourselves to pointing to the page from Rameau's *La Dauphine* (plate 44) in which there appear no less than seven different signs for graces.

Small grace notes that indicate long appoggiaturas are not actually labor-saving devices; it does not take less time to write a small note than to write a full-sized one, and the question then arises why appoggiaturas were not always written out in large notes. There seem to be several factors which may account for the visual distinction of the appoggiatura: it helped to clarify the phrasing by establishing an unmistakable, unbreakable link with the main note. It also contributed to the immediate understanding of the harmonic foundations of the melody. The continuo player, who had before him melody and bass, figured or unfigured, needed to consider for his realization of the harmony only the main notes of the melody.[20] Still another problem concerning appoggiaturas is that of their correct execution. This problem, at least as far as Mozart's scores are concerned, is touched upon in the comments to plates 65-66.

One cannot conclude these few words about shorthand devices without mentioning that in a sense even the fully written-out musical script is a shorthand direction for the performer, simply because even the sum of these written or printed signs do not of themselves tell the whole story. This is particularly true of periods such as the Baroque where improvisation was not only tolerated but usually required and the accompaniment by improvised continuo was an essential element of style. It is in this sense that the gradual increase in expression signs, tempo indications, articulation marks and other directions for performance, which can be followed throughout the plates of this book, is only the graphic equivalent of the gradual restriction of the performer's freedom of improvisation.

DISTINCTION OF PARTS IN KEYBOARD POLYPHONY. Still another evolution in writing methods is closely related to the gradual change of keyboard style from strict polyphony, with its separation of single parts, to free chordal texture. Frescobaldi's style, of course, already showed homophonic elements, and in Froberger's Toccatas and Phantasias we find strict part-writing considerably modified by full chords (plate 11); in these chords, the "extra" notes each have their separate stems, just as do those notes which belong to the contrapuntal lines. Separate stems in part-writing are still used, in general, by the founders of the Classical Viennese school. The transition reveals itself most clearly in Haydn's keyboard sonatas. In sections of lighter

---

Ornamentation, 1893; E. Fowles, *Studies in musical graces*, 1907; H. Schenker, *Ein Beitrag zur Ornamentik*, 1908; A. Dolmetsch, *The Interpretation of the Music of the XVIIth and XVIIIth Centuries*, 1915; J. Arger, *Les agréments . . . dans la musique vocale française du 18e siècle*, 1920; P. Brunold, *Traité de signes et agréments employés par les clavecinistes français des 17. et 18. siècles*, 1935; R. Kirkpatrick, Preface to his edition of J. S. Bach, *The Goldberg Variations*, 1938; and P. Aldrich, *Ornamentation in J. S. Bach's organ works*, 1950.

[20] According to the continuo practice of the second half of the eighteenth century and the theory of harmony implied in it, tones which were not components of the basic harmony, i.e., the chords indicated by the figured bass, were regarded as foreign to these chords and were distinguished from them as tolerated aliens by smaller writing. C. P. E. Bach, in his *Versuch über die wahre Art das Klavier zu spielen*, 1753 and 1762, chapter 25, par. 3, says that the appoggiaturas delay the harmony which actually is determined by the root—"Die Vorschläge halten die Harmonie auf, welche der Grundnote eigentlich zukommt."

texture he usually keeps to strict part writing; even passages as simple as runs of parallel thirds for one hand (plates 55, 56) are written with separate stems for the notes of the upper and lower lines. But let a full chord appear (plate 54, third system), and the stems with their cross-strokes are simply attached to the top and bottom notes, while those in the middle stand free. Such compromises perfectly illustrate the transition from the polyphonic idiom of J. S. Bach to the pseudo-contrapuntal style of the Viennese classics. Beethoven progressed a step farther toward chordal writing; particularly in sections of his piano works which are neither fugal nor in pseudo-string-quartet style, he sometimes seems to think—or at least to write—more in terms of "hands" than of parts.

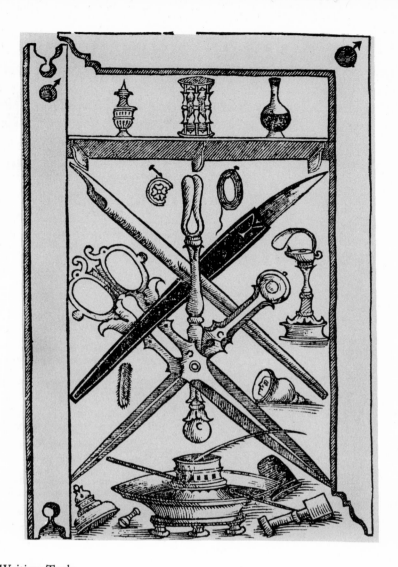

FIG. A. Writing Tools.

Giovambattista Palatino, *Libro . . . nelqual s'insegna à scriver ogni sorte lettera, antica e moderna . . .* Rome, 1540.

Left: Ruler

Top and right: Square

On shelf: Container for pounce;[1] hourglass; bottle for storing ink.

Upper center suspended on nails: Piece of sealing wax; roll of string.

Middle: Quill; knife with straight cutting edge for shaping quills; scissors; dividers; pincers, for attaching the sheet to the "false ruler" beneath which served as a guide.

Middle right: Oil lamp with cap over the flame for "concentration of the light." Oil lamps were preferred to candles which were considered too flickering and too smoky.

Lower middle

Left: Rabbit's foot for spreading the pounce evenly on the paper; *Right*: Metal mirror used at night to concentrate the light from the lamp on the spot where the calligrapher was writing.

Bottom

Left to right: Cover for the inkpot; small seal (?); inkpot with a quill and a stylus used to hold down the paper while writing; thimble worn on the third finger when shaping the point of a quill (black thimbles were preferred as providing a sharper contrast to the color of the quill); large seal.

[1] A fine powder made of ground eggshell and pulverized sandarac which was used to prepare the paper surface for writing. Since it prevented the ink from spreading over an erasure or an unsized paper, the use of pounce made the writing sharper and more precise.

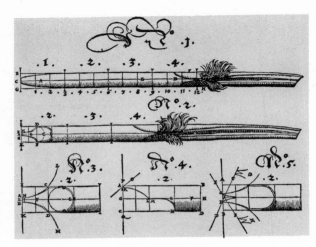

FIG. B.

Instructions for cutting the quill. (from: Wolfgang Fugger, *Ein nützlich und wohlgegrundt
formular mancherley schöner schriefften. . . .*
Nuremberg, 1553)

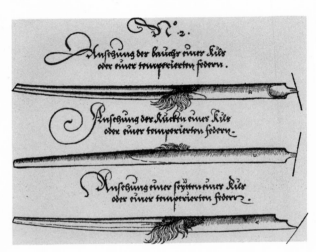

FIG. C.

Lower, upper and side view of a cut quill.
(from: Wolfgang Fugger—same as in B)

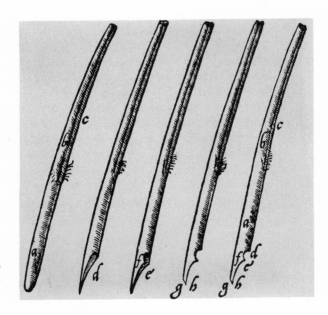

FIG. D.

Stages in shaping the quill. (from: Ludovico
Vicentino [Arrighi], *Il modo de temperare le
penne*, Rome, 1523)

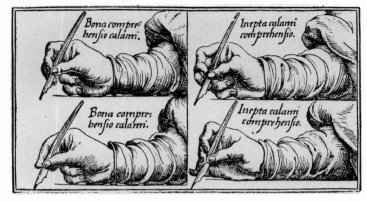

FIG. E.

Correct and incorrect ways of holding the quill. (from Urban Wyss, *Libellus valde doctus, elegans et utilis, multa et varia scribendarum literarum genera complectens*, Zürich, 1549)

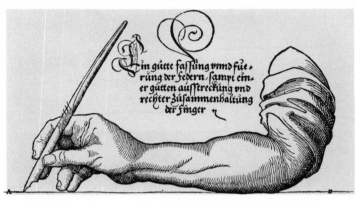

FIGS. F & G.

Correct (top) and incorrect position of the hand and arm. (from: Wolfgang Fugger—same as in B)

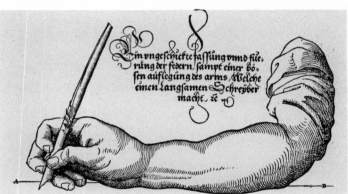

FIG. H.

Hand with quill and example of early seventeenth century writing. (from: Jan Van de Velde, *Spieghel der Schrijfkonste*, Rotterdam, 1605)

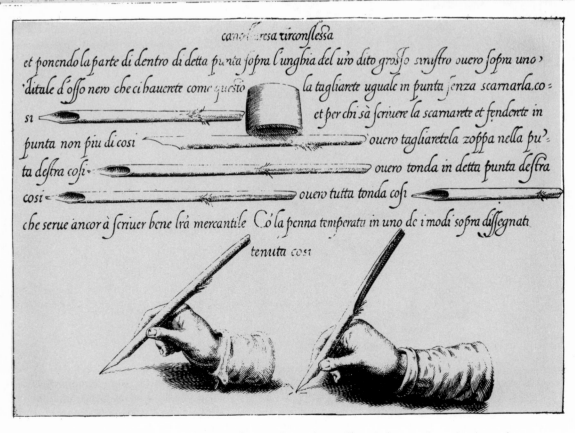

FIGS. J & K. Instructions on how to clean and cut the quill and sharpen its point in various ways; showing two correct ways of holding the quill and a model of one of the late sixteenth century hands, the "Cancelleresca Circonflessa." (from: Giuliantonio Hercolani, *Lo Scrittor' utile e brieve Segretario*, Bologna, 1574)

FIG. L. Portrait of Joseph Haydn. Engraving by L. Schiavonetti after a painting by L. Guttenbrunn.

FIG. M. Beginning of Brahms' *Vergebliches Ständchen*.

FIG. N. Brahms, *Händel Variations*, variation V, bars 5 and 6.

FIG. O. Brahms, *Waltzes*, Op. 39, Waltz II, bars 5-7.

II. THE WRITING ACT

1. THE TOOLS OF WRITING

Sir Toby to Sir Andrew:
"Let there be gall enough in thy ink,
though thou write with a goose-pen."
SHAKESPEARE, *Twelfth Night*

WE HAVE DEALT up to now with script as the vehicle of meaning, that is, the graphic embodiment of musical thought. But script is also the result of the many actions of body and mind which we comprehend under the name "writing." Any analysis of script would be superficial if it did not consider the process of writing which involves as its physical elements the arm, the hand, the fingers, and, last but not least, writing tools such as quill or metal pen, ink and paper.

As for tools, a discussion of them is not without importance, for the same signs take on a different shape if they are made with a quill or with a metal pen. Take, for instance, thick cross strokes like those occurring in Handel's and J. S. Bach's scripts (plates 30, 33, 37, 38). Graphologists today would tell us that such lines were produced by pressure of the pen and they would also—with more or less caution—link this pressure either to qualities of character such as vigor, energy, resolution, virility, excitability, or to temporary emotions such as vehemence, impatience, or the rage of inspiration. But this assumption implies that more strength is expanded on heavy lines than on thin ones. In reality this is true only of certain writing tools. With a steel pen, for instance, thick lines can be produced only by pressure, that is, by bearing down harder on the paper with the tool. With a chisel-pointed goose quill,[1] however, thickness can also be produced simply by turning the quill so that the full broad edge travels over the paper. In this case the physical strength needed for the broad lines is not appreciably greater than that for a hair stroke.

QUILL PEN. The quill has a long history. When papyrus was replaced by paper, a need arose for a finer tool than the reed pen, and such a tool was found in the shaft cut from the feather quills of certain birds such as geese, swans, turkeys and crows. Some quills were very soft, particularly those of the barnyard goose, some very hard, some more or less elastic. After the shafts were trimmed, they had to undergo many processes. They were bathed and scraped to remove their outer skin, then the barrels were dipped into various chemicals to harden them, and so forth. Everyone cut his own quill and kept it, sharp or rugged, fine or coarse, according to his needs or likings, to write out his thoughts, fast, slowly, hesitatingly, timidly, jerkily, tentatively, dominatingly, or passionately.

Cutting quills must have been quite a routine job for most of the older composers and one which was not done for writing purposes alone. Most of them played the harpsichord, if not as virtuosi, at least as providers of the continuo. For plucking the strings the harpsichord action employed a large number of crow quills, or, more precisely, small, pointed segments of crow quills—about 180 of them in large harpsichords with several stops. These quills wore out just as easily as the ones used for writing and had frequently to be replaced by newly-cut ones. Many harpsichords had little drawers or boxes built in for extra quills and other paraphernalia. We may easily imagine J. S. Bach requilling his famous Silbermann Flügel—we are told that he could do this with record speed—and then, with the same knife cutting or

[1] And a modern stub pen.

sharpening his writing quill. Periodical reshaping was necessary, for the point of the quill, unlike that of the metal pen, wore down pretty fast. Changes from thin to coarse writing in a manuscript may mean a worn quill more often than a change of mood. In Mozart's *Serenade KV 361* the first page of the *Adagio* (plate 62) was evidently written with a new or freshly sharpened pen; in plate 63 the point has noticeably dulled. With this in mind, we can often observe cycles of gradual thickening of the lines up to the next resharpening. In many early calligraphy books we can see that the writer began each page with a resharpened quill.

The quill, with its flexible point, permits many motions and tricks of which the modern steel pen is not capable. Modern pen drawings, for instance, have, as a rule, less sensitivity than those made with a quill. It was just as easy to begin a stroke at the bottom and go upward as to do it from top to bottom. The lines produced, however, differ in swing and swell, and thus permit us a good guess at the motions which produced them. The quill also permitted a variety of shadings not possible with the steel pen. The flexible point allowed shadings in different directions up to almost a right angle without appreciably changing the position of the pen, and this was naturally a great advantage for rapid score writing. Dots for black noteheads, thin stems, and ascending or descending cross strokes, for example, could all be made with a quill kept in almost the same position (Handel, plates 38-40; J. S. Bach, plate 33).

Anyone who is seriously interested in the matter of old penmanship is strongly advised to try a quill for himself. In Europe, where geese abound, a goose quill is the natural choice. In the duck-eating United States and Canada a turkey quill is probably the best answer, or, if hunter's luck is favorable, that of a Canada grey goose. A few experiments with a quill pen will suffice to correct some common misconceptions. It is often believed, for example, that disconnected—or, to use a more musical term, staccato-writing—is by its very nature slower than legato-writing. This is not true of quill writing. An elastic, well-shaped quill is capable of bouncing on and off the paper with dancelike strokes, yet with amazing speed; and a connected script is faster only if the writer allows it to degenerate into a scarcely legible scrawl. Another factor, easily overlooked by writers accustomed to steel or fountain pens, is the caution entailed by the little ink blob which hangs threateningly on the point of a quill for some time after it has been dipped in the ink. To avoid black mishaps one has to write away from the blob; otherwise, two adjacent lines easily merge into one thick one or into a blot. This means, as far as score writing is concerned, that a "white" note may turn into a "black" one. The more freely flowing the ink, the greater the peril. Various writers had, of course, their different habitual ways of coping with these peculiarities of quill and ink, and it may be well to bear this in mind when later, in the chapter on characteristics of single signs, an attempt will be made to classify note shapes by degrees of connectedness and initial quill motion.

These somewhat lengthy comments on the quill pen may be of value because many present-day statements about writing in general and writing music in particular seem to be based upon familiarity with the metal pen alone. And now let us turn to the steel pen.

STEEL PEN. Progressing industrialization at the end of the eighteenth and the beginning of the nineteenth century led to a gradual replacement of the quill by the steel pen. The way to its adoption had been paved by various experiments. By 1809 quill nibs were being made to be inserted into penholders. Still earlier pens had been made of gold or horn or tortoise shell and tipped with ruby or other hard substances. The first handmade steel pens appeared in England around 1808. But not until the invention of the cheap machine-made steel pen in

Birmingham (1822) was the reign of the quill pen seriously threatened. Liszt and Chopin still used the quill. Breitkopf & Härtel owned a daguerreotype, made in 1848 during Chopin's visit to Edinburgh, which shows an inkwell with a large quill pen, the down still on its shaft. Wagner received as a present from Mathilde Wesendonk's husband an American gold pen made in New York; with it he wrote the whole calligraphic orchestral score of *Die Walküre*.[2]

From this time on the metal pen asserted itself. Its name in different languages, however, still points to the feather (*pen*, from the Latin *penna; plume, Feder*). Through this transition the variety and individual range of script (which had been facilitated by the "personalized" quill) was greatly reduced; the machine-made metal pen afforded the writer a much smaller range of individuality, and the types of pen on the market determined the possible types of script. Wagner did not live to see the fountain pen, invented in 1883 by L. E. Waterman in New York, and *Rheingold* was written without benefit of the latest achievement of machine-age ingenuity, the underwater ball-point pen. A good fountain pen, with its even ink supply, does away with the periodical script-variations from wet to dry which can be observed throughout the manuscripts of the quill and steel pen eras.

2. CHANGING FASHIONS OF WRITING

FASHIONS in writing move in faster cycles than fashions in writing tools. Every connoisseur of the history of script will, as a rule, readily identify a manuscript as typical seventeenth or eighteenth century writing, English or Italian as the case may be, according to the shape of its script elements and their arrangement on the page. His attribution may be reliable and precise even without conscious reasoning. This process is the same as in the history of art; the connoisseur of graphic art will not only recognize *a prima vista* the individual features of a Mantegna, Rembrandt or Goya, but can also attribute anonymous items to certain periods of print making because of their particular line-work.

A most interesting problem arises here for the student of musical autographs: are these also linked to current fashions of writing in general, and are both of them linked to other phases of graphic art and even in some degree to all the visual arts? This would certainly be a very inviting assumption and at least worth considering as a hypothesis. Anyone who examines contemporary specimens of drawing, print making and letter writing, will not require too much self-persuasion to perceive some similarity in the elementary linear patterns and their combinations into designs of black on white. Rembrandt's handwriting has not only something in common with his style of drawing and engraving, but with any seventeenth century hand.

If this is true, it would seem that throughout the evolution of graphic expression certain basic ideas of form succeed each other, marking and tinging all forms of graphic expression: representational art, handwriting, and musical manuscript alike. As we have said, score-writing imposes infinitely more restriction on the free motion of quill or pen than does ordinary script. Still there is enough of it left, as one can easily perceive from a comparison of the remarkable differences in our various examples. Art historians who knew nothing of music, on being confronted with some of these musical autographs, were often able to relate them correctly to their proper periods. For instance, plate 59 showing a composition by Salieri evoked the

[2] Wolfgang Golther, *Richard Wagner an Mathilde Wesendonk*, Leipzig, 1922, p. 12.

immediate response "Guardi or post-Guardi," and the page written by Paganini was immediately associated with "Delacroix."

3. INDIVIDUAL HANDS

> Malvolio to Sir Toby:
> "By my life, this is my lady's hand!
> These be her very C's, her U's, and her T's;
> and thus makes she her great P's. It is, in
> contempt of question, her hand."
> SHAKESPEARE, *Twelfth Night*, Act II, Scene 5

IN ANALYZING the most important aspects of musical autographs, such as the qualities of single signs, their sequence on the page, their arrangement, and the consistency and regularity of their use by the composers, we shall consider the following factors:

A. *Characteristics of individual signs*:

a) Size (absolute and relative)
b) Width
c) Quality of line (degrees of pressure)
d) Slant
e) Shape
f) Direction
g) Connectedness (continuous or broken hand)
h) Interrelation between shape, direction and connectedness, and suggestions for classification

B. *Relationship between signs*

a) Space sensitivity
b) Evenness
c) Visual harmony and rhythm

C. *Constancy of features* throughout the various manuscripts and throughout the life of a composer[3]

It is obvious that certain features of script which are of central importance for the analysis of ordinary handwriting play no role in musical notation. Among these are alignment and those favorites of graphology—the "arches" and "sways"—produced by concave or convex rendering of letters.

A. *Characteristics of Individual Signs*

a) Extremes of size may be seen in Handel's large and freely sweeping lines on the one hand and Chopin's and Debussy's delicate patterns on the other. Beethoven's scripts alternate between the extremes.

b) As for width Handel (plates 37-43) is usually generous with space; J. S. Bach is eco-

[3] Of eminent value for the analysis of script is one source not often used by psychologists or graphologists; it is the literature on the detection of forgeries of documents which abounds with systematic and detailed observations. Here we should mention only that classic example, *Questioned Documents*, by A. S. Osborn, Rochester, N.Y., 1910.

nomical, often even crowding his notes into a minimum of space (plates 30, 31); Chopin condenses wherever he can.

c) Handel's lines are usually broad and heavy, Beethoven's very often so, J. Haydn's thin and pointed. Noteworthy in this respect are the florid, sinuous cross strokes written, for instance, by Froberger, Handel and Bach.

d) As the term "slant" is ambiguous, it should be explained that we shall designate as "forward slant" a vertical whose top is more to the right than its foot, and the opposite as "backward slant." J. S. Bach, Schubert and Brahms keep to a neat, precise vertical in their bar lines. Mozart, after his early works, tends more and more to backslant for bar lines (see, for instance, the striking examples from the *Coronation Concerto*, pl. 75-80). An extreme forward slant in the stems of the notes is represented by Handel's script for the *Messiah* (pl. 40). Beethoven's bar lines and stems often show an extreme forward slant (pl. 87, 89, 90). This characteristic was already marked in the *Septet* and in his *Piano Sonata*, Op. 26.

e) The shape of notes has already been touched upon in the section on the written sign (p. 12); but only along general lines and only to trace the rudiments of sixteenth century tradition in later periods of notation. We now have to deal with the shapes of notes as determined by local tradition, and with the form that they assume in the scripts of individual composers. One easily detected feature which determines to a great extent the graphic character of any given score page is the relation of note heads to their stems. Here we find divergent practices. Note-heads are turned to left or right; their stems may be attached to either side of the heads, or it may spring from their centers. Thus the available

standard forms are ♩♩♩ ♩♩♩ ♩♩♩ ♩♩♩

Combing through manuscripts of about 1600 to 1800, one comparatively seldom finds a half-note with left downward stem; a quarter-note with right downward stem is frequently used indiscriminately with a quarter-note with left downward stem[4] since both are products of almost the same pen motion; half-notes with left upward stems and the corresponding quarter-notes are extremely rare. Thus the preferred shapes are half-notes with stems pointing either upwards or downwards on the right and quarter-notes with an upward stem on the right or a downward stem on the left. Extreme consistency is exemplified by Handel and Rossini in whose scripts the note-heads turn left, for half-notes as well as for lesser time values and regardless of whether the stems run up or down.

f) The shape of notes is influenced by the habitual main motion of the quill, and especially by its initial direction. The direction of the single strokes forming the notes is again determined largely by the position in which the pen is held. A consistent position of the pen often leads to apparent inconsistencies in script. Mozart, for example, writes quarter-notes with heads turning right on the same page as half-notes with heads left. Evidently he jotted down the heads of his quarter-notes with the point of his quill pointing toward the left, and then drew the stem down still holding the pen in the same position. His half-note is drawn in two motions (fig. 2). The position of his pen was the same whichever way the note-heads were turned.

g) One of the most characteristic features of musical script is connectedness; it is apparently

---

[4] A case in point is Alessandro Scarlatti.

determined to a great extent by the rate of speed in writing. Most of the notoriously fast writers like J. S. Bach, Handel, Mozart or Brahms, it seems, wrote an unbroken, flowing hand, often drawing notes, stems and flags in a single motion without lifting the quill from the paper; while others, Haydn, for example, required several motions for them.

Chopin is an example of the happy medium. Debussy leans towards disconnectedness in writing his scores (pl. 173, 174, 175) as well as in his letters. The increasing disconnectedness noticeable in the scores of Schumann and Hugo Wolf will be discussed later under *Letterhand and Musical Notation*.

h) The last three factors discussed above—the shape of notes, the preferred direction of quill motion, and the degree of connectedness—are closely related and they can be studied profitably only in their interrelation. The actual shapes of notes are the result of two writing habits: the initial quill direction, and the preferred degree of connectedness between the strokes which form single notes. Perhaps one example (fig. 1) may help to show the forms that result when graphic preference, like that for turning note-heads to the left or right, meets with ingrained writing habits, such as connectedness and a tendency to patterns formed by one or more motions. Obviously the more complex shapes, graphically speaking, are more rewarding for our analysis. Thus we turn to half-notes rather than to the relatively simple lesser time values.

FIG. I

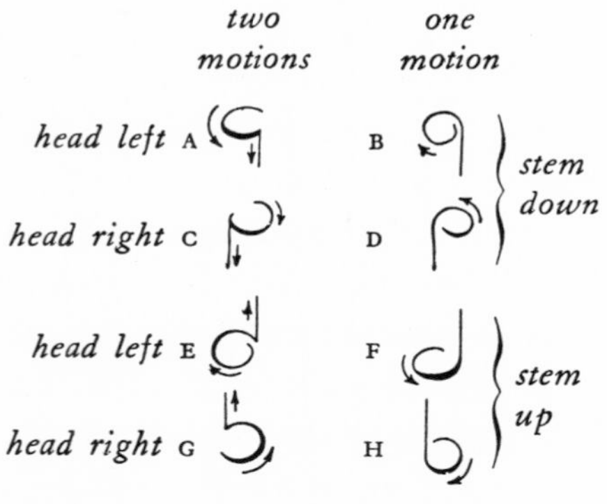

J. S. Bach, assuming that he usually writes his note-heads before drawing the stems, has still a choice among four patterns for half-notes with stem down (A, B, C, D), and four patterns of half-notes with stem up (E, F, G, H). As he does not usually favor heads turned toward the right and as his habitual pen motion is predominantly from left to right, only two forms are left to him: A and F, the first produced by two connected motions, the second by a single round motion. Similar analyses could be made of quarter-notes, etc.

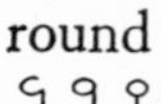

Similarly, different shapes in his script, such as these may be explained as variants resulting naturally from his basic habits of writing.

This approach may then be taken as the point of departure for a methodical comparison of individual scripts in order to disentangle and classify their varieties. Let us compare, for example, the scripts of seven composers, Handel, J. S. Bach, Gluck, Haydn, Mozart, Beethoven, and Schubert, a sequence spanning about 150 years. All are in the traditional German orbit of writing fashions, and several of them are contemporaries.

The first step is the determination of the shapes preferred by each composer:

a) The most frequent types, not only among the seven composers mentioned above, but generally between 1700 and 1830, are A, B, C, D; these shapes are favored by Haydn, Mozart and Schubert.

b) Not quite consistent are J. S. Bach, who also uses E; Gluck, who uses D and F indiscriminately; and Beethoven, who prefers F but also uses D.

c) Extreme uniformity, with all heads pointing toward the left, is represented by Handel's script: A, B, C, F.

The comparison of these shapes, however, remains superficial, as we have emphasized above, unless one asks what type of habitual quill motion produces such shapes, and above all, which is the preferred direction of the single strokes of the quill, especially of the initial motion.

This initial direction can be seen most clearly in the half-notes since quarter-notes and shorter time values are produced, as a rule, simply by touching the paper with the point of the quill (fig. 2).

FIG. 2

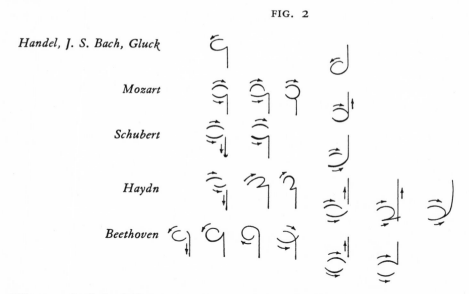

Handel, J. S. Bach, Gluck

Mozart

Schubert

Haydn

Beethoven

Thus we find the following varieties in initial direction:

a) Toward the left: Handel, J. S. Bach, Gluck. The direction of the quill's motion is not entirely a matter of choice of the individual writer. It is frequently related to the direction predominant in ordinary, that is, letter-writing and thus to the position of quill and hand which can best produce the currently fashionable type of script.

b) Toward the right: Haydn, Mozart, Schubert.

c) Inconsistent: Beethoven.

In simplified form, fig. 2 shows various degrees of connectedness and illustrates some outstanding variants. Bach's and Mozart's scripts are well connected, Schubert's less so, and

Haydn's still less, Handel's and Gluck's extremely well, Beethoven's always alternating between extremes. The reader browsing through the autographs reproduced will have little trouble in detecting there all the shapes corresponding to the diagrams in fig. 2; moreover, he will find there numerous variants in addition to the standard forms.

A synopsis of the basic factors that we have discussed may be used for a summary classification, for instance, in the following manner:

Handel: all note-heads toward left, initial quill motion toward left, extreme connectedness.

Haydn: all note-heads toward left except for the quarter-note with stem down, initial quill motion toward right, fairly disconnected.

Beethoven: all note-heads left, occasionally a quarter-note with downward stem has the note-head on the right; initial quill motion variable, connectedness variable, and so forth. Beethoven, therefore, is the only one among the seven who is inconsistent in every respect, a quality, by the way, which is also inherent in other elements of his score writing, such as quality of line, width and size, and which appears also in his letter-hand.

B. *Relationship between Signs*

a) SPACE SENSITIVITY. For those who write and read music the approach to it is auditory and visual at the same time, and the fusion of these two worlds of perception is a very complex matter. In a certain sense one "hears" the score by "reading" the music. Gestalt-psychology tells us that if one looks at human beings under certain conditions, they do not appear diminished in perspective in the same ratio as other equally distant objects but appear larger because of the special pragmatic interest the onlooker bestows upon them. The human eye is not a mere photographic lens or screen upon which optical perceptions are recorded. Perceptions are determined by expectations and memories, in fact, by a whole frame of reference formed by pre-established interest. Likewise with hearing. The listener can select one familiar voice from a great mass of sounds; the ear also can "focus"; it concentrates on anticipated sensations.

The issue becomes even more complicated when one considers that written music is translated through the eye of the performer not only into anticipated sounds but also into motor impulses that affect his voice or his fingers. Thus a pianist when reading A will imagine a smaller musical interval than when reading B and will automatically arrange his fingers for it. He does this even though the visible spatial distance between the two notes forming the interval on paper is equal in both cases. William James distinguished between auditory, visual, and motor types of imagination.[5] These qualities seem to vary from one individual to another according to predominant tendencies. It seems likely that such individual differences have a bearing on the attitude of a score-writer toward his script and affect the manner in which he commits music to paper. Obviously the presence of the staves limits his freedom to express pitch and duration in spatial terms, but within

[5] William James, *Principles of Psychology*, 1910, vol. II, p. 60. Sir Francis Galton, in his *Inquiries into Human Faculty and its Development*, 1883, quoted by James, says: "I have many cases of persons mentally reading off scores when playing the pianoforte, or manuscripts when they are making speeches. . . . Some few persons see mentally in print every word that is uttered; they attend to the visual equivalent and not to the sound of the words, and they read them off usually as from a long imaginary strip of paper such as is unwound from telegraphic instruments."

these restrictions there remains a considerable scope for variety. Any comparison between scores by Mozart and Beethoven shows a striking difference in space-sensitivity.

Mozart realized to the full the possibilities of space for expressing musical relations. He indicates duration and pitch through the greatest possible exploitation of spatial symbolism. His arrangement of groups of notes corresponds quite accurately to their time values. The same is true of pitch relations, although this correspondence can occur only where ledger lines are used. He usually draws these at nearly the same intervals as those between the regular stave lines.[6]

Beethoven is quite different. For him the shapes of notes and rests suffice to express duration, and he attempts no correspondence between time values and graphic lengths (see plate 94). As for pitch: his ledger lines are sometimes very narrow, sometimes extremely wide with little regard for spatial symbolism (see plate 89). His crescendo and decrescendo wedges, however, are usually placed with greatest accuracy, and his combined wedges of diamond shape indicate precisely, as a rule, the peak of the swell (see plate 91).

These observations may help to explain why Mozart's music can be played with great ease from his autographs. But try this with most of Beethoven's manuscripts! True, they were, as a rule, not written for the performer but for the copyist, and these copyists were a pitiable lot indeed. Beethoven's constant, continuous quarrels with them came to be proverbial.

Closely connected with differences in space-sensitivity is another aspect of script arrangement; this is what we might call the "aura of space" surrounding notes or groups of notes, and which with many composers is a characteristic trait, as may be seen by a comparison of the scripts of Handel and Mozart.

In Handel's writing the size of the notes is constant throughout. Groups of notes, whenever he takes the time to write them out in full, come in formalized units like companies of soldiers. The space between them varies, but not that between the single notes of one unit. No doubt this accounts, in part at least, for the monumentality of Handel's script. It also tallies well with his incredible writing speed.

Mozart likewise wrote with fabulous rapidity, yet his is a much more flexible and variable script. The size of the elementary signs, such as notes, rests, and accidentals is less uniform, though never reaching Beethovenesque extremes. The aura is elastic. This makes for a script of ever-changing physiognomy, with its groupings constantly adapting to the progress of the music. The whole graphic texture is much more versatile and colorful in its spatial articulation. And for all this flexibility of script, there is an unsurpassed clarity and neatness, a neatness which, however, is far removed from stereotyped calligraphy.

b) EVENNESS. Among the most remarkable examples of evenness are the autographs of Mozart and Debussy, which go to show that speed by no means prevents regularity. The extreme case of irregularity is that of Beethoven.[7]

The handwriting of an individual is, of course, modified by many circumstances, such as

---

[6] An astounding example of masterly graphic rendition of cross-rhythms is furnished by the famous pages with the three superimposed dances from *Don Giovanni* (plates 70-71).

[7] Two of the foremost graphologists see in irregular writing quite different symptoms: "Les inégalités de l'écriture indiquent les jeux de tendances qui se contrarient" (Crépieux-Jamin, *L'écriture et le caractère*, p. 258); "Das Ebenmass der Handschrift entspricht dem Grade des persönlichen Gleichmuts, der Mangel an Ebenmass dem Grade der persönlichen Erregbarkeit" (Ludwig Klages, *Handschrift und Charakter*, 23. ed., 1949, p. 26).

biological factors, working conditions, and current writing fashions. Perhaps the most important of these are the following:

Education. The type of writing learned from teachers or fellow musicians and the system of ordinary writing prevalent in the local circle of an individual composer, form the foundation upon which the characteristic traits peculiar to his hand develop. It is often not easy to distinguish between individual traits and characteristics merely typical of a current writing vogue. The florid, swelling cross strokes so favored by J. S. Bach, for example, are largely traceable to the common writing practice of the Baroque.

One of the mistakes frequently found in graphological literature is a comparison of scripts from different centuries or different local schools of writing. Not even Klages[8] escapes this danger when in investigating the form level of script, he tries to match the writing of Oscar Wilde, Pope Alexander VI, and Nietzsche. Matching a Renaissance hand with a nineteenth century script may make sense in an analysis of writing technique; but comparing such different patterns to draw conclusions as to the character of the writers shows little historical sense and overlooks the evolution, through successive periods, of expressive patterns in general and of graphic forms in particular.

Age. Examples of the tremor of old age may be seen in pages by J. Haydn and Cherubini (plates 54, 56, 81). Verdi's hand remained remarkably untouched by progressing years (plates 124, 125).

Fatigue or Disease. It may not be entirely accidental that Schumann's hand becomes progressively more erratic and disconnected in the years before his mental collapse. Hugo Wolf, however, always had a tendency toward broken, spasmodic writing. Handel's failing eyesight is clearly reflected in his writing (plates 41-43).

Speed. When Schubert wrote six songs for the *Winterreise* in a single morning and Hugo Wolf composed three and even four songs in one day, they were creating as free, independent masters, urged on only by inner compulsion. In the seventeenth and eighteenth centuries when the composer had not yet become an emancipated artist in his own right, but was commissioned or employed to write his works, his working conditions often demanded speed, and reliable sources tell of well-nigh fantastic production. A case in point is Mozart, whose rapidity was evidently aided by his oft-cited ability to complete a composition in his mind before starting to write it down. For him the act of writing must have been a comparatively automatic procedure. In a famous letter to his sister (April 20, 1782) he apologizes for the reversed order of the music he sent her, because he "put the fugue to paper while composing the prelude." The well-known story about his *Don Giovanni* Overture is probably as legendary as it is characteristic. Writing to his father on the composition of the "Entführung," he said: "Since now the rage for work (*Passion*) is upon me, I would now need four days to accomplish what otherwise would require fourteen. It took me one day to compose the aria in A for Adamberger, the one in B flat for Mme. Cavalieri, and the trio, and one and a half days to write them out."[9] And on another occasion when he was invited to dinner and reminded that he had promised to write some *contredanses*, in less than half an hour he wrote four of them and all in score for large orchestra.[10]

[8] *Handschrift und Charakter*, p. 42.
[9] Letter of October 6, 1781.
[10] Reported by Nissen (Leitzmann, *Mozart in seinen Briefen und Berichten der Zeitgenossen*, n.d.).

The neatness of musical script is dependent to some degree on the purpose for which it was written. There are four cases, each requiring different degrees of neatness and legibility:

1. *Sketches of various phases of a composition.* These are notes for the composer's own use and can afford to be just legible enough so that he will be able to decipher them (see plate 57, Haydn's sketch for the *Creation*, and plate 87, Beethoven's *Piano Trio* Op. 97).

2. *Scripts intended not for performance but for the copyist or printer.* (Beethoven, *Piano Sonata* Op. 109, plates 88, 89, 90; Chopin, plate 109.)

3. *Scripts serving directly for performance.* If the composer himself was to participate in the performance, he could explain and direct, and therefore needed to be less explicit in his score. This was the case, for instance, in the cantatas written by J. S. Bach for his choir at St. Thomas. Scores for performance by other musicians, however, naturally required a higher degree of legibility and precision.

4. *Dedication copies, or scripts for presentation* are often calligraphic, and even "click the heels," as it were. Of this type is the famous autograph of the *Brandenburg Concerti* and the great mass of the *Albumblätter* of the sentimental and romantic era, such as our examples from Salieri and Rossini (plates 59, 103).

It is not quite true that copies written by the composer himself lack interest because they are separated from the act of creation. If a composer is forced to produce a fair copy, he is frequently compelled to re-examine his own composition, and this is likely to result in increased clarity of graphic expression (see, for instance, plate 151, Brahms, Op. 118).

To what degree neatness can vary within the work of one composer can be studied by comparing pages from *Die Meistersinger* and from *Tristan* (plates 126, 127).

c) Visual harmony and rhythm. These features are of central importance in the respective systems of graphology of Crépieux-Jamin[11] and Klages. Their application to musical script could be developed only within the philosophical terminologies of these systems.

C. *Constancy of Features*

For a long time Beethoven retained his irregular hand as a permanent trait; in his late works, however, his writing became somewhat thinner and more regular, although even there it neither gained in legibility nor lost its nervous impulsiveness.

Mozart, whose script was formed very early, retained his clear, springy hand to the end. J. S. Bach's hand varied in several respects: it changed noticeably throughout his life; it varied also from neat calligraphy to a speedy scrawl, according to the immediate purpose of his score. As mentioned above, on pp. 27-30, even the single note shapes vary; usually the heads turn toward the left, but heads pointing toward the right also occur. With Handel it is different; it will be hard to find in his pages notes whose heads do not turn toward the left.

4. GRAPHOLOGY AND MUSICAL SCRIPT

No study of musical autographs can afford to overlook the extensive literature of graphology, which attempts to interpret handwriting as symptomatic of character. Script is the result and record of a motion of the hand of which the beginning and impulse lies deep in the creative

---

[11] ". . . qu'on peut définir le portrait graphologique le produit de l'appréciation première de l'harmonie ou de l'inharmonie de l'écriture. Il n'y a pas d'autre moyen pour apprécier sûrement le caractère d'après l'écriture." Crépieux-Jamin, *Les éléments de l'écriture des Canailles*, Paris, 1923, p. 120.

mind. Does it reflect basic consistencies of personality? If the gait and gestures of an individual, the movements of the muscles of his face, his speech, his laughter and tears are to be regarded as "expressive" movements indicative of character, should not the same be true also of his handwriting? Or is handwriting merely the product of external habits, determined by conditions peripheral to the personality? Graphology is based upon the first of these assumptions.

The status of graphology is still under debate today. European graphology, a discipline with a considerable if somewhat shady past in the old country, has been accepted only recently and reluctantly into American scientific circles. Three principal factors have contributed to the low esteem in which it has often been held: it has been exploited commercially; it has been connected with such pseudo-sciences as palmistry and phrenology; and lastly, the most radical and penetrating approach toward methodical graphology has been made by intuitional rather than quantitative methods and has been expressed in a philosophical terminology which cannot easily be reduced to the vocabulary of the experimental psychologist.

It is not possible to trace here the fascinating evolution of graphological ideas from their origins. Only the briefest outline can be given.

The first steps toward the association of script with character occurred solitarily and at long intervals. The first instruction in script interpretation, as far as I have been able to learn, was published in Bologna in 1622 by the professor of philosophy, Camillo Baldi, under the title *Trattato come da una lettera missiva si conoscano la natura e qualità dello scrivente* (Treatise on how to recognize from a letter the nature and qualities of its writer). The date of publication coincides significantly with the spreading fame of Giambattista della Porta's *De humana physiognomia* (1586) and the beginnings of the *stile nuovo espressivo* in music.

The next advance in graphological speculation occurred 150 years later and was likewise prompted by a wave of interest in physiognomy: Lavater, in his *Physiognomische Fragmente* (1775-1778) discusses the physiognomical implications of handwriting after his analysis of design and color in art.[12] Soon thereafter similar inspiration came from another pioneering branch of physiognomy: it was Gall's phrenology which occasioned further graphological treatises in late eighteenth century Germany.

The translation of Lavater by Moreau de la Sarthe (1806) and the important work by the Belgian Edouard Hocquart, *L'art de juger de l'esprit et du caractère des hommes sur leur écriture* (1812) soon led to the organization of the first graphological society in France about 1830, which in turn, by extensive collecting of material and wealth of single analyses, prepared the ground for the standard work of Jean Hippolyte Michon. His treatises, *Les mystères de l'écriture* (1870) and *Système de graphologie* (1875), represent the first discipline of graphology based on psychological principles and on a consistent method of analyses, the "signes fixes," or typical isolated elements of script that correspond to typical traits of character.

Michon's books caused a sensation among French and Italian physiologists as well as psychologists, inspiring, among others, Lombroso's *Grafologia* (1895). But the great system of modern graphology emerging from discussions of Michon's theories are in the writing of Crépieux-Jamin, beginning in 1885. His ideas exerted their greatest influence in Germany; among their most important fruits were the books of the physiologist William Preyer, the

---

[12] Moreau de la Sarthe, in his French translation of Lavater's work, supplements these remarks by a long chapter entitled *Réflexions sur les caractères physionomiques tirés de la forme de l'écriture.*

Graphologische Monatshefte published by the *Deutsche graphologische Gesellschaft*, founded in 1896, and, since the beginning of our century, the solid body of the works of Klages.

Most of the European treatises are based predominantly upon intuitional methods and a certain innate confidence in the results of introspection. In them graphic movement is regarded as "the quintessence of expression, a 'crystallized' form of gesture, an intricate but accessible prism which reflects many, if not all, of the inner consistencies of personality."[13]

Their basic optimism is rarely shared by American psychologists. With these we find a more cautious attitude, ranging from complete scepticism, regarding graphology as humbug, to a grudging reserve which would not accord the status of true science to any research not founded upon broad experimental grounds and conducted by inductive empirical methods. If American psychologists reproach their European colleagues for vagueness, if not mysticism, European scholars retort by frowning upon "quantitative" statistical methods as insufficient and inadequate for any research into personality. Any scholars who have tried to combine both approaches, have exposed themselves to criticism from both sides.

It is certainly not the business of an anthology of musical autographs to take sides, and yet these autographs are in a way the embodiment of creative thought, of artistic inspiration, and from this angle at least a question may be raised as to the natural limitations of the statistical or quantitative experimental approach. The essence of genius is its uniqueness. Research by experiment presupposes typical conditions. We can hardly hope to reduce genius or its essential trait, recurrent inspiration, to conditions favorable for experimental investigation.

Both schools of thought, notwithstanding their differences, have developed a more or less common tabulation of relevant qualities of scripts—the "graphic elements"—through which the peculiarities of an individual hand can be investigated separately and interpreted as manifestations of personality and character.

Graphological studies of musicians have dealt mainly with their ordinary handwriting and have not included analyses of their scores. This is quite natural, considering the technical limitations imposed on music-writing by the pre-established structure of the score.

It remains for us to pose the question to what extent musical script can be a rewarding subject for graphological analysis. Let us first consider which of the elements of scripts, interesting for the graphological interpretation of ordinary writing, are to be found in musical script. The arrangement of words on a page of ordinary writing, a letter let us say, is determined in Occidental writing by a minimum of rules: the words proceed from left to right in horizontal lines. Everything else, the size of the letters, their relative proportions, the way in which they are linked together, their shape and slant, as well as the alignment of the script—rising or falling as it may be—is entirely up to the writer. The range of individual freedom, however, is quite limited in musical script. There are the staves; there is also the exact significance of up and down on the paper as an expression of pitch relations. In musical script the writer is not free to connect single notes or to write them separately; he is bound by a strict framework determining the spatial arrangement for those operational instructions known as the score. Considering all these restrictions, it is surprising that within them there can flourish the amazing variety of individual hands which the reader will find in our plates.

Among the features of script missing from musical notation are some which are of central

---

[13] Allport and Vernon, *Studies in expressive movement*, New York, 1933, p. 186.

importance for the interpretation of character, in some of the outstanding graphological systems at least. One of these features is alignment, that is, the relation of single letters or words to an actual or imaginary base line resulting in rising, falling, or undulating, or bridge-like lines.[14] Another feature is the employment of connecting links: notes are naturally separate from each other, and when they join into groups, their spatial combinations are strictly regulated by notational requirements which do not apply to word-writing. Thus there is no equivalent in musical script for the various ways of linking the single strokes that form a letter or again, the single letters that form a word. Klages, for instance, distinguishes several aspects of these "Bindungsformen" (links); they may be sharply angular, pointed, thorny, rounded, or arched;[14] likewise, curved, connecting lines may have a garland shape, opening toward the top, or an

[14] The interpretation of these diverse features of script as symptoms of character traits cannot, of course, be expounded here in detail. Just a few random examples may suffice to show types of such interpretations: rising alignment has been taken as indicative of optimistic, falling alignment as indicative of pessimistic tendencies; sharp angular connecting lines as suggesting stability of character, rounded ones as mutability; "garland" connections as symptomatic of open-heartedness, frankness, kindness, or of susceptibility and lack of decision or initiative; "arcade" connections as indicative of a closed, reserved, cautious character, or a lack of openness or sincerity; a preponderance of longer strokes above the line is thought to indicate idealistic tendencies, a preponderance of long strokes beneath the line to suggest materialistic tendencies.

Quite different from these methods of interpretation is the technique to be found in Louis M. Vauzanges, *L'écriture des musiciens célèbres*, Paris, 1913. The book is the only one, as far as I know, that concentrates exclusively on the handwriting of musicians, and for this reason it should be mentioned here. It confines itself to letter-writing; occasionally a few staves of music are reproduced with samples of letter-writing, but it does not attempt an analysis of notational script. The first part (*Etude analytique des écritures*) is a tabulation of the elements of script interesting to graphology, the second and briefest section (*L'imagination musicale; psychologie et graphologie*) gives some conventional remarks on creative imagination, on the emotional nature of music, on musical creation and the nature of genius; the third part, perhaps the most interesting as a type of script analysis frequently met with, presents a large number of studies of the handwritings of composers, ranging from Lully to Bizet.

The method is strikingly simple and of persuasive elegance. A few representative quotations may suffice: ". . . L'écriture grande, lorsqu'elle est suffisamment active, signifie: sentiment élevé de la personnalité, grandes aspirations. L'écriture petite—chez les gens supérieurs et cultivés—veut dire finesse, soin du détail. . . ." (p. 29). Again, in the chapter on J. Haydn: ". . . La dimension généralement petite de l'écriture atteste la finesse de l'esprit et aussi le soin et le souci des détails . . ." (p. 113); and on Mozart: ". . . Il y avait en lui une finesse native (écriture petite) . . ." (p. 120); on Beethoven: ". . . La grandeur de l'imagination est visible dans l'ampleur des mouvements, dans la forme arrondie de l'écriture; sa puissance dans l'énergie, dans la fermeté du tracé . . ." (p. 13). On Schubert: ". . . L'inspiration délicate, élevée et même empreinte de mysticisme (écriture légère, ponctuation élevée, finales montantes) . . ." (p. 154); and on Bizet: ". . . Par moments, certaines poussées d'idéalisme (ponctuation assez élevée) donnent de la hauteur à l'inspiration (notamment dans *L'Arlésienne*) . . ." (p. 225). On the musician in general: ". . . Son intelligence est claire (écriture claire, espacée) . . ." (p. 66).

The formula for these interpretations is simple, too simple, it appears. Take an adjective which applies to the appearance of the script—preferably a spatial term, such as "small," "grand," "rising," "descending," "elevated"—or a qualifying word like "powerful," "fine," etc., and apply it in its metaphorical meaning to the character of the writer. Nothing could be easier.

But is not this basically the same naive technique that is employed by graphological systems like that of Klages, especially when they rely on spatial symbolism, such as "closed" patterns indicating "closed" character, "open" patterns "open" character, or when the predominance of long strokes above the line is interpreted as unstable equilibrium, waywardness, enthusiasm, or idealism, and the predominance of long strokes beneath the line as realism or materialism? Actually, however, the two methods are radically different. For, according to Klages, the symbolic connotations of "closed" and "open" and of "up" and "down," naive as they may be, are not inventions of the graphologist, but correspond to notions inherent in all our minds and thus they can be taken as a legitimate starting point for graphological interpretation.

arcade shape, closing toward the top.[14] In a written page there may be a preponderance of pen movements above or beneath the lines which result in a large proportion of long upstrokes and short downstrokes or vice versa.[14] Finally, one aspect inherent in ordinary script, and perhaps the most important characterological symptom, is the spatial arrangement of the page resulting in varying degrees of "rhythm" and "harmony," terms of paramount importance in Klages' system of graphology, which is based, to a great extent, on "allgemeines Formniveau" (general level of forms).

What then are the graphic elements of ordinary writing which are also to be found in musical script? The size of notes and other musical symbols can vary almost as much as those of characters in ordinary script. Likewise, pressure and shading and many other habits of pen motion, such as directness, firmness, smoothness, tremor, speed, continuous or broken design of single symbols, slant of single script elements (such as stems and bar lines in musical notation) vary almost equally in both fields of writing.

Certainly this situation leaves a sufficiently wide range for individuality in musical script. Whether these graphic elements, taken by themselves, are indicative of the character of the composer, is another question, and obviously one of little relevance. No graphologist is likely to restrict his analysis of a composer's personality to musical script. In general, letter-writing may be more revealing. On the other hand, musical script is of no mean value as supplementary evidence, as perhaps has become clear in our earlier chapter on space sensitivity. Many graphological treatises show a particular interest in the handwritings of musicians as especially gifted or particularly emotional and sensitive individuals, or as individuals afflicted by other "déformations professionnelles"; and it seems all the more surprising that these books do not observe them in the very center of their professional domain, their scores.

To say that the ordinary hand and the musical notation of the same writer are related to each other would amount to a commonplace. If personality manifests itself at all in writing, it must do so in any type of writing. Any comparison of the scores and letters of a composer bears this out. And often one can trace in minute detail certain ingrained habits of pen motion, shading, etc., recurring in both types of writing. An example is Richard Wagner's sketch for the *Ride of the Valkyries* (see plate 131). After the first two staves written in pencil, notes and words continue in ink—and here the text shows a striking resemblance to the notes: in the words of the text the long vertical strokes are all thin, the short horizontal strokes fat (see the *z* in "ziehen," "zu," "zeugen"; the *d* in "Süden," "kämpfenden," "das"; and the *h*'s and *k*'s). The same distinctive shading appears in the notes: the note-heads, set down with the pen touching the paper, are fat, of course, but so are also the horizontal ledger lines, whereas the stems are thin. Evidently letterscript as well as notes were produced by the same motion of the pen: that is, with the pen pointing toward the left margin and producing marked shading when travelling toward the right, but thin upward and downward strokes when moving sideward. Pen motions like these were quite frequent among musicians, for they facilitated— with the steel pen at least—the drawing of the fat flags or cross strokes for eighth-notes and smaller time values. There was less of a problem with the feather quill which could travel with equal ease in any direction except directly against its point. As plate 131 reveals, the peculiarities of the ink writing hardly appear at all in the pencil-script.

Observations like these, matching notation with letterhand, can be made by the reader throughout virtually all the plates of this book; they are of technical rather than psychological and musical interest. More rewarding are the instances in which letterscript is affected by its use in the score. Words or single characters, when used continuously for notational purposes, as expression marks, for instance, may gradually change in form. Repeated over and over again throughout the same score or even on the same page, they gain speed and fluency, they are condensed and simplified and may end up in shrunken form as shorthand signs, which may then remain confined to the scores of an individual composer or be taken over by others and become universally accepted symbols. Such gradual condensation we find, for instance, in the dynamic marks of Mozart. *Forte-piano* is indicated in the violin concerto K 219, composed 1775, by half words, such as *for:pia:* sometimes underlined and, occasionally, by *f:* and *p:* (plate 61); in the score of *Don Giovanni*, composed 1787, *f:* and *p:* suffice, and *fp* is written either in two detached letters or condensed into a beautiful compound sign written without lifting the pen (plate 72). The climax is reached in elegant monogram-like patterns, such as the *sfp*, likewise in *Don Giovanni* (plate 67), *s* and *p* are written in one continuous line, then the *f* cuts through; the second *sfp*: even shows the two dots connected—transitional forms in this evolution may be found in plates 63, 67 (upper staves), 68 (throughout).

A similar case of condensation is the simplification of *col B* into *ColB* (plates 62, 63), or later into *CoB* (plates 75, 80).

Condensations of *ff* or *fff* into a one-line pattern are frequent; plate 122 shows an example from Verdi's *Attila*.

In the example from Richard Wagner we saw both scripts, in letter-writing and score-writing, produced by the same way of holding the pen. In the examples from Mozart we saw letter-hand influenced by its musical environment, or, more precisely, the transformation of certain letterhand signs by their use for musical purposes. A third example will illustrate another and deeper seated phenomenon: the origin of new and highly individual note shapes in accord with the peculiarities of a composer's letterhand. In this respect Brahms' writing is most characteristic. Let us turn first to his musical script. In plate 150 from the *Vergebliches Ständchen*, composed in 1882, the eighth-notes which are crossed by ledger lines are written in an ingeniously simplified form (see bass staff of the pianoforte part). The notehead is represented by a short vertical; this is crossed by the ledger line which then curves downward into the stem in an uninterrupted motion. The advantages of this procedure are obvious. The notehead is likely to flow out into a blot when crossed by the ledger line. This danger is avoided, or at least diminished, if two lines cross each other at a right angle. Furthermore this condensed design is time-saving. Normally the writing of head, ledger line, and stem would require three quill motions. Brahms manages in two. A strikingly similar procedure can be observed in the script where the small hook over the *u* merges with the letter that follows it, in one uninterrupted line, for instance in the words "gut" of the tempo indication and "Guten," "auf," and "aus" of the text.

The practical advantage of these contrivances—not to call them tricks—appears even more clearly when two ledger lines occur, as in the first note of bar 3 (piano bass); here the stem is not even attached to the notehead but travels out from the lower of the two ledger lines, thus reducing to a minimum the dangerous crossing of wet strokes. Variants of these shapes with the stems going up can be seen in fig. N (*Händel Variations*).

Different in shape but following precisely the same principle of simplification are the half-notes crossed by ledger lines (fig. *O. Waltzes*, Op. 59). Here the usual oval notehead is replaced by a double hook resembling a question mark. This necessitates only one crossing instead of two, again saving one motion of the pen. One may assume that such a writing habit evolved gradually through the following stages:

The writing peculiarities mentioned became fixed very early in Brahms' life—no wonder, since even as a boy he was accustomed to copy any music of interest to his curious mind. The reader will find them consistently employed in our plates 143 to 151, dating from 1861 to 1892. It would require a monograph on Brahms' script to analyze the numerous similar writing devices with which the scores abound. Two more may be pointed out here, both again illustrating extreme connectedness: the simplified G-clefs (pl. 151, 148) and the resolute fusion of the G-clef with the C-clef (fig. *M.* and pl. 151).

Let us now turn to Brahms' letterhand. The few bars from the *Vergebliches Ständchen* in fig. *M* give us one glimpse of the peculiarities manifested side by side in his letter- and score-writing. The relation between these two types of script is by no means as obvious as in Wagner's writing. Actually, however, Brahms' letter-script abounds in devices that correspond to his score writing: firmness, straightforwardness, vigor and regular though entirely unpedantic spacing. We recognize in it the same consistent tendency to extreme connectedness[15] achieved by the same little shortcuts of pen motion. Trying to establish whether his score influenced his letter-script, or his letter-script the score, would amount to asking the time-honored chicken and egg question. The gradual evolution in both fields of script which may be observed throughout Brahms' life proceeds along parallel lines—a characteristic and gradually progressing tendency toward reduction to the essentials. Fig. 3, a section from the copy of folksongs made by the fifteen-year-old, shows the beginning of his devices for simplification. Text and notes are still predominantly schoolhand. *I*-dots and *u*-hooks are for the most part still detached; half-notes are of disconnected two-motion design; but some traces of legato-writing appear, especially in the eighth-notes crossed by ledger lines and in the connected clefs.

Fig. 4A, from a letter written in 1862, may be compared with the *Händel Variations* and *Waltzes*. The writing has gained in connectedness. *I*-dots remain still detached in words like "ich," "ein," "mir," "die," "sind," but appear connected in "Begriff" (line 1), "lieb" (line 3), "anzubieten" (line 5), "Variationen" (line 6), "Preis" (line 8), etc. Hooks over the *u* appear connected not only where the link is invited by the shape of the next letter, as for instance, in

[15] Increasing disconnectedness in single signs can be recognized in the scripts of Schumann and Hugo Wolf parallel with the change in their letterhands. Here the progressive clouding of their minds can be clearly followed in the disintegration of their scripts. Notes and other musical signs assume a more and more pointillistic character, and single words dissolve more and more into detached syllables, and these again into separate letters. Often the degree of connectedness changes abruptly, sometimes within the same page. Thus in Hugo Wolf's last letters, even long words appear in connected script while others nearby are completely broken up into separate characters. According to Ludwig Klages, *Handschrift und Charakter*, 23rd ed. p. 126: "Inconsistency in the degree of connectedness indicates a much more central proclivity towards disturbance than the one that we have found manifested by variability of slant, alignment, etc. . . ."

Not to be confused with this phenomenon is the frequent and variable disconnectedness that appears in Beethoven's score- and letterhand. It occurs only sporadically and is occasionally contrasted by extreme connectedness; not only are long words sometimes written in one single unbroken line, but several words may be linked together without the quill ever leaving the paper (in many letters and in the *Heiligenstädter Testament*; see also the *alla breve* in plate 89).

"anzubieten" (line 5), but also in words like "neues" (line 1), whereas "unterlassen" (line 3) and "zum" (line 4) show them detached.

FIG. 3. Detail from a collection of folksongs, made by Brahms at the age of fifteen.

A late letter (1891, FIG. 4B) shows connectedness even further developed; especially characteristic are "hieraus" (line 1) and "voraus" (line 9); the combination of *u* and *p* in "Reichs-Haupt-Bank" (line 15) and the connection of *i*-dots not with the next but with the second following letter, as in "einfachen" (line 7).[16]

It is not easy to sum up in a few words the highly individual flavor of a script like this in both scores and letters. But if one may for once yield to temptation and go beyond technical observations, one may say that this script, taken in its complexity, shows the practical mind of a craftsman who knew how to shape his tools to serve his craft. And, like his art itself, this tool is restricted to the bare essentials. It tries to say much with little. Averse to mannerism

[16] It is neither accidental nor irrelevant that Brahms—unlike Wagner even in this respect—preferred the goose quill to the modern steel pen, even in his mature years (see, Alfred von Ehrmann, *Johannes Brahms*, Leipzig, 1933, p. 14). And when he occasionally resorted to the steel pen, he was made unhappy by its impersonality and lack of responsiveness. On January 28, 1859, he wrote to Joachim: ". . . I am trying to force this sharp and hard steel pen from the *Sahr* to describe to you. . . ." This is not conservatism in a narrow sense but a deep reverence for the voices of the past which made this master collect and arrange old folksongs, edit Handel, gather a remarkable collection of musical autographs, among them Mozart's G minor Symphony and several Quartets by J. Haydn, prefer the natural horn to the modern valve horn in the Horn Trio, and end his last symphony with a *Passacaglia*.

A. Brahms' letter to Breitkopf & Härtel March 1862   B. Brahms' letter to Simrock May 1891

and ostentation, it reflects the artistic honesty and self-restraint of the master who once re-minded the young Richard Strauss that many melodies, all piled up on the same triad, still do not make counterpoint.

SELECTIVE BIBLIOGRAPHY

I. HISTORY OF WRITING IN GENERAL

Karl Faulmann, *Illustrierte Geschichte der Schrift*, Vienna, 1880
———*Das Buch der Schrift*, Vienna, 1878
H. Fichtenau, *Mensch und Schrift im Mittelalter* (Veröffentlichungen des Instituts für österreichische Geschichtsforschung), Vienna, 1946 (review in *Speculum*, October 1947)
Carroll Gard, *Writing, Past and Present*, New York, 1937
Hans Jensen, *Geschichte der Schrift*, Hannover, 1925
Georg Lang, *Die Technik der Feder; der Weg zur Schreibkunst, sachlich begründet und methodisch erläutert. Ein Vortrag mit ergänzenden Abhandlungen zur Federtechnik, Schriftästhetik und Schreibmethodik*, München, 1905
Georg Mendelssohn, *Der Mensch in der Handschrift*, Leipzig, 1928-1930
Adele Millicent Smith, *Printing and writing materials: their evaluation*, Philadelphia, 1901
Jan Tschichold, *Geschichte der Schrift in Bildern*, Basel, 1940

II. NOTATION SINCE 1600

Putnam Aldrich, *Ornamentation in J. S. Bach's organ works*, New York, 1950

Willi Apel, *Notation of Polyphonic Music 900-1600*, Cambridge, Mass., 1944 (second edition)

Adam Carse, *The Orchestra in the XVIIIth century*, Cambridge, 1940. (See Chapter V, "Score and Parts")

Friedrich Chrysander, "*Abriss einer Geschichte des Musikdrucks vom 15.-19. Jahrhundert*" (*Allgemeine Musikalische Zeitung*, 1879, no. 11-16)

E. David and M. Lussy, *Histoire de la notation musicale*, Paris, 1882

Arnold Dolmetsch, *The Interpretation of the Music of the XVIIth and XVIIIth Centuries*, London, 1915

Guido Gasperini, *Storia della semiografia musicale*, Milan, 1905

R. E. M. Harding, *Origins of musical time and expression*, London, 1938

Archibald Jacob, *Musical handwriting or how to put music on paper*, New York, 1949 (see especially chapter 5 dealing with "spacing" and p. 61 ff.)

Ralph Kirkpatrick, "Eighteenth-Century Metronomic Indications," *American Musicological Society Papers*, 1938

Edward E. Lowinsky, "On the use of scores by sixteenth-century musicians," *American Musicological Society Journal*, Spring 1948, pp. 17-23

Hugo Riemann, *Studien zur Geschichte der Notenschrift*, Leipzig, 1878

———"Notenschrift und Notendruck," *Festschrift zur 50 jährigen Jubelfeier des Bestehens der Firma Röder*, Leipzig, 1896

Heinrich Schenker, *Zur Ornamentik*, Vienna, 1908

Willy Tappolet, *La notation musicale et son influence sur la pratique de la musique du moyen âge à nos jours*, Neuchâtel, 1947

Charles Francis Abdy Williams, *The Story of Notation*, London, 1903

Johannes Wolf, *Handbuch der Notationskunde*, Leipzig, 1913-1919

———*Musikalische Schrifttafeln*, Bückeburg, 1923

———*Die Tonschriften*, Breslau, 1924

III. PHYSIOLOGY AND PSYCHOLOGY OF WRITING; GRAPHOLOGY

Gordon W. Allport and Philip E. Vernon, *Studies in expressive movement*, New York, 1933

Gordon W. Allport, *Personality, a psychological interpretation*, New York, 1937 (especially the analysis of "expressive features," p. 481)

R. Astillero, *Grafologia scientifica*, Milan, 1928

H. H. Busse, *Die Handschriftendeutungskunde*, Leipzig, 1902

J. Crépieux-Jamin, *Traité pratique de graphologie*, Paris, 1885

———*L'écriture et le caractère* (3rd ed.), Paris, 1896. Translated under the title *Handwriting and Expression*, London, 1892

———*The Psychology of the Movements of Handwriting* (translated and arranged by L. K. Given-Wilson), London, 1926

June E. Downey, "Graphology and the Psychology of Handwriting," *Educational Psychology Monographs*, no. 24, Baltimore and New York, 1919

Kurt Goldstein, *Language and language disturbances*, New York, 1948 (especially p. 126)

A. Gross, "Untersuchungen über die Schrift Gesunden und Geisteskranker," *Psychologische Arbeiten*, vol. 2, 1899

Edouard Hocquart, *L'art de juger de l'esprit et du caractère des hommes sur leur écriture*, Paris, 1812

Emile Javal, *Physiologies de la lecture et de l'écriture*, Paris, 1905

Ludwig Klages, *Ausdrucksbewegung und Gestaltungskraft*, Leipzig, 1913

———"Begriff und Tatbestand der Handschrift," *Zeitschrift für Psychologie*, vol. 63, 1912

———*Einführung in die Psychologie der Handschrift*, Heilbronn, 1924

——*Graphologie*, Leipzig, 1932

——*Die Grundlagen der Charakterkunde* (10th ed.), Zürich and Bonn, 1948

——*Handschrift und Charakter* (23rd ed.), Zürich, 1949

——*Die Probleme der Graphologie, Entwurf einer Psychodiagnostik*, Leipzig, 1910

Cesare Lombroso, *Grafologia*, Milan, 1895

S. V. Margadant, *Eine tiefenpsychologische Grundlage zur Klages'schen Graphologie*, Amsterdam, 1938

Georg Meyer, *Die wissenschaftlichen Grundlagen des Schreibens* (2nd ed.), Jena, 1925

Jean Hippolyte Michon, *Méthode pratique de graphologie*, Paris, 1878

——*Les mystères de l'écriture*, Paris, 1870

——*Système de graphologie*, Paris, 1875

William Preyer, *Zur Psychologie des Schreibens* (3rd ed.), Leipzig, 1928

Rudolf Pophal, *Grundlegung der bewegungsphysiologischen Graphologie*, Leipzig, 1939

Max Pulver, *Symbolik der Handschrift*, Zürich und Leipzig, 1931

L. Rise, *Character reading from handwriting*, New York, 1927

Robert Saudek, *Experiments with handwriting*, New York, 1928

——"The methods of graphology," *British Journal for Medical Psychology*, vol. 7, 1927

——*The psychology of handwriting*, London, 1925

James Wardrop, *Some Aspects of Humanistic Script 1460-1560*, three discourses given at King's College, Strand, 1952 (not yet published) (reviewed in *Times Literary Supplement*, March 28, 1952)

IV. HANDWRITING OF MUSICIANS

Otto Edwin Albrecht,[1] "Adventures and discoveries of a manuscript hunter," *Musical Quarterly*, 1945, vol. 31, pp. 492-503

Bernard Champigneulle, *Les plus beaux écrits des grands musiciens*, Paris, 1940

Jean Chantavoine, "On the handwriting of Beethoven," *Le Manuscrit Autographe*, no. 22, Paris, July 1929, pp. 62ff.

Alfred Einstein, "Mozart's Handwriting and the Creative Process," *Papers read at the International Congress of Musicology*, New York, September 1939; published by the Music Educators' National Conference for the American Musicological Society, New York, 1944.

Hans Gál, *Wolfgang A. Mozart, Zwei Rondos, D dur und A moll, nach den Handschriften*, Universal-edition, Vienna, 1923

Oswald Jonas, "Musikalische Meisterhandschriften," *Der Dreiklang*, nos. 1 and 2, Vienna, 1937

——"Adventures with Manuscripts," *Music Library Association Notes*, vol. 3, March 1946, p. 135

Georg Kinsky, *Musikhistorisches Museum von Wilhelm Heyer in Cöln; Katalog*; vol. 4 (Musik-Autographen), Cologne, 1916

Hermann Kretzschmar, Preface to vol. 44 of the *Collected Works of J. S. Bach*

Heinrich Schenker, *Erläuterungsausgabe der letzten fünf Sonaten Beethovens op. 101*, Vienna, 1920-1921

Ludwig Schiedermair, *W. A. Mozarts Handschrift in zeitlich geordneten Nachbildungen*, Bückeburg and Leipzig, 1919

Wolfgang Schmieder, *Musiker-Handschriften in 3 Jahrhunderten*, Leipzig, 1939

Georg Schünemann, *Musikerhandschriften von Bach bis Schumann*, Berlin and Zürich, 1936

Donald Tovey, *A Musician talks I. The Integrity of Music*, London, 1941 (pp. 112ff.)

Max Unger, *Beethovens Handschrift*, Bonn, 1926 (*Veröffentlichungen des Beethovenhauses*, no. 4), (see also: *Bericht über den musikwissenschaftlichen Kongress in Basel, 1924*)

Louis Vauzanges, *L'écriture des musiciens célèbres; essai de graphologie musicale*, Paris, 1913

---

[1] While this book was in press Prof. Albrecht's *Census of Autograph Music Manuscripts of European Composers in American Libraries*, University of Pennsylvania Press, 1953, appeared. Its title should be added to this bibliography.

DESCRIPTION OF THE PLATES

Claudio Monteverdi (1567-1643)

L'INCORONAZIONE DI POPPEA[1] (1, 2)

Opera musicale in three acts with a prologue. Text by Giovanni Francesco Busenello. 108 folios, 10 staves to a page. Size: 21.2 x 29.1 cm.

No autograph heading. On the back of the volume is written "Nerone."

Undated. Composed 1642 in Venice.

First performed 1642 in the Teatro SS. Giovanni e Paolo, Venice. Later performances of the opera were given at Naples in 1651 under the title *Nerone*.

Published in Hugo Goldschmidt, *Studien zur Geschichte der Italienischen Oper im 17. Jahrhundert*, Leipzig, 1904, Vol. II, p. 56ff., and arranged by G. Francesco Malipiero, Universal Edition (No. 9608), 1931. Facsimile edition by Giacomo Benvenuti, Milano, 1938.

Collection: Biblioteca Nazionale di San Marco, Venice.

The *Incoronazione* is the last dramatic work of Monteverdi, composed when he was seventy-five. The manuscript in the library of San Marco was for a long time the only copy known; in 1930 another one turned up in the Conservatorio di San Pietro a Majella in Naples which may have served for the performance of 1651 in Naples.[2] Its authenticity as a manuscript by Monteverdi's own hand has been questioned. Goldschmidt[3] maintained that it was written by a copyist in the first half of the seventeenth century; Malipiero claimed the first and third acts as autograph and attributed the second act to a copyist's hand.[4] On the basis of a careful investigation of the manuscript, Giacomo Benvenuti[5] distinguishes in it no less than seven hands, four of them musical ones and three which wrote only words. Among the very few staves of music convincingly attributed to Monteverdi's hand is the first leaf of the manuscript which is only six staves high, while all the rest of the manuscript (213 written pages) is in ten staves.

PLATE IA and IB show recto and verso of this leaf containing the *sinfonia*.

The *sinfonia*, for three instrumental parts, consists of two sections, both of them with the same bass. The first section is in duple time, the second is a rhythmic transformation of the first into triple meter marked 3/2, as was customary in Monteverdi's time in combinations

[1] The reader might have expected our first plate to be the famous page with the "Lasciatemi morire" from the *Lamento d'Arianna* from the Biblioteca Nazionale Centrale, Florence, which would have carried the sequence of illustrations in this anthology back to the year 1608. In the literature on Monteverdi this page has been reproduced again and again for generations and apparently accepted as his autograph. Even Monteverdi connoisseurs like Louis Schneider in his *Claudio Monteverdi*, Paris, 1921, had not questioned its authenticity. Since then Giacomo Benvenuti has made a careful study of Monteverdi's script for the facsimile edition of the *Incoronazione* manuscript in the Biblioteca Marciana and has established convincingly—though with little explanation of the single characteristics of Monteverdi's hand—those few lines of music and other passages in the score of the *Incoronazione* which can reliably be attributed to Monteverdi's hand. Using this investigation as a starting point, and also taking into consideration the signed letters of Monteverdi for comparison, one is led inevitably to conclude with scarcely a doubt that the *Lamento* was not written in Monteverdi's hand.

[2] See the preface to the edition by Malipiero, pp. III and IV.

[3] *Studien zur Geschichte der Italienischen Oper im 17. Jahrhundert*, Leipzig, 1901, Vol. II, p. 56.

[4] Pp. III and IV.

[5] Preface to the facsimile edition of the manuscript of the *L'incoronazione di Poppea* in the Biblioteca Nazionale di S. Marco.

of two dances of different meter. A dance in duple meter was followed by a quicker after-dance in triple meter; such dances were the Passamezzo and Saltarello in the seventeenth century, and earlier, in the sixteenth century, the somewhat slower Pavane and Gaillarde. The signature 3/2 does not indicate triple time in the modern sense. Rather it is the sign for the old proportio tripla[6] or proportio sesquialtera indicating (in accordance with the old tradition of mensural notation still alive in Monteverdi's time) the duration of the time units of the second section in exact ratio to those of the preceding section. In this case the signature shows that three time units after the signature equal in duration two of the same time units before

the signature. In other words: ♩ ♩ ♩ of section 2 = ♩ ♩ of section 1, and not ♩ = ♩ The effect, thus, is a quickening of the tempo in the second section.[7]

The black notes in the second section have exactly the same duration as if they were white; they are used to make clear the shifts of accent involved in the hemiole relation

♩ ♩ ♩ ♩ ♩ ♩ = ○ ○ ○

The writing is forceful and clear, in large fluent notes, and yet it shows those fine, almost imperceptible irregularities which are absent, as a rule, from the neat and regular scripts of professional copyists. Also the character of the few corrections (bars 3 and 11) seems to suggest that they would not have been made by a copyist.

♩ ♩ ♩ ♩ (♩) This is consistently the shape of the notes. The heads of the half-notes are oval-shaped and written obliquely, slanting up to the right. All this points to a comparatively upright position of the quill and to an initial quill motion and predominant tendency from right to left which, by the way, is evident also in the lettering of *Sinfo:* and tallies with the script of the ascertained letters of Monteverdi. The script is well connected with the note-heads written in a single round motion and the stems drawn out without lifting the quill from the paper[8] (see also the *4* in the bass part of the bars 8, 22, 29). The clefs and braces are amazingly round and firm for the writing of a seventy-five-year-old man.

The bass is only scantily figured; except for the indication of *7 6* in the fourth bar, only the cadences are marked by *4 3*. After the last bar in the bass part of page 1, a custos musicus[9] forewarns the eye as to the position of the first note on the corresponding staff on the following page. Differing from general practice of the time which employed the custos at the end of every staff, Monteverdi uses this sign sparingly.

PLATE 2 shows the third page of the manuscript. Its first two staves again contain the bass part of the *sinfonia*; the remainder, in an entirely different hand, comprises the beginning of the *Prologo* with the recitative of *Fortuna*, which in the succeeding pages is followed by the appearance of *Virtù, Amore* and a *Coro di amori*. The bass, unlike that of plates 1A and 1B, is entirely unfigured; the sharps above the notes indicate a major third. Here the bar lines

[6] Thus the after-dances, such as the Gagliarda and the Saltarello were called Proportz or Tripla.

[7] Curt Sachs, "Some Remarks about Old Notation," *Musical Quarterly*, July 1948. Arthur Mendel: edition of Heinrich Schütz, *The Christmas Story*, New York, 1949, preface, p. XII ff.

[8] It is precisely this high degree of connectedness which helps to distinguish the few passages written by Monteverdi from the other hands in this manuscript.

[9] An explanation of the custos musicus is found in a source as late as Leopold Mozart, *Versuch einer gründlichen Violinschule*, I. Hauptstück 3. Abschnitt, §26.

occur after each 11th note only, dividing each of the two sections into four parts. The extremely condensed writing in these two staves suggests that they were inserted after the recitative of *Fortuna* was written. A comparison of the notes in the first leaf of the manuscript (plates 1A, 1B) with this bass part leaves no doubt that they are by the same, that is, Monteverdi's hand. There is the same connected script, the same time signatures, the same sharps with approximately upright verticals, the same custos.

The hand which wrote the recitative of *Fortuna* is strikingly different. The writing is less connected, the sharps are slanting, the C clefs differ and likewise the custos which is added here to each staff individually. There is, moreover, a certain uneasiness in the individual shapes and the whole configuration, quite different from the firm script of the first two staves and of plates 1A and 1B. *Fortuna's* admonition is written for soprano and unfigured bass. The text runs: "Deh' nasconditi o virtù già caduta in povertà non creduta Deità Nume, ch'è senza Tempio. Diva senza devoti e senza Altari disusata disprezzata Abborita (sic!) malgradita et in mio paragon sempre. . . . [schernita]."

Michael Praetorius (1572-1621)
EUPHEMIA HARMONICA[1] (3-6)

Cantata, for eight voices divided into two four-part choruses, dedicated to the Elector Johann Georg I of Saxony and celebrating the birth of his daughter Maria Elisabeth (November 22, 1610).

Eight folded leaves (one for each voice), upon which only the inside pages are written, in a folder with an autograph title page. 9 staves to each page. Size of page: 32 x 20 cm.

Composed 1610.

Collected Works (Ed. by Friedrich Blume), G. Kallmeyer Verlag, Wolfenbüttel, Berlin.

Collection: Sächsisches Hauptstaatsarchiv, Dresden, Germany.

The present manuscript is a typical example of the notation of a polyphonic vocal piece in single parts, before the notation in score arrangement had become generally adopted.

The plates show: the title page, the tenor part of chorus II, the continuation of this tenor part, the second and last page of the bass part of chorus II.

There are no bar lines employed, although they were quite common, long before, in lute and keyboard tablatures.[2] Coordination between the single parts is helped by cues such as *voce* (see Plate 4), indicating a single vocal entry; *omnes* (plates 4, 5, 6) indicating simultaneous entry of all eight voices together and *Instrumento* indicating instrumental entries.

Occasionally, ledger lines are extended to form a short sixth staff line (see plate 6). The brevis is always designed with great care. The semibrevis signs (whole-notes), and also the minims (half-notes) that have downward stems, preserve the old lozenge shape. Continuation signs appear at the end of each staff. In the bass part (plate 6) the ♭ is written between the half circle and the two dots of the bass clef. Note the large initial *A* in plate 4 taken from the first text word.

---

[1] Friedrich Blume, in his "Revisionsbericht" *Collected Works* p. XVII, considers this manuscript the only known, and probably the only preserved musical autograph of Praetorius.

[2] Already in Conrad Paumann's *Fundamentum Organisandi*, Nuremberg, 1452.

Dietrich Buxtehude (1637-1707)

ECCE SUPER MONTES (7)

Cantata for 2 sopranos, alto, tenor, bass, 2 violins and continuo.

6 pages. Size: 20.5 x 32.5 cm.

Autograph heading: "Ad pedes/ J-N-J [In Nomine Jesus]/ Ecce super montes / à. 8:/ Dieter: Buxtehude:"

Composed 1680.

Collection: Kungl. Universitetsbibliotek, Uppsala, Sweden.

The manuscript is written in German keyboard tablature, a method of notation used from about the middle of the sixteenth century until as late as the time of Johann Sebastian Bach. Each vocal and instrumental part is indicated by two superimposed lines of symbols. The upper line indicates the time values of the notes using symbols like A for single notes, and B for groups of notes. The lower one indicates, by means of letters, the pitch of the notes. The words of the text are written beneath each vocal part; the hooks attached to some of the letters indicate accidentals.

PLATE 7 shows 1) an introductory sonata for instruments; 2) a choral section; 3) part of a soprano aria. The sonata (top system from left to right on the plate) consists of four instrumental parts. The choral section (two sopranos, alto, tenor, bass, and three instruments) occupies the next two sections, always from left to right. It begins with the voices and continuo; the instruments enter later. After the double bar there follows a cadence in long sustained chords. The aria is written in two lines, the upper for the soprano (text beneath), the lower for the continuo.

Dietrich Buxtehude (1637-1707)

APERITE MIHI PORTAS JUSTITIAE (8, 9)

Motet for alto, tenor, bass, and two violins. Dedicated to the Royal Swedish Commissarius and Postmaster Cristoffer Schneider.[1]

13 pages. Size: 32.5 x 20.5 cm.

Autograph[2] heading: "Aperite mihi portas iustitiae/ a - 5 - A: T: B: et 2 Violini/ D.B. JJ. [Jesu Juva]."

Undated. Composed before 1662.[3]

Collected Works, Vol. VII. No. 71.

Collection: Kungl. Universitetsbibliotek, Uppsala, Sweden.

PLATE 8 shows the part for the *Bassus Continuus*. The page opens with a short *Sinphonia* (12 bars) marked C_4^6. Then on "Aperite," the voice enters with the mark C_2^3. The continuo is numbered. Notice the repeated *Tutti* and *Presto*. The ♭ signs are now, unlike plate 7, placed after the bass clefs.

---

[1] See André Pirro, *Dietrich Buxtehude*, Paris 1913, p. 500.

[2] Pirro refers to the manuscript as "aspect d'autographe."

[3] According to Pirro, p. 84, the date is unknown.

PLATE 9 shows the alto part. *Sinphonia* and *12* refer to 12 bars of the instrumental introduction. The 2. (voices) preceding the entry of the alto refers to the *a-2* after "Aperite" in the part of the basso continuo.

⌒⁚⌐ The signs call for repetition of phrases of the text.

While the bar lines are fully drawn out through the five-line stave, in the *sinphonia* section of the continuo part, they are only suggested by little dashes in the alto part and in the corresponding section of the continuo.

Score and letter-writing show calligraphic elegance, with the spacing adapted most sensitively to the corresponding time values of the single notes. Note the beautiful continuation signs at the right margin and the direction to turn the page (*Verte*) at the lower right hand corner of the page.

Johann Jacob Froberger (1616[1]-1667)

SUITE NO. 6 AND TOCCATA NO. 1 (10, 11)

From the Second Book of the Toccatas and Suites for Keyboard.

108 folios, in leather binding. Varying number of staves. Size: 26.5 x 18 cm., 18 x 26.5 cm.

Autograph heading: "Libro secondo / Di Toccate, Fantasie, Canzone, Allemande, Courante, Sarabande, Gigue, et altre Partite. / Alla Sac.ᵃ Caes.ᵃ M.ᵗᵃ / Divotissim.ᵗᵉ dedicato / In Vienna li 29. Settembre A° 1649 / Da Gio: Giacomo Froberger."

Composed 1649.

Denkmäler der Tonkunst in Österreich, Vol. XIII and VIII.

Collection: Österreichische Nationalbibliothek, Vienna Ms. 18706.

The two examples chosen from this autograph volume illustrate various methods of notation which Froberger employed. We find there side by side the typical "new" German keyboard tablature, and staff notation with from five to seven staff lines.

PLATE 10 showing the theme, *Prima Partita*, of the famous variations "Auff die Mayrin" forming *Suite No. 6* is in the German keyboard tablature customary from the middle of the seventeenth century up to J. S. Bach. It is written in free three part polyphony, each part consisting of two lines. The upper line contains the symbols indicating the time values, the lower the letters indicating the pitch. No vertical bar lines are used, but the horizontal line beneath the time symbols define each bar. There are four bars in the first section, eight bars in the second; each section is to be repeated. The whole variation suite consists—besides the theme, *Partita 1*— of five more Partitas, among them a Courante, its Double, and a Sarabande.

PLATE 11 shows the opening (first three double staves) and the close (last two double staves) of the first *Toccata* (in A minor) of the Libro Secondo. The script employs six lines for the upper staff, seven for the lower, and can easily be read even today, if the upper five lines of the upper staff are read in the G clef, the lower five lines of the lower staff in the bass clef, the remaining lines being considered as ledger lines. Bar lines occur only sporadically. The writing

---

[1] The year of Froberger's birth has been disputed. Kurt Seidler, *Untersuchungen über Biographie und Klavierstil J. J. Frobergers*, Königsberg 1930, points to the entry in the birth register of Stuttgart as May 19, 1616.

is extremely neat and well spaced and aims at calligraphic elegance, especially in the waving cross strokes. The quaint ornamental embellishment of the initial of the title occurs in many of Froberger's autographs; likewise the playful *m's* (*manu*) preceding the final flourish that terminates in a *pria* (*propria*).

Johann Jacob Froberger (1616-1667)

LAMENT ON THE DEATH OF FERDINAND IV, KING OF THE ROMANS (12, 13)

From Suite No. 12 of the Fourth Book of Toccatas and Suites for Keyboard.
114 folios, in leather binding. Varying number of staves. Size: 26.5 cm., resp. 18 x 26.5 cm.
Autograph heading: "Libro Quarto/ di/ Toccate, Ricercari, Capricci, Allemande, Gigue/ Courante, Sarabande/ Composto et humilissm[te] dedicato Alla Sacra Cesarea/ Maestà/ di/ Fernando/ Terzo/ da Giov: Giacomo Froberger. . . ."
Composed 1657.
Denkmäler der Tonkunst in Österreich, Vol. XIII.
Collection: Österreichische Nationalbibliothek, Vienna, (Ms. 18707).

The Suite No. 12 of the *Fourth Book* consists of three pieces, the second being a Courante, the third a Gigue. The first, which is reproduced in full in plates 12 and 13 is the famous *Lament* on the death of the young Roman king Ferdinand IV who died April 2, 1657 ("Lamento/ Sopra la dolorosa perdita della/ Real M.[stà] di/ Ferdinando/ IV. Rè de Romani"). It is a mournful Allemande, by its very style obviously intended for the clavichord. Froberger was very fond of such "character" pieces,[1] thus contributing to a line of program music that leads through Denis Gaultier's *Tombeaux*, François Couperin's *Ordres* depicting physiognomies and temperaments, Kuhnau's *Biblische Historien*, and Schumann's *Wald* and *Kinderszenen* to Virgil Thomson's *Musical Portraits*, such as those of *Dorothy Thompson* and *Fiorello La Guardia*.[2] In the present composition the programmatic character is strongly enhanced by Froberger's drawings at the opening and close of the little piece. The first shows an hourglass flanked by two mourning putti under bare trees. The second illustrates by clouds and angels the heavenly glory ready to receive the king's soul that slowly ascends toward it upon a ladder of three unbroken octaves in C major.[3]

Notice the little *t's* (trills) added to the treble melody. In the *Denkmäler der Tonkunst in Österreich* additional bar lines are added to establish a 4/4 notation.

---

[1] Another famous piece of this kind by Froberger is his *Plainte, faite à Londres pour passer la mélancolie.*

[2] Mattheson, in his *Grundlage einer Ehrenpforte,* Leipzig, 1732, reports that Froberger was able to play on the "clavir" entire stories depicting the persons involved with their mental characteristics ("Abmahlung der dabey gegenwärtig gewesenen Personen, samt ihren Gemütheigenschaften").

[3] Another dirge by Froberger, composed for his friend the French organist Blancheroche, the *Tombeau fait à Paris sur la mort de Monsieur Blancheroche; lequel se joue fort lentement à la discrétion sans observer aucune mesure* terminates also in a diatonic scale of three octaves but here in the minor and leading downward, evidently to the grave.

Henry Purcell (ca. 1659-1695)

THE EPICURE (14)

Two part song for treble (or tenor) and bass. Words by Abraham Cowley.

Four pages, six double staves to each page. Size: 32 x 20.5 cm.

Autograph heading: "The Epicure by Mr. Cowley." At the end, signature: "Mr. Purcell."

Undated. Date of composition unknown. Printed in *The Banquet of Musick/ or / A collection of the newest and best songs / composed by several of the Best Masters*, VI, in 1692; and later in *Orpheus Britannicus*, II, in 1702.

Collected Works, Vol. XXII, no. XXVII, p. 100.

Collection: The Library of Congress, Washington, D.C.

PLATE 14 shows the first of four sections the second and fourth of which are in triple time while the third section is a recitative for the bass in duple time. Characteristic are the G clefs. Separate sixteenth notes are designed in the usual way, A, those which follow dotted notes are written as B.

Observe the care given the musical phrasing with respect to the text: a musical passage has one long slur if it accompanies one syllable (bars 7 and 8), and several slurs if it accompanies several syllables (bars 14-17). The text, in which some words are abbreviated in the old manner ("w" in bar 9ff., i.e., "what") reads as follows: "Underneath this Mirtle Shade on Flowry beds Supinely laid w[i]th O'drous oyls my head ore flowing & around it Roses growing what sho'd I do but drink away the heat and troubles of the day."

Alessandro Scarlatti (1660-1725)

QUANTE LE GRAZIE SON (15)

Cantata in E minor for alto and continuo.

5 pages, 12 staves to each page. Size: 20.1 x 27 cm.

On the cover, in eighteenth century script: "Cantata in E mol/ per la Voci [sic] di Alto/ coll' Basso continuo/ comp: 4° Giug: 1703./ di/ Cavagliere Allessandro Scarlatti./ M. di Capella a Napoli./ (Nato 1659. † 24. Ottobre 1725.)/ Partitura Autografa."

Signed and dated on the first page.

Composed June 4, 1703.

Collection: Maria and Rudolf Floersheim, Wildegg (Aargau), Switzerland.

PLATE 15 shows the opening recitative and the beginning of an aria marked *grave*. The text of the recitative reads: "Quante le grazie son, ch'hai nel bel viso o Soride mio ben Idolo mio; tutti Legami son onde Amor crudo m'avvinse si, che sola te desio; e se dagl'occhi tuoi resto diviso ricco d'affanni son di gioie ignudo. Ogni tuo riso alfin ogni tuo sguardo all'acceso mio Cor è fiama, e dardo." On top of the page the remark "Fortunato Santini al Sig. Aloisio Fuchs."[1]

[1] Abbate Fortunato Santini (1778-1862) was a composer, and musical scholar, who had assembled a famous collection of early music. Aloys Fuchs (1799-1853), an employee in the Austro-Hungarian

As was customary at the time, a large ornamental initial *Q* (beginning of the word "Quante") is placed before the clefs.

Short ties, usually crossing the bar lines, connect sustained bass notes. The bass is numbered throughout.

In the vocal part, the eighth and sixteenth notes are usually not connected by cross strokes, except when several of them correspond to one syllable of the text, as is the case in bar 14.

Sixteenth-notes are usually written as A, but after dotted notes in the older manner B (bar 3 and 7 of the recitative and bar 3 of the aria). Here as always in Scarlatti's scores (see the following plates) notes with upward stems have their heads to the left, whereas those with downward stems have the heads placed on either side.

War Department, and singer in the Imperial Court Chapel in Vienna, was likewise an enthusiastic and successful collector of musical books and scores, particularly autographs. Apparently Santini presented this cantata to Fuchs for his collection.

Alessandro Scarlatti (1660-1725)

ARIA PER CAMERA (16)

For soprano and figured bass.
2 leaves (4 pages), 12 staves to each page. Size: 20.8 x 28.3 cm.
At top of first page: "20. Agosto 1706 // d'Aless° Scarlatti."
Apparently unpublished.
Collection: Accademia Filarmonica, Bologna.

PLATE 16 shows the first page of the manuscript with an opening recitative and the beginning of an aria in *andante lento*. The freely flowing, sinuous writing is echoed by the vigorous brackets and clefs and above all, by the undulating cross strokes, especially in bars 1, 3 and 6 of the aria.

A comparison with the preceding plate shows a difference in the shape of the bass clefs. While in the first plate they open toward the right, in this plate they open—with one single exception (beginning of the aria)—toward the left. But actually both these variants are produced by the same motion of the quill: Scarlatti starts the bass clef with a dot from which the curve is then drawn upwards. If the curve turns out to be short, a half circle is formed, opening toward the left; if the curve turns out longer, a full circle results (see second stave); if the curve turns out even longer and more spirited, a spiral results, opening toward the right.

Alessandro Scarlatti (1660-1725)

LA GRISELDA (17)

Opera in three acts, with "symphonies" and accompaniments for trumpets, horns, flutes, oboes and strings, and a figured bass for harpsichord. Text by Apostolo Zeno.
128 folios, ten staves to each page. Size: 28 x 21 cm.

Autograph heading: "Griselda, opera 114, Posta in Musica Dal Cav^e Alessandro Scarlatti per sua Eccellenza Sig^e Principe Ruspoli In Roma. Xbre 1720 e Genn° 1721."

First performed in 1721 at the Teatro Capranica ("Sala delli illustrissimi signori Capranica") in Rome.

Collection: British Museum, London.

The page shows part of an *Andante* aria in F major sung by *Gualtiero*. Notice the rapid alternation between *tutti* and *solo*, a highly dramatic method of accompaniment. The short and gentle instrumental solo passages in bars 9 and 18 are of especially delicate effect.

Directions like *solo, tutti, piano* are usually emphasized by curves above or beneath. The braces connecting the staves terminate in playful flourishes.

The v signs in bar 3 are equivalent to dots augmenting the time value of the given note.

Repetition is indicated by these signs after the short six-bar instrumental ritornello. The continuo is figured.

The writing at first glance appears strangely different from that in the preceding plates. It seems stiffer and has lost much of its former vigour, but an interval of fifteen years accounts for this sufficiently. A closer inspection reveals the same basic characteristics: for example, the absence of a slant in bar lines and stems, and the cross strokes that thin out toward the right (cf. the last bar of this plate, with the bottom stave of Plate 15, *Quante le grazie son*). Curiously the lettering has changed less than the score writing.

Antonio Vivaldi (ca. 1680-1743)

ARSILDA REGINA DI PONTO (18, 19)

Opera in 3 acts. Text by Domenico Lalli.

Composed 1716. First performance 1716, at the *Teatro S. Angelo*, Venice.

Collection: Biblioteca Nazionale, Turin.

The manuscript consists of 294 leaves and includes two scores of the opera in different hands; the second copy is undoubtedly written by a copyist and lacks the introductory sinfonia; the first copy is in all probability almost entirely written in Vivaldi's own hand. The two pages reproduced are from this first copy which consists of 323 written and 20 blank pages, size 23 x 30 cm.

A monogram in the upper left corner of plate 18 is a composite of many letters. Three of them, D, A and V, most likely stand for Don Antonio Vivaldi. If the others are interpreted as A, R and P, they would seem to represent the initial letters of *Arsilda Regina di Ponto*, but Vivaldi uses the same monogram in several other operas as well as in some works of sacred music.[1]

Plate 18 contains the beginning of a recitative by *Cisardo* (bass) to the text: "Questo, ò Popoli, è il giorno in cui si deve con rinovati voti giurar fede al Regnante: quella, dà cui dipende il

---

[1] For a list of the works in which this monogram appears see Olga Rudge, "In Margine ai Mss, Vivaldiana," in *La Scuola Veneziana*, Note e Documenti, Siena: Libreria Editrice Ticci, 1941, pp. 60-62.

comun bene, e d'ogni regno e'l Nume:..." The accompanying bass is not figured. The braces which join the two staves intersect the large bass clefs, producing a flamboyant pattern.

PLATE 19 shows the beginning of an *Allegro* aria for alto in 3/8 time with the text: "Perchè veggo nel tuo volto l'Idol mio che il cor m'ha tolto per te peno, per te moro e ti chiamo mio tesoro, mà, mà, non parlo già con te."

The energetic writing shows extreme connectedness. The quill is never lifted when it turns from the note head to the stem or from the stem to the flag. The flags, however, that indicate sixteenth-notes (see plate 18, vocal part) are drawn as separate cross strokes not connected with the main flag.

Antonio Lotti (ca. 1667-1740)

LAUDATE PUERI (20, 21)

For two sopranos and alto with instrumental accompaniment. 29 leaves, 10 staves to each page. Size: 23 x 31 cm.
Undated. Unsigned. Apparently unpublished.
Autograph heading: "Laudate Pueri A.B./ 2 Canti, e Alto, con Istromenti."
Collection: Biblioteca Nazionale di San Marco, Venice.

PLATE 20 shows the first page of the manuscript, the beginning of an *Allegro* instrumental introduction in 2/4 time. See *Pian* indicating the beginning of a "concertino" section. The ♭ in bar 9 serves as a ♮.

PLATE 21 shows page 38, a section from a *Gloria* in D minor, in Siciliano rhythm. The preceding page is marked *Largo* and the time given there *12*, i.e. 12/8. The vocal part (alto) moves between two instrumental parts, one of them in the alto clef, the other an octave lower in the bass clef. The bass is unfigured.

The : signs in the vocal part indicate repetition of the text. The text is apparently not in Lotti's hand. The score writing is hasty and vigorous.

Benedetto Marcello (1686-1739)

CHURCH MOTET (22)

With instrumental accompaniment.
Six pages, sixteen staves to each page. Extremely thin paper, some corners missing. Size: 30 x 21.7 cm.
On the first page: "Bened. Marcello" (autograph?).
Undated. Date of composition unknown.
Apparently unpublished.
Collection: Accademia Filarmonica, Bologna.

There is no indication of the type of instruments required. The part between the voice and the continuo apparently is for *violoncello obbligato*.

PLATE 22 shows page 5 of the manuscript. The bass is figured only in a few places. The writing is hasty and irregular, but fluent. There are no bar lines at the right margin.

Benedetto Marcello (1686-1739)

LUCIO COMMODO (23, 24)

Intermezzi and choruses for the tragedy. 54 leaves; 8 staves to each page. Size: 15 x 20 cm.
Autograph heading: "Intermezzi e Cori per la Tragedia di Commodo recitata da Nobili Accademici l'anno 1719, di Benedetto Marcello N.V."
Composed 1719. Performed 1719, probably Venice.
Collection: Biblioteca Nazionale di San Marco, Venice.

PLATE 23 shows page 2 of the manuscript, containing the opening of a *sinfonia* in D major, marked *presto*, for a body of strings. The bass is unfigured. Note the time-saving device of combining the sharps into one single pattern. Unlike Alessandro Scarlatti (see plate 15) Marcello writes notes which have downward stems always with their heads to the right, and those which have upward stems with their heads to the left.

PLATE 24 shows page 7 of the manuscript, the first page of the first *Intermezzo*, with the beginning of a bass recitative. The bass is unfigured. The text (*Spago* deploring the cost of his wedding) is in darker ink. The writing is widely spaced, the single elements of the script-patterns are highly connected. At times the sixteenth-notes have a flag crossing the stem in the older manner, at times the flag is drawn out of the stem so that the whole symbol approximates the modern sign ℓ

Niccolò Antonio Porpora (1686-1766)

GLI ORTI ESPERIDI (25)

"Azione teatrale" in two parts, with "symphonies" and accompaniment for trombe da caccia, oboes, bassoons, strings, and figured bass.[1]
108 leaves, 10 staves to each page. Size 21.5 x 29 cm.
Unsigned. Dated at the end: "22 Agos.to 1721."
Collection: British Museum, London.

PLATE 25 shows the end of a duet (*Allegro*), sung by Venus and Adonis. It is the last page of the first part of the opera, and signed at the right hand lower corner "Fine della p:ma p:te/15. Agosto/ 1721." The manuscript was written while Porpora was still in Venice, eight years before he left for London to lead the opera in the Haymarket Theatre, competing with the King's Theatre, for which Handel was composing at the time.

The score-writing is round and buoyant, quite in accordance with the letter writing. The swelling cross strokes resemble Handel's. Note the ⌣ at the end.

[1] The title given by François Joseph Fétis, *Biographie Universelle des Musiciens*, 12. ed. 1875, Vol. 7, p. 100.

Johann Sebastian Bach (1685-1750)

CLAVIERBÜCHLEIN VOR WILHELM FRIEDEMANN BACH (26-29)

A small bound volume. 138 pages. Size: 17 x 19.5 cm.

Autograph heading inside the front cover: "Clavier-Büchlein/ vor/ Wilhelm Friedemann Bach/ angefangen in/ Cöthen den/ 22. Januar/ Ao. 1720." At the head of the first page the inscription: "I.N.I." [In Nomine Iesu]. At the back of the book the signature of Wilhelm Friedemann Bach at the age of nine.

Compiled by Johann Sebastian Bach in 1720/21.

First published in its entirety in 1927 by the Bärenreiter Verlag, Cassel.

Schmieder, thematic catalogue, p. 659.

Collection: Library of the School of Music, Yale University, New Haven, Conn.

This little book was written by J. S. Bach for his eldest son Wilhelm Friedemann and was possibly also used by others of his pupils. It contains 62 pieces, among them the *Little Preludes*, the *Two and Three Part Inventions* and a number of *Preludes* from *Das Wohltemperierte Clavier*. It also includes several pieces by other composers.

A great number of the pages are beyond any doubt in J. S. Bach's hand; some are just as certainly not written by him, the rest are controversial.[1] Of the four pages selected for reproduction, three are generally accepted as written by J. S. Bach; the first (first *Praeludium* from *Das Wohltemperierte Clavier*) has been widely debated.

PLATE 26 shows the first eleven bars of *Praeludium 1* from *Das Wohltemperierte Clavier*. Several of the hand-ruled staves are reinforced by the quill. The first five bars, with the figuration written out in full, can hardly be attributed to J. S. Bach's hand: the writing is heavy and awkward, like that of a hesitant and little-experienced hand, the brackets are wobbly, the clefs, especially the soprano clef, of pedantic regularity. All this is different in the one bar inserted after bar 4, and also in the last five bars which show the figuration abbreviated by chords. The script is free and flowing; and particularly the clefs resemble those in J. S. Bach's manuscripts. The last four bars are written over erasures.

PLATE 27 shows the second half of *Inventio IV*. Note the vigorous, flowing cross strokes, many of them undulating and tapering toward the right end; and the brisk ties that connect the bass notes throughout the pedal point from bar 4 to 9. Mordents are found in bars 4 and 12. The last three bars are written on a freehand staff added underneath.

PLATE 28 shows the second half of *Inventio XIV* entitled in the autograph "Praeambulum 8." It is one of the most evenly written pages in the *Clavierbüchlein*. However, Bach does not hesitate to break a bar in its middle and continue it in the next staff. The orderly aspect of the page is helped by the visual symmetry of the pattern that forms the main motive:

PLATE 29 which reproduces the close of *Praeambulum 13* is a typical example of increasing condensation in space because of lack of paper. The first staff has 3½ bars, the second, 4½, the third, 4¾, the last added one, 7¼. Here, as in the preceding two plates, ledger lines are frequently extended, thus creating a six or even seven line staff.

[1] Collected Works, Jahrgang 45, Vol. 2, p. LVIII ff. and 213 ff.

Johann Sebastian Bach (1685-1750)

ES IST DAS HEYL UNS KOMMEN HER (30-31)

Cantata for four part chorus, soli, transverse flute, oboe d'amore, two violins, viola and continuo. Text arranged after a song by Paul Speratus.

17 pages; 19 to 24 hand-drawn staves to each page. Size: 36.5 x 23 cm. (including cloth cover).

Autograph heading: "J. J. [*Jesu juva*] Do[meni]ca 6. post Trinitatis. Es ist das Heÿl uns komen her. a 4 Voci. 1 Trav. 1 Hautb./ 2 Violini, Viola e Cont." At the end of first page, probably in the handwriting of Wilhelm Friedemann Bach: "di J. S. Bach/ Propria manu scrpt." At the end in J. S. Bach's hand: "Fine D S Gl." [*Deo soli gloria.*]

Unsigned and undated.

Composed in Leipzig about 1731.[1]

Collected Works Vol. 1, No. 9.

Schmieder, thematic catalogue, No. 9.

Collection: The Library of Congress, Washington, D.C. (Acquired in 1931 from Mrs. Werner Wolffheim in Berlin, with the aid of funds jointly provided by the "Friends of Music in the Library of Congress" and the "Beethoven Association.") The manuscript once belonged to Wilhelm Friedemann Bach.

The manuscript shows several alterations; the entire recitative preceding the final chorale has been re-written. The writing is extremely rapid, with no attention to elegance of appearance. In general Bach's writing ranges from the scrupulously careful to the hasty and casual. The scores of most of the great monumental works, such as *The Art of the Fugue*, the *Brandenburg Concertos*, dedicated to the Margrave of Brandenburg, and the *Musical Offering*, dedicated to Frederick the Great, are of admirable neatness; the *Passions*, the *B Minor Mass*, and the *Sonatas for unaccompanied violin* are marvels of calligraphy. But most of the *Cantatas*, to judge from the autographs or facsimiles I have been able to see, were written for the ordinary routine of performance by his own chorus and orchestra, and accordingly look rather hurriedly written with no more than scant attention to legibility for performers who were used to Bach's handwriting, and who could ask him questions about anything doubtful. Among these latter is the present score.

PLATE 30 shows the first page of the cantata. In the first six-staff system the instruments are indicated as follows: *Travers., Hautb d'Amour, Violino 1, Violino 2.* The next two staves, which are not marked, are intended for viola and continuo. As the page has only 23 staves, this leaves only five staves at the bottom (the last drawn freehand), so Bach writes the two violin parts on one staff.

The smudged passage in bars 10 and 11 is clarified by tablature signs and reads in the *Complete Works* which were prepared from the parts of the cantata:

The page presents the whole ritornello with which the first versus of the cantata opens and closes. The ⌒ in the third bar of the bottom staff indicates the final chord of this versus. The following notes lead over to the entry of the chorus (on the second page of the manuscript).

[1] See Spitta, *Johann Sebastian Bach*, 2nd ed., 1916, II, p. 292.

There the soprano begins with the choral text "Es ist das Heÿl. . . ." Bach quotes the first word "Es" at the bottom of the page under the ⌒ mentioned.

PLATE 31 shows page 7 of the manuscript beginning with bar 94 of the introductory chorus. The four vocal staves, added to the six instrumental ones, result in a ten-staff system. This page shows the three strata typical of a chorale cantata:

    I.   The cantus firmus with the words of the chorale
    II.   The rest of the chorus
    III. The orchestra.

In I. the soprano presents in long notes the chorale melody: "Der Glaub' sieht Jesum Christum an, der hat gnug für uns all getan." II. The other vocal parts move in eighths and enter successively in imitation. III. The instruments move partly with the accompanying voices, partly in patterns involving syncopations and sixteenth notes.

Johann Sebastian Bach (1685-1750)

IN ALLEN MEINEN TATEN (32-34)

Cantata for mixed chorus, soli and orchestra. Words by Paul Fleming (1609-1640).

Twenty pages; 18-20 staves to each page. Size: 34.4 x 22 cm.

Autograph heading: ". . . In allen meinen Thaten/ a 4 Voci, 2 Hautb, 2 Violini, Viola/ Continuo." At the end, in the composer's hand: "Fine. S.D.Gl. [*Soli deo gloria*]/ 1734." The signature "di J. S. Bach" and the designation "Trauungs Cantate" and "nach der Trauung" over the title of versus 7 are not in the composer's hand.

Composed in 1734, in Leipzig.

Collected Works, Vol. XXII, No. 97.

Schmieder, thematic catalogue, No. 97.

Collection: The New York Public Library, New York (presented by the Bliss and Herter families). Previous owners: J. A. Stumpff, Vienna, a friend of Beethoven's, and Frederick Locker, London, who permitted the publication of the cantata in the edition of the *Bach-Gesellschaft*. The inventory of the estate of Carl Philipp Emanuel Bach lists only the autograph parts of the cantata, but not the score.

PLATE 32 shows page 2 of the manuscript, with a section from the first versus of the cantata. This versus consists, in the manner of a French overture, of a short *grave* introduction and a *vivace*. In bar 5 of this *vivace* the chorus enters with the choral tune as cantus firmus in the soprano. Eight bars later the page reproduced begins.

> "In allen meinen Thaten
> lass' ich den Höchsten rathen,
> der Alles kann und hat.
> er muss zu allen Dingen
> soll's anders wohl gelingen,
> selbst geben Rath und That."

In the fifth staff the soprano part is written above the viola and separate from the other vocal parts. Lack of space causes numerous irregularities: groups of notes frequently cross the bar line and trespass into the following bar (see, for example, bar 4, viola, alto, tenor; bar 5, viola; bars 10 and 11, tenor); a small vertical dash usually clarifies the situation. Often more than the regular four sixteenth-notes are joined together (see: bar 3, continuo; bar 4, alto).

PLATE 33 shows page 5 of the manuscript, with the end of versus 2, versus 3 in full, and the beginning of versus 4.

Versus 2 is an aria for basso and continuo to the text: "Er mag's mit meinen Sachen nach seinem Willen machen, ich stell's in seine Gunst." The articulation of the bass motif is carefully indicated.

Versus 3 is marked *Recit*[*ativo*]. Text: "Es kann mir nichts geschehen, als was er hat vorsehen,[1] und was mir seelig ist; Ich nehm es wie er's giebet, was Ihm von mir beliebet, das hab ich auch erkiest."

Versus 4 is marked *Violino Solo* and *Largo*. This solo part is written in the same style and requires the same virtuoso technique as the composer's sonatas for solo violin; double stops abound and passages in linear harmony (bar 7 ff.) are frequent. There are some precise dynamic directions for the violin part: bar 2, *piano*; bar 4, *f*; bar 5, *piano*; bar 6, *f*. The sign at the second beat of bar 5, beneath the second staff, is a B flat (not an F), lower tone of the double stop. Notice *tr*[*illo*] in bars 2 and 6. The dance-like grace of the violin melody is reflected in a writing of similar verve and elegance.

PLATE 34 shows the last page of the autograph headed *Versus ultimus*. It contains the closing chorale score in the following order from top to bottom: 1 and 2, two oboes; 3, first violin; 4, second violin; 5, viola; 6, soprano; 7, alto; 8, tenor; 9, bass; 10, continuo. The two oboes double the soprano, and the continuo doubles the bass; thus the polyphonic texture consists of seven parts.

The text of this versus (printed in the *Collected Works*) is:

> "So sei nun, Seele, deine, und traue dem alleine,
> der dich erschaffen hat;
> es gehe wie es gehe, mein Vater in der Höhe,
> weiss allen Sachen Rath."

In several places added letters clarify the notes. Almost all of the corrections deal with the register of notes; certain passages are transposed an octave higher: see bars 1 and 2, second violin; bar 9, tenor.[2] Several passages are smudged: bar 5, alto[3]; bar 9, viola[4]; and last bar, tenor.[5]

---

[1] Collected Works incorrect: "ersehen."

[2] The Collected Works give bar 9 of the tenor part:

[3] Given in the Collected Works:

[4] Given in the Collected Works:

[5] Given in the Collected Works:

Johann Sebastian Bach (1685-1750)

MEINE SEEL' ERHEBT DEN HERREN (35-36)

Cantata for 4 part chorus, soli, trumpet, 2 oboes, 2 violins, viola and continuo. Words after St. Luke by an unknown author.

12 leaves including wrapper; music on leaves 3-11; verso of leaf 11 blank; as the wrapper is included in the pagination, the back of the wrapper would be leaf 12. 23 staves to a page. Size: 36.5 x 21.5 cm.

Heading on front of the wrapper: "Festa Visitationis/ Mariä/Meine Seel erhebt den Herren/ à/4 Voc:/Tromba/2 Hautbois/ 2 Violini/Viola/e/Continuo./di Sign:/I S Bach."

Undated.

Composed ca. 1740.[1]

Collected Works, Vol. I, No. 10.

Schmieder, thematic catalogue, no. 10.

Collection: The Gertrude Clarke Whittall Foundation Collection, The Library of Congress, Washington, D.C.

PLATE 35 shows leaf 3 verso with the first entry of the chorus *Meine Seel erhebt den Herren*. "Erheben" (to elevate) is depicted by the ascending scale motif in tenor and bass (bars 4-9) both of which are doubled by instruments. On the preceding page, this scale motif appears in inversion (bars 1 and 2 of the continuo). Bar 4 of staff 1 and bar 8 of staff 2 contain corrections; in bars 9 and 10 of the bottom staff the names of two notes (H and C) are added for clarification; in bar 5 of the staves 5 and 8, half-notes have apparently been filled in to make them quarter-notes.

The scoring follows the order, from top to bottom: oboe 1, oboe 2, violin 1, violin 2, viola, vocal parts, continuo; there is no staff for the trumpet, which was probably intended to double the soprano, thereby reinforcing the choral-tune.

PLATE 36 shows leaf 10 verso with a recitative for tenor, accompanied by strings and continuo, with the text: "Was Gott den Vätern alter Zeiten geredet und verheissen hat, erfüllt er auch in Werk und in der That...." The figures of the accompanying strings have phrasing slurs only at their first appearance in bar 10. The bass is for the most part unfigured; only a few accidentals are marked: see the $4\natural$ beneath the B on the third beat of bar 13 and the $7\sharp$ beneath the D in bar 20. In bar 16 clarifying letters *fd* are placed over the part of the first violin.

Strange patterns occur in places where in groups of sixteenth-notes the cross strokes intersect stems that alternatingly run up and down (see bars 12 and 16 of the viola part).

Both plates are characteristic examples of Bach's habit of utilizing the score paper to the last inch, even to the extent of dividing measures between one staff and the next.

[1] According to C. S. Terry, *Bach's Orchestra*, London 1932, p. 191 ff.

Georg Friedrich Handel (1685-1759)

CANTATA FOR ONE VOICE AND INSTRUMENTS (37-38)

10 pages, the last one partly blank. 6 to 8 staves to a page. Size: 17.6 x 23.9 cm.

Autograph heading: "Cantata."

Unsigned and undated.

Collected Works, Vol. 52b, No. 28.

Collection: The New York Public Library, New York. Presented in 1932 by the Bliss and Herter families.

The first page contains an amorous recitative: "Languia di Bocca lusinghiera e bella," written on two staves, the upper for voice, the lower for an unfigured bass.

PLATES 37 and 38 show pages 3 and 4 of the manuscript with parts of the aria which is accompanied by oboes, violins and bass. The text runs: "Dolce bocca labra aurate questo cor non catenate piu non brama liberta." The text has been corrected: "amate" replaced by "aurate"; "perchè brama" by "più non brama"; "ch'incatenate" by "non catenate." The corrected version is retained throughout the rest of the aria. The writing is of the usual Handelian speed and vigour, with the stems drawn out of the heads of the notes in one single unbroken motion. The energetic and curving cross strokes swell in the middle. Of the bar lines, some run through all four staves of the system, others merely through one staff, while others are omitted.

Georg Friedrich Handel (1685-1759)

LOST IN ANGUISH, QUITE DESPAIRING (39)

Aria for soprano with accompaniment of strings.

Four pages, two quintuple staves on a page. Size: 22.4 x 29 cm.

Unsigned and undated. On the contemporary paper cover, the mounted inscription: "The song —Lost in anguish is Handels own handwriting in the Oratorio of Theodora/F. N."

Date of composition uncertain. This Aria differs from the version in the Collected Works, vol. 8, pp. 165-169.

Collection: The Library of Congress, Washington, D.C.

PLATE 39 shows the first page of the manuscript. At the beginning *Sentza Hautbois* and *Largo Assai*, and indications of the orchestration: *Viol[in] 1°, 2°, Viol[in] 3° e Viola*. The part of the second violin has the indication *in unis[on]* with the first violin. The bass is not figured. In bar 1, bass stave, Handel evidently changed A into B. Since the notes became blurred, he added on top "*e e d*." A similar clarification became necessary in bar 5, first violin. There are numerous other corrections.

Only the notes are written by Handel; the balance of the manuscript was prepared by his amanuensis, Smith.[1]

The writing shows Handel's usual strong right slant. The bar lines are separate for each staff. In bars 9 and 11, in the vocal part, he uses the old writing for sixteenth-notes: A and B, while bar 3 shows the modern notation, C.

The highly connected writing shows every evidence of rapidity.

[1] I am indebted for this information to Dr. J. M. Coopersmith.

Georg Friedrich Handel (1685-1759)

MESSIAH (40)

Oratorio. Text selected and arranged from the Scriptures by Charles Jennens.
260 pages; 10 staves to each page. Size: 25.4 x 32 cm.
Signed on the last page: "Fine dell Oratorio./ G. F. Handel. Septemb 12./1741."
Composed August 22 - September 14, 1741.
First performed April 13, 1742, in Dublin.
Collected Works, vol. 45. Facsimile Edition, Deutsche Händelgesellschaft, Hamburg 1892.
Collection: The King's Music Library, British Museum, London.

The *Messiah* is one of the famous examples of incredibly fast composition. Handel wrote the score in 24 days. Even the mere technical task of putting this gigantic work on paper—not to mention composing it—would seem inconceivable, if one were not aware of the many time-saving devices which Handel employed in his writing. Of his musical shorthand the plate reproduced is a typical example. It shows page 179 of the manuscript, containing bars 36-45 from the aria for basso near the end of the second part of the oratorio. The text, no less fitting today than in Handel's time, reads: "Why do the nations so furiously rage together, why do the people imagine a vain thing?"

Handel employs many simplifications and shorthand devices: groups of four sixteenth-notes are frequently represented by one single quarter note without stem (see bars 1, 2, 5, 6, 7, etc.). Ledger lines are not restricted to single notes but extended sometimes for the full length of the bar (bar 9). Signs for doubling of instruments also save time (see bar 11, second violin). The bar lines are drawn arbitrarily, at times through all five staves, usually embracing periods of two or four bars; at other times, only through single staves; and sometimes even omitted (see, for example, measures 2-3 of the vocal part, and 1-2 of the continuo).

There are no expression marks, except for very scarce dynamic marks such as the *forte* on top of bar 5, which evidently is meant only for the G major chord, bars 5 and 6.

The writing, itself furiously raging, has the strong forward slant typical of Handel, and seems to press on with irresistible impetus. One thing, however, is consistently preserved in all this hurry: the note-heads, unlike those in J. S. Bach's scripts, point without exception to the left, no matter whether the stems run up or down. The clefs are sketchy: the alto and bass clefs hastily scrawled, the G clefs reduced to simple hooks. The text, apparently filled in later, in places runs far ahead of the music.

Georg Friedrich Handel (1685-1759)

JEPHTA (41-43)

Oratorio. Text by Thomas Morell.
268 pages; 10 staves to each page. Size: 25.1 x 31.7 cm.
Dated on page 9 (beginning of the Menuet): "Oratorio Jephta / angefangen den 21. Jan^r. 1751."
Signed and dated at the end of the manuscript: "G F. Handel. aetatis 66. Finis. ♀ Agost. 30. 1751."

Composed 1751.

First performed February 26, 1752, Covent Garden, London.

Collected Works, vol. 44.

Collection: The King's Music Library, British Museum, London.

Ten years after writing the *Messiah* Handel began the composition of *Jephta* with his usual drive. In thirteen days the first part was just about finished; twelve days later he had arrived at the final chorus of Part II. Then his eyesight failed; he had to stop working and noted this in the score on February 13. Ten days later, on February 23, he noted on the following page that he had somewhat improved and had taken up work again, "den 23. dieses, etwas besser worden / wieder angefangen." Yet he never regained his full strength, and only by working at intervals and with great effort, did he complete the work by August 30. Thus the composition took seven months, a very long time for Handel.[1]

The struggle between the creative impulse and the failing body can be traced throughout the score. The manner of writing ranges from the energetic and forceful to the staggering and tremulous; and a comparison between the different scripts provides a rare insight into his method of working. It is because of this that the following three pages were chosen.

PLATE 41 shows page 91 containing a section of the chorus "When his loud voice" that closes the first part of the oratorio. The lower five staves which contain the vocal parts and the bass are written in a determined and resolute hand; the upper five staves containing the instrumental parts which double the chorus, are in an unsteady and tumbling script.

The eighth-notes in bar 3 of the vocal bass have cross strokes as well as individual flags, the latter possibly added as correction.

PLATE 42 shows page 182 containing a section of the chorus "How dark, O Lord, are thy decrees!" that closes the second part of the oratorio. It was while writing this page that Handel suffered an attack of blindness. By what some people would call a coincidence the words of this page read: "All hid from mortal sight." In the right lower corner Handel remarks, mostly in German script, "bis hierher komen den 13 Febr. 1751 / verhindert worden wegen des Gesichts meines linken Auges / relaxation [crossed out] / so relaxt." The deterioration of the writing is apparent in the unsteady and hesitant patterns of the script.

PLATE 43 shows page 251, containing the recitative of *Jephta's* wife, *Storge*, "O let me fold Thee," and the beginning of her aria, "Sweet as sight." The aria is set in two-part writing throughout, the upper staff for voice and violins in unison, the lower staff for continuo. In the right lower corner the text is corrected: "Still I'm of Thee possessed" is crossed out and replaced by "Sweet as Sight to the Blind" in large and shaky letters.

The bass is unfigured.

In page 251 the writing has regained a little bit of its original strength, but the notes still stagger and totter, with their stems in different directions. The writing is precisely of the same kind as in the upper five staves of plate 41 (page 91) which proves that these have been filled in by Handel after failing sight impaired his hand. Thus a comparison of our three plates alone

---

[1] In the extensive literature on Handel, various reasons are given for the interruptions in the composition of *Jephta*. R. A. Streatfeild, *Handel*, London 1909, assumes that they were caused by returns of mental disorder; E. J. Dent, *Handel*, London 1934, p. 127, refers to the fact that Morell supplied the text to Handel in installments.

offers an insight into Handel's working method.[2] He evidently drew first the essential contours, usually treble and bass and contrapuntally important lines, and only after the completion of this essential structure did he fill in all the rest, especially the doubling instrumental parts.

[2] An extensive discussion of Handel's working habits is found in Chrysander's preface to the fac-simile edition of *Jephta*, published by the *Deutsche Händelgesellschaft*, Hamburg 1885.

Jean Philippe Rameau (1683-1764)

LA DAUPHINE (44)

For the harpsichord.

2 pages, 10 staves to each page. Size: 26.7 x 20.5 cm.

Autograph heading: "La Dauphine."

Undated. Composed 1747 to celebrate the second marriage of the Dauphin with Marie-Josèphe of Saxony. Published in 1895 by A. Durand & Fils in the *Oeuvres complètes* under the direction of C. Saint-Saëns, in the volume containing the Pièces de Clavecin, p. 100.

Collection: Bibliothèque Nationale, Paris.

Characteristic are the G clefs without the lower loop, the two flats joined by one stem and the continuation marks at the right margins. The first two bars of the lower staff are written in the alto clef.

The piece is studded with ornaments:

Cadence appuyée, see bar 1;

double cadence, see bar 1, lower staff;

cadence, throughout;

coulé, bars 30, 33, etc.;

Pincé et port de voix, bars 5, 34, 36 ff.[1]

The meticulous organization of the script reveals great space sensitivity.

[1] A careful tabulation of the symbols for ornaments used by Rameau is given by C. Saint-Saëns in the *Oeuvres complètes*.

Giambattista Martini (Padre Martini) (1706-1784)

IN CONVERTENDO (45)

Church cantata for alto and instrumental accompaniment.

51 pages, 10 staves to each page. Size: 21.9 x 29.5 cm.

Unsigned. Undated.

Apparently unpublished.

Collection: Accademia Filarmonica, Bologna.

PLATE 45 shows page 25, with a section from an aria for alto. The bass is figured. The ♭ in the first bar of the bass before the F is marked there in order to insure a harmonization in accordance with the melody.

The writing is in a fluent, economical and forthright hand with straight cross strokes.

Carl Philipp Emanuel Bach (1714-1788)

FANTASIA IN B FLAT MAJOR (46)

Published by the composer as the third piece of the *Sechste Sammlung für Kenner und Liebhaber*, which appeared under the title *Clavier-Sonaten und freye Fantasien nebst einigen Rondos fürs Fortepiano für Kenner und Liebhaber, Ihro Hochgräflichen Gnaden Mariæ Theresia, Reich-Gräfin zu Leiningen-Westerburg unterthänig gewidmet und componirt von Carl Philipp Emanuel Bach. Sechste Sammlung. Leipzig, im Verlage des Autors. 1787*. The six pieces included in the *Sechste Sammlung* are: *Rondo I, Sonata I, Fantasia I, Rondo II, Sonata II, Fantasia II*.

Four pages, seven double staves to each page. Written in black ink on heavy paper. Size: 33.5 x 21.5 cm.

Autograph heading: "Fantasia, allegretto. Von mir, C. P. E. Bach No. 208."

Wotquenne thematic catalogue, No. 61.

Collection: The Library of Congress, Washington, D.C.

PLATE 46 shows the first page of the *Fantasia*.[1] The aspect of the page, with its disrupted and variegated texture is a true mirror of the structure of a free fantasy, with its alternation between rapid passages, recitativos, and broken chords, and its constant changes of time, as well as of rhythm. The bar lines are drawn separately for the upper and for the lower staff. The recitative-like passages are not divided by bar lines, although in bar 5 the upper staff is subdivided. The many little upright wedges above the notes indicate rigid staccato.[2]

∿ (bar 14) is explained in the treatise as "Prallender Doppelschlag" (a turn combined with an appoggiatura and a short trill): The dynamic signs (*f, p*) are sometimes followed by dots.

Bar 12 shows erasures and corrections.

The writing, shaky yet clear, shows the hand of the master at the age of 74, one year before his death.

---

[1] C. P. E. Bach composed for all the stringed keyboard instruments—harpsichord, clavichord, and pianoforte. The wording of the title of the *Sechste Sammlung* leaves some doubt as to whether "fürs Fortepiano" refers to all six pieces of the collection or only to the rondos, and the word "Clavier" tells little, since it means, simply, keyboard. His earlier sonatas were expressly marked "per cembalo" (for harpsichord). The style of the present Fantasia, however, and especially the dynamics and the frequent *ten[uto]* marks point, past any dispute, to the pianoforte. In his treatise *On the true manner of playing the Clavier* C. P. E. Bach explains: "The notes which are neither detached nor *geschleift* (legato), nor *ausgehalten* (held) should be sustained for half of their value; unless the word *ten* (gehalten) is marked above, in which case they must be held for their whole value."

[2] According to C.P.E. Bach's treatise.

The *Urtext Ausgabe* of Breitkopf & Härtel differs in many respects from the present manu-script.[3]

The notation A (below) which appears in the *Urtext Ausgabe* (bars 1ff.) is only seemingly equivalent to B in the manuscript. When Bach draws some stems up and others down from the beam, he does it for a very good reason, for in this way he manages to explain to the performer the hidden antagonism between the 4/4 meter and the recurrence of the three-note motive C that is embedded in it. Thus the *Urtext Ausgabe*, which presents the first four bars as in notation D (see below, right), actually falsifies the aim of the composer. The point in question is a matter of principle, as can be seen from many similar passages in C. P. E. Bach—the Fantasia in E flat major of his *Vierte Sammlung*, for instance—and from countless passages in J. S. Bach's works. Similar rhythmical effects were used by Mozart in such works as the *Piano Concerto in C major, K.503*, and in the Rondo of his *String Quartet in F major, K.590*.

Jean Jacques Rousseau (1712-1778)

SOLFÈGE À DEUX VOIX ÉGALES (47)

26 pages of very heavy paper; 7 double staves to each page. Size: 34.5 x 24 cm.

Unsigned. Undated.

Collection: Harvard College Library.

The manuscript contains 13 solfèges, each filling two pages. The first is headed *Premier Solfège*, the following eleven with numbers only. The last one (No. 13) is entitled: "Non sunt loquelae. Duo de M. Mondonville" and had a text added which, however, has been erased and can be deciphered only in spots.

PLATE 47 shows page 11 with the first page of *Solfège no. 6*. The design of the notes as well as the spacing is done with an accuracy that borders on pedantry. The braces for the double staves are decorated, the time signatures ornamentally drawn. Rousseau had a passion for drawing. In his *Confessions* he reports how coloring surveyors' charts awakened his old lust for design, and how he would have been capable of passing whole months among his pencils and brushes without leaving the house.[1]

[1] J. J. Rousseau, *Les Confessions*, Partie 1, Livre v: ". . . Le lavis des mappes de nos géomètres m'avait aussi rendu le goût du dessin. J'achetai des couleurs, et je me mis à faire des fleurs et des paysages. C'est dommage que je me sois trouvé peu de talent pour cet art, l'inclination y était tout entière. Au milieu de mes crayons et de mes pinceaux j'aurais passé des mois entiers sans sortir. Cette occupation devenant pour moi trop attachante, on était obligé de m'en arracher. . . ."

Christoph Willibald Gluck (1714-1787)

ORFEO ED EURIDICE (48-49)

Opera ("Azione teatrale per Musica") in three acts. Text of the Italian setting by Raniero de' Calzabigi. Text of the French version by Pierre Louis Moline.

59 sheets. 16 staves to each page. Size: 30 x 22.5 cm.

No autograph heading. Unsigned.

Composed 1762.

First performed October 5, 1762, at the Burgtheater, Vienna. The first performance of the French version took place on August 2, 1774, at the Paris Opera.

Denkmäler der Tonkunst in Österreich, Jahrg. xxi, vol. 44a.

Collection: Bibliothèque Musicale de L'Opéra, Paris.

PLATES 48, 49 show pages 26 and 27 of the manuscript (French version), with a section from *Amour's* aria from Act I (*Lent et gracieux*) to the text "Soumis au silence, contrains ton désire, fais toi violence, bientôt à ce prix tes tormens vont finir. Tu sçais qu'un amant discret et fidelle, müet et tremblant aupres de sa belle en est plus touchant." The six staves contain: violin I, violin II, bassoons, oboes, the vocal part, and the violoncello and double bass. Occasionally the score is compressed into five staves. This is achieved by writing the oboe part in together with other parts: either with the second violin, or the vocal part, or the first violin (see on page 26, bar 8: *Unisono con il P[ri]mo Viol [ino] in 8va* and *Oboè con il Primo* in the first staff of the last system).

The aria begins in 3/4 time with pizzicato in the strings, and turns at the beginning of page 26 (plate 48) to 3/8 time and *Coll'arco*.

Note the staccato signs and the appoggiaturas combined with mordents ($\sim$).

Gluck uses the traditional signs ♩ for sixteenth notes in the vocal part.

These pages are a characteristic example of the new flexible dramatic orchestration that follows closely the emotional vicissitudes of the action. Observe especially the change between coll'arco and pizzicato (p. 26, bar 3 and last bar; p. 27, bar 13), the echo effects (*piano- forte-piano* in p. 27, first system), and the fortissimo outburst that coincides with coll'arco (p. 27, bar 13).

The end of plate 49 contains the first bars of *Orfeo's* recitative (marked *Orf-*).

Christoph Willibald Gluck (1714-1787)

OVERTURE TO ARMIDE (50)

Opera in five acts. Text by Philippe Quinault.

Six sheets; 11 written pages; 16 staves to each page. Size: 31 x 23 cm.

Unsigned.

Opera composed 1777. First performed September 23, 1777, at the Paris Opera.

Collection: Bibliothèque du Conservatoire National de Musique, Paris.

PLATE 50 shows page 2 of the manuscript with a section of the Overture, starting with bar 27. The instruments employed are: (1) flute and violin I; (2) violin II; (3) viola; (4) oboe; (5) horns; (6) kettledrums; (7) trumpets; (8) violoncello solo, and from bar 5 (marked *forte Tutti*), double bass and bassoon. In the parts for the second violin and the viola, Gluck crossed out three bars, and wrote the correction beneath into the stave reserved for the winds.

There are meticulous phrasing marks—slurs and staccato dots—in the leading parts. The first staff (flute and violin I), in darker ink and provided with separate bar lines, was apparently written first.

Johann Christian Bach (1735-1782)

CEFALO E PROCRI (51, 52)

Cantata for three voices and orchestra.

81 leaves, 12 staves to each page of music. Size: 23.5 x 29 cm.

Title page: "Cefalo e Procri/ Cantata/a/tre voci/ del Sigr. G. C. Bach/Londra 1776." Signed at the top of page 1: "G. C. Bach 1776."

Apparently unpublished. The Cantata is not listed in the index of J. C. Bach's works in Max Schwarz, *Johann Christian Bach* in the *Sammelbände der Internationalen Musikgesellschaft*, Jahrgang II, Heft 3, pp. 442-454, April-June 1901, nor in the *Thematic catalogue of J. Chr. Bach's works* in C. S. Terry's *Johann Christian Bach*, London 1929.

Collection: The Library of Congress, Washington, D.C.

Johann Christian Bach, Johann Sebastian's eleventh son, known as the "Milanese" or "English" Bach, was a pupil of Padre Martini, and like Handel and many others, imported Italian music to England. Bach composed the part of *Procri* in the present Cantata for his wife, the Italian prima donna Cecilia Grassi.

PLATE 51 shows the first page of the composition, an introduction to a recitative of *Cefalo* marked *allegro maestoso*. Note the sharp dynamic contrasts, and within the dynamic range of the loud chords, the gradation between *f[ortissi]mo* in the basses, and the *sforz[and]o* in the violins. *cB* in the viola part indicates "coi bassi."

The handwriting and the dynamic marks are characteristically Italian (see, for instance, the *violini, Vni.*).

PLATE 52 shows the fourth page of the larghetto with *Aurora's* part: "Vo cercando in queste arene il pastor che m'innamora. . . ."

Scoring: stave 1 and 2) violins; stave 3 and 4) clarinets in C; stave 5) horns in F; stave 6) viola; stave 7) Aurora; stave 8) basses.

Note the use of the two dots after most of the directions, such as *p* and *pizz*. Note also slight divergencies between the vocal part and that of the first violin: the latter has more phrasing slurs and a mordent in bar 4, while the former has the mordent in the last bar where the violin has the ornamentation written out.

Franz Joseph Haydn (1732-1809)

ANDANTE IN F MINOR, OP. 83 (53, 54)

Usually reprinted as "Andante con Variazioni."

Eleven pages. Four double staves to each page. Size: 23.1 x 31 cm.

Autograph title page: "Sonata." Heading of first page: "In nomine Domini / di me Giuseppe Haydn m[anu]p[ropria] 793." There are several erasures, corrections and insertions.

Composed in 1793. First published in 1799 by Artaria & Co., Vienna, as "Variations pour le Clavecin ou Pianoforte, composées et dediées à Madame la Baronne Josephe de Braun, par Joseph Haydn. Oeuvre 83."

Collection: The New York Public Library, New York. (Presented as a gift in 1932 by the Bliss and Herter families.)

PLATE 53 shows the first page of the manuscript, which contains the variation theme; two sections, each repeated.

Only the first double stave contains clefs and key signatures. There are very few expressions signs—bar 2: *cres*; bar 3: *f*; bar 12: *p*; bar 25: *ten*[*uto*] *f*—not *fz* (the apparent *z* is actually the two dots which Haydn usually places after the dynamic signs) bar 29: *p*. These dynamic marks, especially the *cres*, are impracticable on the harpsichord and were clearly intended for the pianoforte. True, the title announces the piece "pour le Clavecin ou Pianoforte," but such announcements were quite customary when the pianoforte became a serious rival of the harpsichord and the publishers tried to sell their music to the players of either.[1]

The phrasing is fastidiously indicated by slurs and staccato dashes. It is interesting to notice that in bars 14, 15 and 17 the turns are indicated by small grace notes, while bar 5 shows, however sketchily, the sign for the short inverted mordent ⩘ .

Haydn, like C. P. E. Bach, was of painstaking accuracy in his directions to the performer. Letters which he wrote to his publisher, Artaria, complain bitterly of liberties taken by the printer.

PLATE 54 shows the last page of the manuscript. The first double stave contains the end of the composition, followed by "fine / laus Deo." The other staves contain an insertion with = *de*, referring to a *Vi* in page 5 of the manuscript, which contains a considerably less elaborate version of the bars inserted. The beginning and end of the insertion are marked in red pencil by *i* (i.e., 1) and 2.

Haydn meticulously indicates the number of notes in the rapid passages by *20, 19* and *6*; but in bar 12 the four 6-groups contain only 22 notes. Did Haydn miscalculate or did he forget to fill in the two D's which are missing in the diminished seventh chords in the right hand?

Inconsistent is the use of beams in bars 7 ff. of the insertion. In some bars Haydn uses single beams, in others triple beams.

In both pages shown Haydn, as usual, draws the bar lines separately for upper and lower staves. In places where one hand performs two parts, these are consistently written as two independent parts with separate beams for each.

---

[1] *Beethoven's Op.* 2 was still announced by the publisher as for "Clavecin ou Pianoforte."

Franz Joseph Haydn (1732-1809)

SONATA NO. 52 (55, 56)

For the pianoforte in E flat major.

Seventeen pages, four double staves to each page. Size: 23.5 x 29.8 cm.

On the title page, in the composer's hand: "Sonata." Autograph heading of first page: "Sonata composta per la Celebre Signora Teresa de Janson.[1] / In Nomine Domini/ di me Giuseppe Haydn Lond[ra] / 794." At the end of the manuscript: "Fine/ Laus Deo."

Composed in London 1794. Published in 1798 by Artaria & Co., Vienna, as Op. 82, and in 1799 by Longman, Clementi, & Co., London, as Op. 78.

Collected Works: Series xiv, vol. iii, no. 52.

Collection: The Library of Congress, Washington, D.C. (Acquired in 1933 with the aid of funds presented by "The Friends of Music in the Library of Congress.")

The present manuscript represents the complete score of one of Haydn's best known piano sonatas, the sonatas written in England three years after he received a doctorate at Oxford University. As is evident from many added numbers and red pencil marks, this score served as an engraver's copy. The two bottom staves on the last page contain a draft for a cadenza written in darker ink and not related to the sonata.

The manuscript shows Joseph Haydn's thin and tidy hand. There is almost no shading in the various sweeps of the pen; the cross strokes are no thicker than the stems or the bar lines. The writing shows little indication of swiftness. Haydn was not a speedy writer. Several of his letters describe his deliberate method of working.

PLATE 55 shows the first page of the sonata. The words "In Nomine Domini" introduce practically all the compositions of the deeply religious master. Notice the characteristically simplified shape of the clefs. They are used only for the first two double staves. There are many dynamic indications, as usual in Haydn's script, followed by two little dots, side by side like leaders or one upon the other like a colon. These dots are often misinterpreted in editions of Haydn's works. In the Peters Edition of Haydn's *Klaviersonaten*, edited by Köhler and Ruthardt, for instance, *f*: is read as *fz*.

Haydn adheres even in his latest keyboard compositions to the notation traditional for strict part writing: the upper and lower staves have their own separate bar lines, and the dynamic marks are added meticulously to each staff separately (bars 1, 3, 6, 9, 10, etc.). The passages of thirds in bars 3, 4, and 5 have beams above and beneath to indicate their two-part nature.

PLATE 56 shows the beginning of the *adagio* movement in E major, a half step above the key of the first movement. Notice the simple tall 3 indicating 3/4 time. The great wealth of dynamic shadings (*p, f, ff, crescendo*, and crescendo wedges) reveals Haydn's purposeful exploitation of the dynamic resources of the pianoforte and especially of its capacity for gradual increase and decrease of tone volume. A crescendo repetition of the same tone, as the B in the right hand of bar 15, could not have been performed on the harpsichord. Born only a few years after Bartolommeo Cristofori had built the first pianoforte, Haydn was brought up with the harpsi-

---

[1] Miss Janson, later Signora Bartolozzi, was one of Clementi's most gifted piano students. Haydn dedicated a number of compositions to her.

chord and in London in 1794 there were still incomparably more harpsichords than pianofortes.

Haydn placed the dynamic marks with great care: those written between the staves apply to both hands (bars 1, 2 and 3, for instance); in bars 4, 11, 14, 18, 20, they are added to each hand separately. Bar 8, however, has a crescendo wedge only in the bass figure and likewise the *crescendo* in bar 15 evidently applies only to the right hand.

Notice the four-part notation. In bar 3, for instance, the notes are given upper and lower cross strokes in each hand instead of being condensed into one lump chord.

Extremely characteristic of Haydn's handwriting are the frequent drawings of the beams in opposite directions ≪ or ≫ (see bars 3, 4), with no regard to the direction of the melodic line. In bar 15 Haydn takes great pain to add triple cross strokes to the rising passage in the right hand; in bar 21 he contents himself with one single cross stroke.

Notice the zigzag natural signs in bars 11 ff. A trembling hand is especially evident in the slurs and cross strokes of bars 8, 15, and 21.

Franz Joseph Haydn (1732-1809)

DIE SCHÖPFUNG (57)

Sketch for the introduction to the oratorio. German text by Gottfried van Swieten after the English original by Lindley.

1 page; 10 staves. Size: 22.4 x 31 cm.

Unsigned and undated. The name "Joseph Haydn" at the top of the page is not by the composer's hand.

Die Schöpfung was composed 1795-1798, Vienna. First published in Vienna, 1800 (Publisher's name not mentioned in the edition). First performed in Vienna, 1798.

Collection: The New York Public Library, New York.

During his second visit to London, Haydn was given an oratorio text compiled for Handel from Milton's *Paradise Lost*. Haydn took the text back to Vienna, had it translated and adapted, and began to set it to music under a grant of 500 ducats offered to him by twelve members of the Austrian aristocracy. The first performance took place on April 29 and 30, 1798, in the Vienna palace of Prince Schwarzenberg.

Several drafts for the work have survived and show various stages of the composition.

The page reproduced in plate 57 is evidently one of the first drafts for the orchestral introduction to the *Chaos*. Another draft, much more elaborate, and closer to the final score, is preserved in the Vienna Nationalbibliothek. A comparison between these two drafts and the final version as printed in the *Collected Works*, Breitkopf & Härtel, offers a profound insight into the genesis of this famous oratorio.

This page has only ten staves. Besides the usual body of strings are indicated clarinets, oboes 1 and 2, *F* (flutes), and *Fago.* (bassoon).[1] The violoncelli and the doublebasses are both written

---

[1] In his symphonies Haydn used to note the instruments of his orchestra in a different order: the autograph of the symphony "mit dem Paukenschlag" shows: clarini (trumpets), timpani (kettledrums), horns, oboes, flutes, bassoons, body of strings. The prominence given to the trumpets and their association with the kettledrums are deeply rooted in an old tradition.

in the bottom stave. The Vienna sketch has sixteen staves, with the full orchestra of the final score, adding at the beginning a long C played in unison by the whole orchestra. In the final score four more measures are added at the beginning.

The key and the general course of the harmony, with its fluctuation between C minor and E flat major, is already firmly established in the present draft by the figured bass. The sharp dissonance of the D in the flute against the C minor chord of the other instruments in bar 14 of the final version is suggested in bar 10 of the present draft.

A comparison between drafts and final version reveals also a different treatment of the staccato triplet figures which cut through the chromatic chaos like beams of light. In the Vienna draft these triplet figures appear seven times between bars 4 and 11, each time in different instruments. The final version is more parsimonious in this respect; the figures appear no more than three times. In bar 5 of our plate the triplet figure emerges in the top staff, though not yet assigned to a specific instrument. Then it crops up in bars 6 and 9, evidently inserted as an afterthought. Only once in the present sketch, in bar 5, does the triplet figure appear as a broken triad.

Domenico Cimarosa (1749-1801)

CHORUS FROM THE INDICA MARINA (58)

32 pages, 2 of them blank; 12 staves to each page. Size: 23 x 32 cm.

Autograph heading on title page: "Cimarosa/ Coro/ dall' Indica Marina/ Num.° I." Beneath, added by another hand: "In Pietro Burgo p la tavola dell'Imperatrice/ tutto originale, e mano Cimarosa."

Undated. Apparently composed during Cimarosa's stay at the court of Catherine II of Russia, in Petersburg, 1787-1792.

Collection: Chigi Saracini, Accademia Musicale Chigiana, Siena.

Almost all of Cimarosa's autographs are in the possession of the Conservatorio S. Pietro a Majella in Naples. Cimarosa took great care to collect his autographs, and willed them to his friend and patron Cardinal Consalvi, after whose death they were turned over to the Conservatorio.[1]

PLATE 58 shows the first page, with the opening of the orchestral introduction for the chorus. The order of the scoring is: winds, strings, kettledrums, chorus, basses. The writing is neat and fluent. Note the simplified G clefs.

[1] Francesco Florino, *La scuola musicale di Napoli*, 1881, Vol. II, p. 388 ff.

Antonio Salieri (1750-1825)

ORA FA UN SECOLO (59)

Vocal Trio written for the centennial of the erection of a church.

One leaf written on one page, five double staves. Size: 23 x 29.6 cm.

On the margin, almost all the way around the composition Salieri wrote: "Piccolo Terzetto

composto il giorno 25 Sett: 1814 celebrandosi in Liechtenthal[1] il compimento del primo secolo, che fu fabbricato il sacro Tempio detto in lingua tedesca Die XIV Nothhelfer: musica di me Ant. Salieri primo maestro di Capella della Corte Imp. e Reale di Vienna."[2]
Collection: The Library of Congress, Washington, D.C.

The writing, notwithstanding the composer's age, is still vigorous. Salieri held the position of Hof-Kapellmeister at the Court of Vienna from 1788 to 1824. He had written his last opera *Der Neger* in 1804. His music is little known today, but among his most notable pupils were Cherubini, Beethoven, and Schubert.

[1] Liechtenthal is a suburb of Vienna. Franz Schubert was born there and as a schoolboy sang first soprano in the Liechtenthal church of Die Vierzehn Nothelfer.

[2] "Little Trio composed the 25th of September 1814 in celebration at Liechtenthal of the hundredth anniversary of the erection of the holy Church called in German 'Die XIV Nothhelfer': music by me, Ant. Salieri, music director of the Chapel at the Imperial and Royal Court in Vienna."

Wolfgang Amadeus Mozart (1756-1791)

CONCERTO FOR VIOLIN IN A MAJOR, K.V. 219 (60, 61)

46 leaves, all of them written on both sides; 10 staves to each page. Size: 16.5 x 23 cm.
Autograph heading: "Concerto di Violino. di Wolfgango Amadeo Mozart/Salisburgo li 20 di decembre/ 1775."
Composed in Salzburg, December 1775.
Collected Works, series XII, 5. André, thematic catalogue, no. 174.
Collection: The Gertrude Clarke Whittall Foundation Collection, The Library of Congress, Washington, D.C.

PLATE 60 shows leaf 4 verso, containing bars 44-48 of the first movement. The instruments are: solo violin, first violin, second violin, viola (the first bars of the viola part are blank but they do not have rests either. Here the viola, as indicated earlier in the score, doubles the part of the double-bass), first oboe, second oboe, horns in A, violoncello, and double-bass.

The *Collected Works*, which were prepared with no regard to the autograph, omit the wedge-shaped staccato signs in the oboe parts (bar 1), and the staccato dots in the first violin part (staff 3 of the page), and replace the ♪ appoggiatura in bar 5 of the solo violin by a ♪. As usual, the solo part is free of expression marks, leaving the interpretation to the good taste of the performer.

PLATE 61 shows leaf 24 verso, containing bars 85-92 of the second movement (*Adagio*). Here dynamic marks appear in the solo part. Note the subtle difference in phrasing in bar 5:

A ♫♩ in the first violin,

B ♫♩ in the second violin. The *Collected Works* omit the staccato dots in bar 6 in the viola, violoncello, and double bass (staves 5 and 9), and replace the appoggiatura A in bar 7 of the solo violin by B.

Both plates show the writing habits of the nineteen-year-old master not yet definitely established. Sometimes he indicates the dynamic marks by their first syllables, sometimes by their first letters only; occasionally he underlines them. Sometimes the vertical line of the *f* is straight, sometimes curved at the ends, sometimes turning into a loop. The bar lines, unlike those in Mozart's later script, do not yet show any marked slant.

Wolfgang Amadeus Mozart (1756-1791)

SERENADE: GRAN PARTITA (62, 63)

For wind instruments and double bass, in B flat major, K.V. 361.

91 pages. Several pages between the movements and last page blank. 12 staves to a page, top and bottom stave blank. Size: 22.5 x 32 cm. (including binding).

Bound in brown cardboard with a label pasted on bearing the words: "Serenade von W. A. Mozart, Partitur."

Unsigned. Undated.

Marked on top of the first written page: "Gran Partitura" (*sic!*) evidently not in Mozart's hand.

Composed in 1781 in Munich and Vienna.

Published 1803 under the title: "Grande Serenade pour deux Hautbois, deux Clarinettes, deux Cors de Bassette, quatre Cors, deux Bassons et grand Basson ou Bass . . . Oeuvre posthume."

Collected Works, series IX, 12. André, thematic catalogue, no. 170.

Collection: The Gertrude Clarke Whittall Foundation Collection, The Library of Congress, Washington, D.C.

The instruments indicated on the first page and again at the beginning of the single movements are: 2 oboes, 2 clarinets, 2 basset horns, 2 horns in F, 2 horns in B flat, 2 bassoons, and double bass ("contrabasso"; not, as in many editions, "contrabassoon").

PLATE 62 shows page 34 of the manuscript, the first page of the third movement (*Adagio*).

The two clefs in the horn parts indicate that both horn parts are written on one staff. The sign *col B* (col basso) in bars 1 and 2 indicates that the copyist is to fill in the same notes as those written in the double bass part. The solo entries are indicated by *solo*. All marks, such as *pia, solo, col B*, and also the *tr* in the first clarinet, are followed by ":", just as in most scores of Joseph Haydn. Note the careful phrasing slurs. Single sixteenth notes are indicated sometimes by the old sign with the flag crossing the stem, sometimes in the modern way with two parallel short flags (see the end of each bar). There are separate bar lines for each staff.

PLATE 63 reproduces page 40 of the manuscript, showing bars 31-35 of the *Adagio*. The part of the second bassoon bears again the sign *col B*. Note the variety in the shape of the numerous *fp* marks, ranging from separate letters to one single simplified sign.

The three strata of different rhythmic pulsation stand out with great clarity: 1) the solo parts (oboe I, clarinet I, basset horn I), with their spacious, sighing cantilenas; 2) the bass (double bass), with its inexorable, striding figures in equal eighth-notes; and 3) in the middle, the other instruments, supplying the softly tapping background rhythm.

Wolfgang Amadeus Mozart (1756-1791)

QUINTET FOR TWO VIOLINS, TWO VIOLAS AND VIOLONCELLO, IN C MAJOR, K.V. 515 (64)

24 leaves; 12 staves (2 quintuple staves and 2 blank staves) to each page. Size: 23 x 31.8 cm.
Autograph heading: "Quintetto."
Unsigned. Undated.
Composed in 1787 in Vienna. Published 1789 by Artaria & Co., Vienna.
Collected Works, Series XIII, 4. André, thematic catalogue, no. 185.
Collection: The Gertrude Clarke Whittall Foundation Collection, The Library of Congress, Washington, D.C.

PLATE 64 contains bars 355-384 from the last (fourth) movement (*Allegro*). The page is an example of extremely rapid writing, with no attention to elegance, but perfectly clear. Speed is apparent in the many slurs which are almost straight, in the hardly recognizable trill sign in bar 12 of the second violin part (cf. the trill in bar 14), and in the ③ signs indicating triplets, in bars 17 and 19.

The phrasing, however, is indicated most meticulously. Note, for instance, the consistent use of In several places (bars 21-22, 25-26, 29-30) the phrasing slurs for the second violin and the viola become entangled. Note the unequal treatment of the bar lines: in most places they are not drawn in one stroke but separately for the first violin and connected for the other parts. Only the bar lines after bar 20, 22, 23, and 24 run through unbroken. The bar line after measure 21 is drawn separately for each instrument: this is precisely the spot where the three middle parts re-enter while the first violin pauses. The first viola starts a canon at the octave, with the first violin following 2 bars later. Earlier in the movement, in bars 120 ff. the same canon was executed, but there the first violin entered first and the first viola followed. It would seem that in bar 21, Mozart at first decided to repeat the same order and to start with the first violin: two rests are noted in the first violin and crossed out; they correspond to the pauses which precede the entry of the first viola in the third stave. Thus Mozart, unless we assume a slip of the pen, decided on second thought to reverse the order of the instruments which perform the canon.

Wolfgang Amadeus Mozart (1756-1791)

ALLEGRO IN D MAJOR, FOR PIANOFORTE, K.V. 485 (65, 66)

Four pages, of which three and part of the fourth are written on; six two staff-systems to each page. Size: 22.7 x 30.2 cm.
At the end of the last staff: "Mozart mp/ le 10 de Janvier 1786/ à Vienne" (the last two words half erased). Underneath, a hardly legible erased dedication: "Pour Madselle Charlotte de W. . . ." On the cover of the binding: "Franz Nemećzek."

Published about 1787 by Hoffmeister, Vienna, under the title "Sonate (Rondo)."[1]

Collected Works, Series XXII, No. 7.

Collection: The Heinemann Foundation for Research, Educational, Charitable and Scientific Purposes, Inc., New York. Previous owner: Franz Niemetschek (or Nemeček), son of Mozart's first biographer, Franz Xaver Niemetschek, Vienna.

PLATES 65 and 66 reproduce the first and the last page of the manuscript. Throughout the whole score the phrasing (slurs and staccato dots) and the grace notes are meticulously indicated, yet, strangely enough, the first page has no dynamic marks whatsoever. The Collected Works, however, prescribe for the beginning "piano" and "legato." The last page of the manuscript shows most delicate dynamic shading. The bar lines are drawn at times through both staves, at times through each stave separately.

Autographs like this should be studied by the thousands of pianists who rely on editions that are "enriched" like modern breakfast food. They throw some light on the controversial problem of the appoggiaturas. Mozart makes a clear distinction between long and short appoggiatura,[2] the short ones being indicated by a little stroke across the stem of the small note. If there were still any doubt as to whether the appoggiaturas in the first bar were short ones, the last page would remove it, for there we find short and long appoggiaturas side by side: bars 2, 6, and 10 show long appoggiaturas, each connected to the following note by a slur. Thus bars 5 and 6 should be performed as follows:

In spite of the incredible speed with which he worked, Mozart knew how to make himself perfectly clear.

[1] Jahn-Abert, vol. II, p. 277, points out that the present piece, although usually called a rondo, is in form much nearer to a sonata movement than to a rondo.

[2] See also Leopold Mozart, *Versuch einer gründlichen Violinschule*, IX, 3, 9, 17ff.; Robert Haas, *Die musikalische Aufführungspraxis*, pp. 246ff.

Wolfgang Amadeus Mozart (1756-1791)

IL DISSOLUTO PUNITO OSSIA IL DON GIOVANNI (67-74)

Opera buffa ("dramma giocoso") in two acts. K.V. 527. Text by Lorenzo Da Ponte.

534 written pages: Overture, 26 pages; Act I, 272 pages; Act II, 236 pages. Mostly 12 staves to each page. Size: 22.9 x 31.1 cm.

Composed in 1787. First performance, October 29, 1787, Prague. First published, Breitkopf & Härtel, Leipzig, 1801.

Collected Works, Series V, No. 18.

André, thematic catalogue, no. 44.

Collection: Bibliothèque du Conservatoire National de Musique, Paris.

PLATE 67 shows a section from *Leporello's* aria, "Notte e giorno faticar," which opens the first act. The orchestration subtly depicts *Leporello's* self-pity: the winds (oboes, staves 4 and 5; bassoons, staves 6-7; horns, stave 8) are added to the strings gradually bar by bar, until, with "sentinella" we have the full orchestra. The striking graphic expression of this does not come out at all in the modern printed scores which place the winds above the strings. The winds, written in paler ink and with thicker quill were evidently filled in after the vocal and string parts. Note the decorative swing and ornamental balance of the *sfp*, which, in its perfect linear elegance, almost resembles a monogram.

PLATE 68 shows a section from the *Allegro* part of *Leporello's* aria, Act I, scene 4. It is a typical example of dramatic, dynamic shading. The loquacious boasting of the buffone is characterized by a whole chain of *f*'s and *p*'s, which follow each other at half a bar's distance.[1] Then follows as a comic climax, the *p* at "ogni forma" in bar 5 and 6, which then swells into a *forte* in bar 8.

In *Leporello's* part, bar 7, Mozart adds the lower octave in smaller notes as an alternative. While there are dynamic marks in abundance for the orchestra—nearly one to each bar—there are none for the vocal part. The freedom of the interpreter is not hampered.

PLATE 69 shows the recitativo secco preceding the finale of Act I: the dialogue between *Masetto* and *Zerlina*, interrupted by *Don Giovanni* from backstage. The musical symbols and the text are both written as fluently, compactly and evenly as if they were independent of each other. And yet, they proceed in such perfect correlation that it is impossible to discover which of the two was written first.

PLATE 70 shows a section from the last scene of Act I. Of the three orchestras on the stage, two are already under way: the first, and larger one, in 3/4 minuet time (staves 5-8, and 12-13); the second (violin and double bass), in 2/4 contredanse time (staves 3-4). At this point, the third (also violin and double bass) joins in (staves 1-2) by pretending to tune up (*accordano*) and trying empty fifths with the bow, then *pizzicato* (bar 4); and again *coll'arco*, first in the violin, and, one bar later, in the bass. All this "tuning" is still in the minuet time of the first orchestra. Not until three bars after the end of this page, will the third orchestra come into its own with a waltz tune (marked "Teitsch," i.e., "Deutsch," by Mozart) in 3/8 time.

The second violin and the second viola parts (stave 6-7) are written in a conspicuously paler ink and are evidently filled in later—just as in the autograph pages preceding and following. In spite of the condensation of the five vocal parts into only two staves (staff 9 and 11), there was no space left for the horns which had to be added at the bottom of the page in a hand-written staff. Curiously enough, staff 10 is blank, or so it seems at first glance. But there are small bar lines drawn, subdividing every other bar into two, and thus making nine bars out of the six minuet bars, or—in other words—introducing a contredanse metre into this staff. And indeed there are—at closer inspection—nine full rests in staff 10. The puzzle is solved by the preceding page (not reproduced), which shows that the blank staff is reserved for *Don Giovanni* who "si mette a ballar con Zerlina una Contradanza." And three bars after the end of our page, *Don Giovanni* addresses *Zerlina* in 2/4 time: "Vieni con me," while *Leporello* compels *Masetto* in 3/8 time to dance with him the "*Teitsch*." Thus the bar lines and rests in the staff 10 of our page are a hint to the conductor of the impending entry of *Don Giovanni* in 2/4 time. *Don Giovanni* himself, however, does not need any warning, for he is already dancing the contredanse, and besides, it was he who planned all this rhythmical jumble in his presto-aria (the "Champagne aria") no 12: "Senza alcun ordine la danza sia; ch'il menuetto, chi la follia, chi l'allemana farai ballar."

---

[1] The *Collected Works* ignore this precise marking: Mozart carefully distinguishes between *fp* (contracted into one single sign, as used in the half-notes of the winds) and the *f:p:*, as used in the strings. Here the *Collected Works* use *fp* signs in every half-bar.

PLATE 71 shows the closing page of the dance scene. All three orchestras, with their different rhythms, are now in full swing. The last bar contains *Zerlina's* cry for help (see soprano clef). The double bar line which follows ends the dance music. The two horns are now taken from the auxiliary staff into staff 11 and, although noted in minuet time, they actually reenforce the contredanse.

Note how the page is divided into various strata by the different ink and styles of writing: staves 6 and 7 are in the same pale ink as in the preceding page; thin and pointed writing appears in the vocal parts; in staff 8 for the oboes a broad inky quill was used and the writing is fat and full.

PLATE 72 shows a section from Act II, Scene 17, the dialogue between the *Commendatore* and *Don Giovanni*. As usual, the vocal parts are free from directions, but with what consummate skill they are set into relief by the dynamic shadings of the orchestra, so as to make sure that the words will be clearly understood! To single out only one point: in bars 1 and 5, the third beat is preceded by *p* to give prominence to the new syllable occurring there; in bars 9 and 11 of the vocal part, however, where the first three beats are covered by the same long syllable, the *f* is maintained longer and replaced by a *p* just in time to avoid drowning out the first beat of the next measure in the vocal part.

The trumpet and kettledrum parts are not included in this manuscript but were written on separate pages.

PLATE 73 shows bars 13-22 after the handshake (*più stretto*) between *Don Giovanni* and the *Commendatore*. There is an almost regular alternation between *f* and *p* in the orchestra, with the *f*'s always on *Don Giovanni's* "No!"

In this page we find, as so often in Mozart's scores, a strong backhand slant in the stems as well as the bar lines. In one spot, Mozart is even compelled to correct the slant: the larger *fp* in the last bar beneath the violas (fourth stave), has crowded two chords of the bassoons so far toward the right that the second chord is outside of its bar. An added vertical bar line sets the situation right.

PLATE 74 shows the next page of the manuscript. Here the alternation of *f* and *p* is condensed into the smallest possible space. Again the *f*'s reinforce the "No's!" Right after this a *pia:* (not the usual *p*), marks the ghastly unison that accompanies the last fateful words of the *Commendatore*: "Ah, tempo più non v'è."

Wolfgang Amadeus Mozart (1756-1791)

CONCERTO FOR PIANOFORTE AND ORCHESTRA IN D MAJOR, K.V. 537, THE "CORONATION CONCERTO" (75-80)

112 pages, of which four are blank; 12 staves to each page. Size: 23 x 31.3 cm.

Unsigned and undated.

Composed 1788. First performed by Mozart during the celebration of the coronation of Leopold II, in Frankfurt am Main. Published 1794, by J. André, Offenbach, as op. 46, with the remark: "Ce Concerto a été executé par l'Auteur à Francfort sur le Mein, à l'occasion du Couronnement de l'Empereur Leopold II."

Collected Works, Series XVI, 26.

Mozart's Autograph Register No. 76: "Ein Klavier Konzert in D dur.- à 2 violini, viola e basso; 1 flauto, 2 oboi, 2 fagotti, 2 corni, 2 clarini et timpany ad libitum." André, thematic catalogue, no. 213.

Collection: The Heinemann Foundation for research, educational, charitable and scientific Purposes, Inc., New York.

Mozart, with but few exceptions, suggests the piano part by filling in the melody only and leaving the lower staff blank. In the score, he needed only this outline to synchronize the piano part with that of the orchestra. For his own performances, thanks to his fabulous memory, he did not require any score at all.[1] The first edition by André[2] contained only separate instrumental parts, which were taken from the present autograph, but no score. It is not known who completed the pianoforte part for this edition.

PLATE 75 shows the first page of the first movement. Mozart indicates only the winds on the margin and, apparently as a later addition, 2 *clarini* [*i.e. trumpets*] *in D* and *Timpany in D* on the top and bottom of the page. Staves 2, 3, 4 contain the first and second violin and viola parts; staff 11 the double bass part; the remaining staves, 9 and 10, the piano part. It is interesting to see how Mozart consistently singles out the piano part by marking it with little brackets and by placing a little circle between its two staves on the left margin of the page. The lower staff of the piano part is marked *coB:* [*coi bassi*], a direction to the performer to follow the double bass or the bassoons. From directions like these, it is clear that Mozart wanted the solo instrument to serve also as a continuo, by doubling the basses of the orchestra, and, most likely, by filling in the harmonies.

PLATE 76 shows leaf 6, recto, with bars 98-107, from the middle of the first movement. Note the seven-part unison in bars 3 and 5, moving against the dotted timpani motive (bottom stave). The dynamic marks in the *tutti* (*sf - p - sf - p - f*) are accurately placed on each beat.[3]

PLATE 77 shows leaf 11, verso, containing bars 183-190, from the development section of the first movement. Here in a highly contrapuntal passage—a two-part canon in the piano solo—not even Mozart takes any chances; both staves are neatly written out.

Note the strong back slant. Typical of Mozart's writing, it is even more striking here, since aside from the two piano staves the whole page is blank. The darker ink appearing in the braces and bar lines of the top and bottom staves again indicates that the trumpets and drums were added later.

PLATE 78 shows leaf 14, recto, with bars 216-225 of the first movement. Again, different shades of ink permit plausible conjectures as to the working method. The first violin part stands out, with its thin, hard, noticeably backslanted writing; it was probably entered first. A broader quill was used for staves 3, 4, and 11 (second violin, viola, double bass); these parts were probably filled in later. Different again are the winds (staves 5-8), written in a sharp hand, with

[1] Friedrich Rochlitz, *Für Freunde der Tonkunst,* 3rd edn., 1868, vol. 2, p. 180ff. tells several anecdotes about Mozart playing his piano part from blank pages or from sheets on which only the bass was noted: "On my travels I have to do it this way; otherwise they steal copies and print them immediately. . . ."

[2] Köchel-Einstein, p. 687.

[3] Different in *Collected Works* which have

thus resulting in short accents that are not warranted by the manuscript.

vertical and even forward-slanted stems. They were most likely filled in still later. Within this complex texture, six different parts move with perfect ease. While filling in the middle parts, Mozart amused himself with some of his little jokes: bassoon and flute (with the two oboes) are written in imitation, and in bar 7, the second violin moves up into the higher octave while the other instruments simply repeat the preceding period.

In the lower stave of the piano part (G clef!) bar 2 is filled out. After the chord concluding the solo, the bass clef is restored, evidently to instruct the performer to follow, in continuo fashion, the bass of the tutti.

The turns after the trills are written out.

PLATE 79 shows the first bars of the *Larghetto*. The *corni* were originally placed over the *fagotti*. At the entrance of the *tutti* the bass was transposed an octave lower, apparently on second thought. It is interesting, moreover, that in the same bar, the *forte* is marked only in the string parts; the wind instruments must therefore have stood out sufficiently against the strings. Such dynamic marks permit conclusions as to the relative strength of the choirs customary at that time.

Even here, where the piano begins solo, only its melodic contour is written out. As the greater part of the page is blank, the backslant of the bar lines is particularly conspicuous.

PLATE 80 shows the end of the *Allegretto*. The order of the instruments differs from that in the first movement (cf. plate 75); they are from top to bottom: 1) violins I; 2) violins II; 3) violas; 4) flute; 5) oboes; 6) bassoons; 7) horns; 8) trumpets (clarini); 9) kettledrums; 10) 11) piano-forte; 12) double bass.

Note the complete absence of dynamic and other expression marks in the piano part.

The final rest is marked with a ⌒ not only on the top and bottom of the page, but also in the middle, evidently to insure that the last chord will not be held any longer than a quarter note, or to show the conductor he need not scramble to turn the page.

Luigi Maria Cherubini (1760-1842)

FRAGMENT OF A STRING QUARTET (81)

Consists of 15 measures of a movement in A minor headed "All.° moderato."
1 sheet of which about one-sixth is cut off, 3 quadruple staves. Size: 22 x 27.5.
On the back of the sheet: "Quatuor 6me/ pour deux violons, Alto et Basso/ par L. Cherubini/ (Paris 1835)." At the bottom: "Commencé le 4 juillet, continué à differentes reprises et terminé le. . . ." Beneath this title a few bars of fragmentary sketches.
Collection: The Pierpont Morgan Library, New York.

This fragment corresponds to bars 8-22 of the first movement of the string quartet in A minor mentioned as No. 427 in the Chronological Catalogue in Edward Bellasis, *Cherubini*, London 1847 and it may be assumed that the fragment is an earlier draft for the beginning of the quartet. This assumption is borne out also by the presence of sketches in the bottom stave. It was perhaps the modulation into the subdominant which appears a little precociously in bar 4, that led Cherubini to invent a longer opening motif.

PLATE 81 shows the front of the sheet. There are few dynamic marks; note the strong accents in bars 3-4 and 7-8. The writing is extremely neat and carefully spaced but the hand of the master at the age of seventy-five is unmistakably shaky.

Ludwig van Beethoven (1770-1827)

TRIO FOR VIOLIN, VIOLA AND VIOLONCELLO IN E FLAT MAJOR, OP. 3. FINALE, *ALLEGRO* (82)

10 pages, 5 triple staves to each page. Size: 22.5 x 31.5 cm.

Unsigned. Undated.

The manuscript represents an earlier version of the *Finale* which was revised in many respects before publication.

Composed 1792 and 1793, in Bonn and Vienna.[1]

Published in 1797 by Artaria & Co., Vienna, as "Gran Trio per violino, viola e violoncello, composto dal Sigr. Luigi van Beethoven. Opera III." Beethoven later rearranged the work which was published in 1807 as *Sonata pour piano et violoncello, op. 64, tirée du grand Trio pour le violon, oeuvre 3.*

Collected Works, Series VII, No. 54.

Nottebohm, thematic catalogue, p. 4; Bruers, thematic catalogue, p. 58.

Collection: The Library of Congress, Washington, D.C. An autograph of other movements of the *Trio* is owned by the Bibliothèque du Conservatoire National de Musique, Paris.

PLATE 82 shows the first page of the *Finale* which is the sixth movement of the work that, with its two minuets, is an offshoot of the divertimento form. The plate reproduced is a typical example of the speedy and thin but fairly clear hand of the young Beethoven. At the same time it shows features which later on will stand out more and more clearly in Beethoven's scripts, such as the simplified G clef, and, above all, the breaking up of the notes into three disconnected elements: head, stem, and flag (see, for instance, the eighth-notes in bars 6 and 7 in the first violin part which are written in three separate strokes of the pen).

[1] According to Alexander W. Thayer, *Ludwig van Beethovens Leben*, Leipzig 1917, 3rd edn., Vol. I, p. 312. Carl Engel, "Beethoven's Op. 3—An 'Envoi de Vienne,'" in *Musical Quarterly* Vol. XIII, No. 2, 1927, p. 261ff., esp. 277, places the composition, with good reason, in the first years in Vienna, 1793 and 1794.

Ludwig van Beethoven (1770-1827)

SONATA FOR PIANO AND VIOLIN IN G MAJOR, OP. 96 (83-86)

Twelve sheets (48 pages, of which 8 and a half pages are blank); 20 staves to each page; written in triple staves, usually with one blank staff between them. Size: 35.5 x 24 cm.

Autograph heading: "Sonate von L. von Beethoven. in Februar/1812/oder 1813."

Composed in 1812.

Published in 1816 by S. A. Steiner & Co., Vienna. First performed January 1813, at the Palace of Prince Lobkowitz in Vienna, by the Archduke Rudolph, to whom the sonata is dedicated, and by the famous violinist Pierre Rode, for whom it was composed.

Collected Works, Series XII, No. 10.

Nottebohm, thematic catalogue, p. 93; Bruers, thematic catalogue, p. 244.

Collection: The Pierpont Morgan Library, New York. Sketches for the last three movements of this sonata were in the *Preussische Staatsbibliothek*, Berlin, before the dispersal of the collection during the last world war.

PLATE 83 shows page 11, containing 29 bars near the end of the first movement. The ♭ preceding the E in bar 16 of the violin part is repeated in bar 18, but not in bars 17 and 19. It is inserted there in the *Collected Works*.

There are meticulous phrasing marks. Note especially the phrasing in bars 9 and 12 in the piano part, right hand, and in bars 13-16, violin part.

The waving line over bars 17, 18 and 19 seems to have consisted originally of three separate single curves which, evidently on second thought, were later joined.

Note also the careful dynamic marks, for instance, the *cresc[endos]* in bars 9 and 13, both leading through lines of dashes to an abrupt *p[iano]*.

PLATE 84 shows page 17 of the manuscript, containing the beginning of the third movement, *Scherzo*. This page presents a strangely consistent pattern because of the large half-circular eighth rests which appear after practically every note.

The fourth staff was used for sketches which were then erased. The G in bar 6 of the violin part was blurred and had to be explained by an added letter. In the fourth staff of bar 18 a slip of the pen is corrected by pencil. In bars 9 and 10 the F sharp and G in the bass of the piano part are not accompanied by the lower octaves, since the compass of Beethoven's instruments did not reach that low.[1]

PLATE 85 shows page 37 of the manuscript containing nine bars from the *Adagio* variation in the last movement. This page is full of corrections, cancellations and erasures. In several erased passages the staff lines are traced over roughly (see bars 6, 7, 8) and the blotched notes are clarified by letters (see bars 2[2] and 8). The staves between the systems for the piano and violin parts are often used as auxiliary staves for experimenting, some in pencil, others in ink: the fifth staff from the bottom, for example, evidently contains a draft for the violin part beneath.

Note the characteristic diamond-shaped crescendo-decrescendo signs. The underlined words *klein geschrieben* in the middle of the page near the right margin are a direction for the copyist.

PLATE 86 shows a section near the end of the last movement.

The slurs in bars 2, 3 and 4 above the violin part apparently were originally separated and then joined together. If so, this would be one of the many instances when Beethoven's imagination went beyond the capacity of the instrument, for so long a slur would far exceed the longest phrase a fiddle bow can sustain.[3]

[1] During Beethoven's lifetime the compass of large pianofortes, such as those built by Johann Andreas Stein and Broadwood, grew from five to six octaves; the lowest tone gradually descended from Contra F to Contra C.

[2] The upper voice in the right hand of the piano part of bar 2, G G B B B B is changed by the Collected Works into G G G G B B.

[3] According to a famous though perhaps apocryphal anecdote, Beethoven's friend, the celebrated violinist Schuppanzigh, once complained of the difficulty of a passage in one of Beethoven's works,

In bar 8 the writing becomes so dense that clarification by the insertion of letters was necessary.

Between the triple staffs, single staffs are left blank for sketches.

Of interest also is the erasure of the sharp before the A in bar 9 of the violin part and—if one may judge from its more thorough erasure—of the corresponding sharp in bar 13 of the piano part. The sharp, however, before the A in bar 14 has no equivalent in the corresponding bar 10. Unless this was an oversight, one may assume that Beethoven wanted the repeat of the passage to be more pungent or wished to prepare for the second A sharp that appears two bars later, as the leading tone in B minor.

The numbers over bars 11 and 12 are fingering marks.

---

whereupon Beethoven shouted: "Does he believe that I think of a wretched fiddle when the spirit speaks to me?" (Quoted in Friedrich Kerst, *Bee-* *thoven, the man and artist, as revealed in his own words*; translated by H. E. Krehbiel, New York, 1905, p. 25.)

Ludwig van Beethoven (1770-1827)

SKETCHES FOR THE PIANO TRIO IN B FLAT MAJOR, OP. 97 (87)

Dedicated to the Archduke Rudolph.

8 pages, 16 staves to each page, with a total of 122 written staves. Size: 22.8 x 31.5 cm.

The first page contains sketches for the variation movement; the second and third for the *Scherzo*; the sixth, seventh, and eighth for the *Trio*; and the fifth for the last movement.

The entire work was composed in 1811.

First performance April 11, 1814, in Vienna, by Ignaz Schuppanzigh, Joseph Linke, and the composer at the piano.

Published 1816 by S. A. Steiner, Vienna.

Collected Works, Series XI, No. 6.

Nottebohm, thematic catalogue, p. 94; Bruers, thematic catalogue, p. 245.

Collection: The New York Public Library, New York (presented as a gift by the Bliss and Herter families).

The manuscript, although well preserved, is not easy to decipher. It abounds in corrections and overwritings. Fragments of ideas are jotted down in certain places, then taken up again in other places, so that quite some effort is required to piece together the related ideas. Meter and key are rarely indicated, clefs and accidentals missing almost throughout. Most of the sketches are written in ink, only a very few in pencil.

Beethoven worked slowly, often painfully so. Only through a long succession of sketches and revisions did the final form take shape. A good example of this method is the present plate: it shows page 2 of the manuscript headed *Scherzo*, and represents an early phase in the genesis of this movement.

The opening theme, which is presented as a dialogue between the violin and the violoncello (corresponding to bars 1-16 of the final version) fills staves 1 and 2. The instruments succeed each other on the same staff and are indicated by the changing clefs in the first staff: while an initial bass clef is not indicated for the first four bars given to the violoncello, we find simplified G clefs suggesting the violin part in bars 5 and 9. The dynamic marks correspond almost precisely to those in the final version: bar 3 has a *crs* (*crescendo*); bar 4 a *sf* (in the final version a *sfp*). The same signs are repeated in the last two bars of staff 1.

The passages with eighth notes slurred together in pairs in staves 5, 6, and 9 of the sketch, correspond to bars 47 ff. of the final version. The first bar of staff 5 seems to foreshadow the little imitation motives in bars 78 ff. of the final version, although the sketch introduces them in countermotion.

The word *oder* occurs several times on the page: a gigantic one in the right margin, over the hand-drawn extension of staff 7; two others in staff 9 and between staves 10 and 11. *Vi=de* marks are planted as road signs through the maze: for instance, the *Vi=1000* towards the end of staff 9, which apparently refers to *=de 1000* in the middle of staff 13. Likewise the *x 1200* in the right margin seems to refer to the *x 1200* in bar 5 of the second staff from the bottom.

Especially interesting is staff 10. It begins with an enormous *=de*, although no corresponding *Vi=* can be detected on the page. Then 11 bars follow, written in fat and powerful strokes over the original much smaller script. At first glance, they look confused enough; but viewed from some distance, they detach themselves sufficiently from the tangled background to be recognized as the passage in bars 32 ff. of the final version.

Ludwig van Beethoven (1770-1827)

SONATA FOR THE PIANOFORTE, IN E MAJOR, OP. 109 (88-90)

36 pages, 8 staves to each page; 1 blank sheet. Size: 23.8 x 30.5 cm.
Autograph heading in the composer's hand: "Sonata für das Hammerklavier[1] von L. v. Beethoven."
Signed by composer on title page. Undated.
Composed 1820. First published 1821, Schlesinger'sche Buch- und Musikhandlung, Berlin.
Numerous corrections in ink and pencil.
Collected Works, Series XVI, No. 30.
Nottebohm, thematic catalogue, p. 105; Bruers, thematic catalogue, p. 272.
Collection: The Gertrude Clarke Whittall Foundation Collection, The Library of Congress, Washington, D.C.

PLATE 88 shows bars 14-20 of Variation IV from the last movement. Dynamic marks provide the finest and most precise shadings:

bar 1: *f - sf - il più forte*
bar 2: *ff: - dimin*
bar 3: *dolce*
bar 5: $\diamond$ *pp*
bar 6: *pp*
bar 7: $\diamond$

---

[1] The original German indication "für das Hammerklavier"—chosen by Beethoven already for the sonatas Op. 101 and Op. 106—was abandoned in the first edition, apparently with Beethoven's consent, for the more customary "für das Pianoforte."

Of unsurpassed clarity are the large lozenge-shaped crescendo-decrescendo signs, which indicate precisely the peaks of volume. In the printed editions much of the accuracy of these signs is abandoned. Pedal marks (*ped.*) in bars 5, 6, and 7, are terminated by o in ink. In bar 5 this mark was crossed out and replaced by a larger one in pencil, further to the left, evidently to ensure that the pedal sustained throughout the dominant would be lifted before the tonic.

The repeat is indicated by a little *1* (1) above bar 5 and a 2 at the beginning of bar 7.

In bars 1 and 6 groups of six notes are abbreviated to groups of two with dots indicating the repetition.

In the printed versions, beats 2 and 3 of bar 3, lower staff, show another, evidently improved, version transferring the passage one-sixth lower than it is in the autograph.

PLATE 89 shows the beginning of Variation V. Beethoven first wrote in ink "All° ma non troppo"; over the "ma non troppo" he wrote "alla breve"; then he crossed out the "alla breve," which evidently was sufficiently indicated by the ¢ and added the "ma non troppo" again in pencil.

It is interesting to compare the crossed-out second double staff with the final version in the third. In bar 1 of the crossed-out section the rhythmical motif ♩♩♩♩, which up to then had been retained, is abandoned and the final version beneath restores it; in bar 3 of the crossed-out section the motion of the middle parts is downward while it is upward in the final version.

In the first three bars the first edition adds *sf* to the half-notes of the bass.

The writing is rapid and impetuous. Frequently the quill had no time to draw the head of the note, and only the beginning of the stem indicates the pitch (see, for instance, the last staff).

PLATE 90 shows bars 20-24 of Variation VI. In spite of the 3/4 time, Beethoven writes the B that forms the pedal point without a dot.

For obvious reasons Beethoven combines eight notes under one cross stroke at the end of the last bar; the printed version mechanically continues the preceding groups of four notes up to the end of the bar.

A waving line continues the trill on the pedal point which was introduced three bars before the beginning of this page, and ends with the turn in bar 5.

The writing, though still passionate and vehement, is somewhat lighter and less convulsive than in earlier scores. The cross strokes are jotted down violently. The quill must have hit the paper with heavy impact (see especially bar 1, second beat, bar 5, and the large sharps before the A's at the end of the last bar).

Ludwig van Beethoven (1770-1827)

SYMPHONY NO. 9, IN D MINOR, OP. 125 (91-93)

For orchestra, solo voices and chorus.

A bound volume and numerous single pages. Movement I: 99 written pages; Movement II: 85 pages; Movement III: 45 pages; Movement IV: 155 pages. Movements I, II, and III on oblong pages, size 23 x 30 cm., 16 staves to each page; in Movement IV the shape and size of the pages change according to need: 105 pages are oblong, similar to the pages in the preceding movement, the size of the remaining 50 pages is 35.5 x 34.5 cm.; 23 staves to each page.

On page 1 of the bound volume autograph heading: "Sinfonie/mit Schluss-chor über Schillers Ode: "an die Freude"/für grosses Orchester 14 Solo und 4 chor-stimmen,/componirt und/ Seiner Majestät dem König von Preussen/Friedrich Wilhelm III/in tiefster Ehrfurcht zugeeignet/von/Ludwig van Beethoven/125tes werk."

Composed 1817-1823, Vienna. Published 1826 by Schott & Söhne, Mainz. First performed May 7, 1824 in the Kärnthnertor-Theatre, Vienna.

Collected Works, Series 1, No. 9.

Nottebohm, thematic catalogue, p. 119 ff.; Bruers, thematic catalogue, p. 279 ff.

The autograph was in the Preussische Staatsbibliothek, Berlin.

Throughout the score many enlarged duplications of dynamic marks are written in red chalk; evidently by Beethoven's own hand and probably inserted as a guide for performance.

PLATE 91 shows the introduction to the third movement entitled, in stumbling letters of ever-growing size, *Adagio molto e cantabile.*

The scoring indications call the trumpets by their old name, "clarini." In the margin the oboes are indicated above the clarinets, but this order is reversed at the beginning of their parts. In the bottom staff, assigned according to the marginal indications to *violoncelli e bassi,* the word *violoncelli* is interpolated to indicate that the basses keep silent.

Striking is the large crescendo-decrescendo sign in bar 2, combined into one single diamond-shaped pattern which marks the dynamic peak with razor-sharp accuracy. The penciled repetition of this sign may have been added on the occasion of a performance.

Note the differentiation between *mezza voce* in the first violin and *p* in the other strings in bar 3.

PLATE 92 shows bars 121-127 of the finale with a section of the first variation on the theme of joy. This variation is written for three parts, the theme being assigned to the violas in unison with the violoncello (the upper voice in the bottom stave) while the basses and the first bassoon (staff 4) both perform cantabile counterpoints.

The long phrasing slurs in the bassoon part (bars 3 and 4, 6 and 7) and the bass part have been replaced by shorter ones in the printed versions, thus substantially changing the melodic physiognomy of these counterpoints; for example, A is replaced by B.

PLATE 93 presents the climax of the choral section of the movement with the first combination of the two main subjects for a double fugue. The soprano carries a rhythmically altered version of the invocation to joy: "Freude, schöner Götterfunken, Tochter aus Elysium," and the alto the counter subject: "Seid umschlungen, Millionen."

The order of the scoring is as follows: 1) flutes; 2) oboes; 3) clarinets in A; 4) bassoons; 5 and 6) four horns; 7) trumpets; 8) trombones; 9) first violins; 10) second violins; 11) violas; 12) violon-cellos and double basses; 13) soprano; 14) alto; 15) tenor; 16) bass. The staves for the chorus are joined by an additional brace.

The dynamic marks are applied with utmost subtlety. There are many shadings: *ff:, f., sf:* in the instrumental parts and *fo* in the vocal parts. Great stress is laid on the effect of the upbeat in the countersubject: an initial *ff* or *f* is immediately softened to an *sf*; only in the first violin part an *f* is maintained after an initial *ff*.

The last note in bar 4 of the flute part is mistakenly written as a half-note instead of a quarter-note.

Beethoven uses latin characters in *All° Energico/ e sempre ben marcato/ le note*, and in *unisono*; gothic script for the words of the German text. The writing, for all its ever changing slant and variations in size, is of the greatest possible connectedness. This page is a good example of one characteristic trait of Beethoven's script, the flagrant incongruity between time-values and their expression on paper. Frequently the note of the first beat is placed in the middle of the measure or even farther to the right (see bars 2-4 of staff 3; or bar 3 of staff 10). In the first bar of the first violin part, on the other hand, he made a correction which cramped the whole passage into the left half of the measure. How different is all this from Mozart's accurate spacing!

Ludwig van Beethoven (1770-1827)

SECOND MOVEMENT (PRESTO) OF THE STRING QUARTET IN B FLAT MAJOR, OP. 130 (94, 95)

Six leaves of greenish paper, eleven written pages, last page blank; ten staves to each page, fifth and tenth stave blank. Size: 23.8 x 30.5 cm. Unsigned. Undated.

Composed in 1825, according to Thayer's *Chronologisches Verzeichnis*.[1]

First performed in Vienna, March 21, 1826 by the Schuppanzigh Quartet.

Collected Works, Series VI, Vol. 2, No. 13.

Nottebohm, thematic catalogue, p. 123 ff.; Bruers, thematic catalogue, p. 313 ff.

Collection: The Gertrude Clarke Whittall Foundation Collection, The Library of Congress, Washington, D.C.

This quartet is the third of the "Galitizin Quartets." The title of the edition published on May 7, 1827, after Beethoven's death, was "Troisième Quatuor pour 2 Violons, Alto & Violoncello des Quatuors composés et dediés a Son Altesse Monseigneur le Prince Nicolas de Galitzin, . . .". The last movement of the quartet was originally the *Great Fugue*, which later was published separately as Op. 133.

Sketches for this quartet are found in the sketchbooks of 1825 and 1826, which were formerly in the possession of Anton Schindler and subsequently went to the Staatsbibliothek, Berlin.

The catalogue of music manuscripts owned by Artaria & Co., Vienna, issued 1893, lists the autograph of the fifth movement (cavatina) as well as sketches for the sixth movement.

PLATES 94 and 95 show pages 1 and 3 of the manuscript. Both are extremely characteristic of Beethoven's hand, especially in the untidiness of the writing, which is irregular in almost every respect: size, spacing, pressure, width, etc. These pages are also typical in the number of corrections. According to Eusebius Mandyczewski, the present manuscript "represents a clean copy, embodying the final version of the work in spite of some minor corrections." Nonetheless some of the corrections are of incisive importance.

[1] According to Nottebohm, thematic catalogue, the finale was composed in 1826.

The first plate (bars 1-12 of the movement) shows Beethoven as usual tirelessly changing and revising the almost completed work. Bars 1-3 and 5-7 reveal an afterthought. The viola part has been erased and replaced in vigorous notes by the present striking counterpoint. The stems of some of the former notes are still visible, especially in bars 3 and 7; what these notes were is open to conjecture; probably they followed a line of less outstanding individuality. In connection with the alteration of the viola part, the violoncello part was also changed: for instance, in bars 2 and 6 the A has been moved an octave higher. The counterpoint returns later, in bar 64 ff., in a slightly different version, but already in the changed form.

Peculiar to Beethoven's hand are the rhombic crescendo-diminuendo signs: they are much smaller or entirely omitted, evidently for lack of space, in some bars of the second violin part. The Collected Works insert them there.

The second plate shows bars 21-29 of the movement, i.e., a part of the section in 6/4 time.

In bar 3 Beethoven abandons the $^{8}\sim\sim$, jots down a gigantic *loco* and resorts to ledger lines. Here the quill leaves too much ink. The writing sand, far from helping, makes things worse. Thus in the end Beethoven must resort to clarifying letters on top of the notes. In his haste he notes the appoggiaturas sometimes by ♪ sometimes by ♪. Against all rational spacing, they often govern a wider area than the notes themselves.

The script is uneven in the extreme; notice bars 3 and 6, where the writing in each of the four parts is different. Only the part of the first violin is written evenly in thin notes, as if in one constant flow.

The double stops in the second violin in the first bar of the second section (bar 6) and the preceding second ending of the first section (bar 5) have evidently been added on second thought. The natural sign in bar 8 was added in pencil. The pencil crescendo in bar 6 is traced in ink; the horizontal dashes in the following bars continue the crescendo up to the forte on the following page of the manuscript.

Beethoven was lavish with space: the measures are extremely wide; only bars 4 and 5 (that is, the first ending of the first section and the second ending, following the repeat of the first section), are crowded. The latter, particularly, seems to have been squeezed in later. It looks as if Beethoven had originally planned to use bar 4 for the first as well as for the second ending, then changed his mind for the sake of the harmony. As bar 4 remains in the Tonic up to the end, while the section (bar 6) begins in the Dominant, Beethoven evidently came to find it more appropriate to anticipate the Dominant by the chords in the second half of the preceding bar; thus he wedged in bar 5 as a second ending, marked 2 above it, and a corresponding *i* (meaning 1) above bar 4. But one should perhaps go even further in the interpretation of this page and try to relate the explanation attempted earlier to two other details, which otherwise would remain isolated puzzles. The *loco* in bar 3 does not seem logical as the page looks now. Why didn't Beethoven continue the 8va sign, which would have required fewer ledger lines? Evidently he originally planned a passage which would not go up so high; with this in mind, one can easily detect some thin stems under the thick ones in bars 3 and 4, and even a note head in bar 4. Thus, it seems that Beethoven, when he first jotted down the part for the first violin, gave it a different turn at the end of the first section. We can no longer decipher the passage now overlaid with heavier notes, but in view of his other changes, especially the one anticipating the Dominant, it would seem logical that the first violin part originally went to f″, perhaps as follows:

And indeed, the original thin stem of the last note in bar 3 reaches up to the third ledger line, corresponding to an e″.

The bottom stave was used for pencil sketches for the part of the first violin.

Notice that Beethoven does not repeat the initial clefs and the accidentals. The buoyant braces, so characteristic of Beethoven's hand, end in a spiral facing outward.

Carl Maria von Weber (1786-1826)

OBERON (96)

Aria for the opera. Libretto by J. R. Planché.

One leaf, written on both sides. Size: 24.5 x 30.5 cm. On the front, an arrangement for voice and pianoforte accompaniment of *Huon's* aria: "Ruler of this awful hour . . ."; three triple staves. On the back, 14 measures of Fatima's song: "Oh Araby, dear Araby. . . ."

Autograph heading: "Act the Second.|: after the storm:|/Preghiera . . . Adagio."

The opera was composed in 1825 and 1826; published in 1826 by Welsh & Hawes, London; first performed April 12, 1826, in London, Covent Garden.

Collection: The Library of Congress, Washington, D.C.

The *Preghiera* is no. 13 of the second act of the opera, and follows immediately after the "Storm," which, after Beethoven's *Pastorale* and Weber's *Freischütz*, is one of the most powerful musical tempests ever depicted by an orchestra. It is this storm to which the heading of the page refers. The text of the present page reads: "Ruler of this awful howr—spare, o spare, yon tender flowr! if thou must strike, o let thy thunder fall on me, on me, the wretched cause of all. . . ."

On the back of the page, five more bars conclude the *Preghiera*. Then follows the opening of the third act, with *Fatima's* song, in B flat major, *andante con moto*: "Oh Araby, dear Araby, my own, my native land."

Observe the range of the delicate dynamic shadings from *fo* to *pps*, the accents in the piano part and the differentiation between *dolce* in the voice, and *dolcissimo* in the accompaniment, in bar 13. Also the dramatic, sudden lapse from *f* into *pp*, at "on me, the wretched cause."

The writing is clear, fluent and vigorous. The stems are drawn out of the heads, and the flags of the sixteenth-notes out of the stems. The staff lines are extended by hand to the right edge of the page.

Franz Schubert (1797-1828)

DIE FORELLE (97)

Song with piano accompaniment, Op. 32. Words by Christian Friedrich Daniel Schubart.

One sheet written on both sides, five triple staves to a page. Size 23 x 31.8 cm.

Autograph heading: "Die Forelle/Von Schubart." In the upper right corner: "Frz. Schubert M[propr]ia/ Oct. 1821."

Composed originally in 1817 or 1818. First printed in 1820, as a supplement to the *Wiener Zeitung für Kunst, Literatur, Theater und Mode*, Vienna. Later published in 1825 by Anton

Diabelli & Co., Vienna, under the title "Die Forelle, Gedicht von Schubart, in Musik gesetzt für eine Singstimme mit Begleitung des Pianoforte von Franz Schubert."

Collected Works, Series xx, vol. 5 (but this version is not included!).

Deutsch, thematic catalogue No. 550.

Collection: The Gertrude Clarke Whittall Foundation Collection, The Library of Congress, Washington, D.C. There are two other copies of the song in the collections of Maria and Rudolf Floersheim, Wildegg (Aargau), Switzerland, and G. Salvini, Porto, Italy.[1] The present autograph, written three or four years after the composition of the song, is evidently a dedication copy or a copy rewritten from memory for some immediate occasion.[2]

This autograph differs from all four versions given in the Collected Works, which gives 1817 as the date of the first. Their tempo indications are: (1) *Mässig*; (2) *Etwas geschwind* (as in the present version); (3) *Nicht zu geschwind*; (4) *Etwas lebhaft*. None of these four versions has the prelude of the present one, but like it they all have a postlude after each strophe. In three of the versions in the Collected Works the sextolets of the accompaniment in the postlude are repeated in the right hand before they are transferred to the bass. In the fourth, however, which is identical in this respect with the present version, they are in the bass throughout; in the present version this pattern is followed in the prelude as well.

Schubert was a teacher, which, no doubt, accounts for the extreme tidiness of his hand and the use of two kinds of script, latin for the title and for the Italian word "Piano-Forte," gothic for the text, tempo indication and poet's name, and for his own signature.

Notice the neat braces and clefs, the unusually large numbers indicating the time, and the consistent meticulous accents and staccato dots.

[1] Alfred Orel, "Kleine Schubert-Studien," in *Archiv für Musikforschung*, Berlin, 1937.

[2] Schubert's friend, Anselm Hüttenbrenner, in his *Bruchstücke aus dem Leben des Liederkomponisten Franz Schubert* reports, ". . . Schubert paid little attention to the whereabouts of his numerous compositions. When he showed some of his new songs to his good friends, they took the copy-books away and promised to bring them back soon, which, however, they did seldom enough." At another place in his biography Hüttenbrenner tells us: "One evening I invited Schubert to my home, since I had received from a distinguished family a few bottles of red wine as a reward for repeated services as an accompanist. After we had finished the precious 'Geyarder' wine to the last drop, Schubert sat down at my desk and composed the enchanting song 'Die Forelle,' of which I still own the original. . . . This was February 21, 1818." The almost fantastic alertness of Schubert's genius is confirmed by many of his contemporaries. Hüttenbrenner again reports: "Schubert, Assmayer, Mozatti and I agreed to sing every Thursday evening a newly composed quartet for male voices. Once Schubert came without a quartet, but when we reproached him, he wrote one immediately in our presence."

Franz Schubert (1797-1828)

RONDEAU BRILLANT IN B MINOR, FOR PIANO AND VIOLIN, OP. 70 (98, 99)

Twenty-eight pages, sixteen staves to each page. The end of page 7 is crossed out; page 8 contains sketches for the continuation of page 6, page 9 is blank; page 10 contains the continuation of page 6. Size: 24.7 x 32 cm.

Autograph heading: "Rondo (op 70 [in pencil, not in Schubert's hand]) Oct. 1826/ Frz. Schubert M[propr]ia."

Composed in 1826. Published in 1827 by A. Diabelli & Co., Vienna, under the title: "Rondeau brillant pour Pianoforte et Violon par François Schubert. Op. 70."

Collected Works, Series VIII, No. 1.

Deutsch, thematic catalogue, No. 895.

Collection: The Heinemann Foundation for Research, Educational, Charitable and Scientific Purposes, Inc., New York.

The manuscript abounds in corrections, most of them evidently not later emendations but radical changes made in the process of composition. The writing is vigorous and tidy in spite of apparent haste. The bar lines are for the most part drawn separately for each staff.

PLATE 98 shows the beginning of the *Rondo*. The braces joining the staves, though fairly carefully drawn in the first two systems, become entirely shapeless later. Note the curious zigzag 4 in the time signature. In bars 15-16, 18-19 and 26-27 the violin part, which was evidently written first, was not spaced out widely enough to allow for the three sextoles of the piano part; so the bar lines had to be connected by S-curved lines.

Whenever possible Schubert uses the time-saving repetition sign ⤢

PLATE 99 shows a page from the Allegro. The page begins seventeen bars before the transition to G major[1] (♮♯‖) .

[1] The Collected Works depart from the autograph, mainly in its dynamic signs. The signs in the violin and piano part, bar 2ff. are *fz* (cf. the more clearly written *fz* in bar 10). The Collected Works use *sf*, adding one to beat 2 of bar 1 and ignoring the one in bar 4. The Collected Works, moreover, add *ff* to the chord in the piano part bar 6, *ff* to the entry of the violin, *sf* to the last chord in the pianoforte in bar 7, and a $<$ in the violin part which passes into a $>$ only at the beginning of bar 15.

The deleted violin melody on the bottom of the page is quite different in the *Collected Works*, but the transition to G major has been retained.

Gioacchino Rossini (1792-1868)

ALMAVIVA OSSIA L'INUTILE PRECAUZIONE (100, 101)

Opera ("dramma buffo") in two acts. Text by Cesare Sterbini, based upon Beaumarchais' *Le Barbier de Séville*.

330 leaves with 642 written pages. 10, 12, 14, or 16 staves to each page. Size: 21.5 x 28 cm.

The first 5 leaves and the guitar accompaniment to the canzone of *Almaviva* "Se il mio nome" are not by Rossini's hand.

Autograph heading: "Teatro Argentina/Opera Terza/Il Barbiere di Siviglia/Del Sig.r Gioacchino Rossini//Atto Primo/Sinfonia/Basso."

Unsigned. Undated.

Composed 1816 for the Carnival in Rome. First performed February 20, 1816, at the Teatro Argentina, Rome. The title "Il Barbiere di Siviglia" was used only half a year later, at performances of the opera in Bologna.

Collection: Biblioteca del Conservatorio di Musica G. B. Martini.

PLATES 100 and 101 show the front sides of leaves 32 and 37 from Act I, with opening and a later section of *Figaro's* famous cavatina.

Leaf 32 recto: the tempo *All: Viv:* is indicated only at the bottom. The violins and violas are written above the winds. The violin part shows careful dynamic shading, diminishing from *f^mo* through decrescendo to *f*, immediately followed by decrescendo. Rossini writes the G clef in a manner that is as ingenious as it is easy and comfortable, by breaking it into two downstrokes instead of executing it in one full round curve. He also avoids loops in his lettering (see the "*l*" in *violini, flauto, clarinetti,* etc.). The F clef, intersected by a vertical line, looks like an "alla breve" sign.

Leaf 37 recto: the clefs are not repeated. Note the phrasing achieved by writing ♪♫♫ in the initial bars of the second violin and viola parts; and by the staccato notes there, and in the vocal part on "di qualità," and also in the last bar (first violin, flute, and solo bassoon).

According to all reports, Rossini composed with fabulous speed. Thus it is not surprising that a close inspection of his script reveals certain peculiar time-saving habits such as are easily and often unconsciously developed by speedy writers. Wherever on the second plate (101) a ledger line is supposed to cross the head of a note, the head itself is omitted, thus saving one motion of the quill. This does not in the least impede the legibility of the script: every draftsman and printmaker is familiar with the fact that two intersecting black lines create, by an optical illusion, a more or less vague dot at the point of intersection. It is interesting, however, that Rossini apparently falls into this habit only when he is in full swing. While Plate 101 shows everywhere the simplification mentioned, the beginning of the cavatina (plate 100) employs the customary dots, with the possible exception of the flute part.

Gioacchino Rossini (1792-1868)

GUILLAUME TELL (102)

Opera in four acts. Text by V. J. Etienne de Jouy and H. L. F. Bis. 1087 pages: Overture and Act I, 392 pages; Act II, 250 pages; Act III, 292; Act IV, 153. 16 staves to each page. Size: 25.1 x 33.3 cm.
Unsigned. Undated.
Composed in 1829.
First performance in Paris, August 3, 1829, at the Opéra.
Collection: Bibliothèque Musée de l'Opéra, Paris.

Guillaume Tell was the last of Rossini's operas and besides the *Barbiere di Siviglia* his most successful. In only five years it reached a hundred performances at the Paris Opera.

PLATE 102 shows a section from the *Andantino* in 6/8 time (Act IV, No. 19) sung by *Arnaldo.* Besides the ordinary crescendo and decrescendo wedges, Rossini uses a small closed wedge (in the shape of a triangle pointing to the right, see bars 1 and 5). What does it mean? In Rameau's *Zoroastre* (1749) and also in Gluck's autograph scores[1] and in their early French editions[2] this sign is frequent, and evidently stands for decrescendo. In the edition of *Iphigénie en Tauride*[3] a triangle pointing to the left occurs, leading from a piano to a forte. In the score of *Guillaume Tell* however, half a century later, the open decrescendo wedge and the small triangle pointing

---

[1] See, for example, *Alceste,* French version.
[2] Ed. Des Lauriers, Paris.
[3] Ed. Des Lauriers, p. 165.

to the right appear side by side:[4] moreover, in bar 5 of our page, such a triangle is superimposed on an open crescendo wedge, the latter leading to a *f*. Thus it seems likely that Rossini's triangle stands for a short diminuendo that is to begin precisely at the point indicated by the vertical line of the wedge. One wonders, however, how this applies to a pizzicato like that in bar 1, staff 3.

[4] Mr. Raffaele Tenaglia, Librarian of G. Ricordi & Company, Milan, draws my attention to the fact that a triangle pointing to the left also appears in Rossini's scores. He believes that this triangle is equivalent to an open *crescendo* wedge followed by a *sf*, and conversely, the triangle pointing to the right equivalent to *sf* followed by an open *decrescendo* wedge.

Gioacchino Rossini (1792-1868)

MI LAGNERÒ TACENDO (103)

For voice and piano accompaniment.
One page, 9 staves. Size: 14.7 x 18.9 cm.
Signed: "G. Rossini" and dedicated to "Al Maestro de' Maestri."
Undated. Composed Paris, 1830 (?).
Collection: Maria and Rudolf Floersheim, Wildegg, Switzerland.

This page is one of countless little vocal and instrumental pieces written by Rossini into the albums of his admirers. Similar pieces are found among the nearly 200 musical "bon mots" composed by Rossini during his Paris time and all preserved in the Liceo Musicale in Pesaro; most of them are of grotesque or parodistic character, such as the "Hygienic Prelude for use in the morning" or the "Miscarriage of a Polka Mazurka" etc.

The text is amorous. But who is "the master of the masters" to whom Rossini dedicated this musical trifle of 8 bars? Is it the god of love? Is it Cimarosa or Cherubini?[1] Or perhaps Brillat-Savarin who must have been dear to Rossini not so much as a musician—he played in a New York orchestra during the French revolution—as for his treatise on the art of dining, the famous *Physiologie du goût?*

Unusual is the 5/4 time. The decrescendo triangles are the same as in the preceding plate. The close of the piano part has the usual decrescendo sign.

[1] Friedrich Stendhal, *Rossini*, Paris, 1824: "Rossini adored Cimarosa; if he speaks of him, tears come into his eyes. . . . He had the highest esteem for Cherubini as the most learned musician."

Niccolò Paganini (1782-1840)

MOTO PERPETUO, IN C MAJOR, OP. 11,
NO. 6 POSTHUMOUS (104)

Title page and two written pages, 24 staves. Size 20.2 x 29 cm.
Autograph title page: "All° Vivace e movimento perpetuo/ per violino con accompto di Chitarra[1]/ Genova li 6 Aprile 1835 / Paganini." Several illegible notes in red ink. The virtuoso solo violin part is very closely written; the accompaniment is missing.

[1] "Chitarra" designates the Italian guitar of Paganini's time. The virtuoso composer was fond of guitar accompaniment. Being an Italian patriot, Paganini withdrew from public life after the in-

Composed 1835.
Collection: The New York Public Library, New York.

PLATE 104 shows the last page. The *Moto Perpetuo*, which has become a showpiece of violinists, consists of 189 bars of rapid and uniform staccato motion without pause, an ideal study for détaché bowing at extreme speed. Movements with such unceasing quick flux were fashionable before Paganini; of similar character is the finale of Joseph Haydn's *String Quartet Op. 64, No. 5.*

Fétis regards the piece as a movement from a sonata for violin and orchestra. The Schott edition includes an orchestral accompaniment, as well as an accompaniment for pianoforte. The violin part coincides with the present autograph.

Autographs of Paganini's works are rare. He jealously guarded the solo part of his compositions and started publishing his works only in later years after he had abandoned his concert tours.

The writing, although perfectly legible, shows every evidence of great rapidity. There are many dynamic and expression marks, such as: *cresc, fe, ff, po, dolce.* In the fourth bar from the end Paganini uses up to five ledger lines instead of employing the 8va sign.

At the end in Paganini's hand: "misure 146[?]e Compreso la Repplica 189."[2]

vasion of Italy by Napoleon and lived for three years in Tuscany in the castle of a lady who played the guitar. It was there that he acquired a virtuoso mastery of this instrument. His *Quartets Op. 4* and 5 were written for violin, viola, violoncello, and guitar, and his *Op.* 2 consists of 6 sonatas for violin and guitar.

[2] 146 bars, or 189 bars including the repeat.

Gaetano Donizetti (1797-1848)

NEL VOSTRO SEN PIÙ VOI RITROVO (105)

Fragment of an aria for soprano with orchestral accompaniment.
Eight pages, four containing the aria, three blank, the last page containing nine bars with a sketch of a *duetto recitativo*. 16 staves to each page. Size: 26.5 x 40.5 cm.
Unsigned. Undated.
Composed in 1827 (?). Apparently unpublished.
Collection: The New York Public Library, New York (presented by Mr. Sam Franko).

The aria is in A major, marked *larghetto* on the top and bottom of the first page. As the names *Elisabetta* and *Potozki* occur in this manuscript, this aria was probably meant for Donizetti's opera *Gli esiliati in Siberia ossia Otto mesi in due ore* which was performed for the first time on May 13, 1827, in Naples. The words of this aria are missing in the published libretto. The composer may well have written it with the intention of inserting it into the opera.

PLATE 105 shows page 4 of the manuscript, with *Elisabetta's* outcry: "Sempre per voi questo mio core palpitarsi. . . ." Note the careful phrasing slurs in bar 1 of the page, the accents (>) in the bass, and the typical coloratura passages of the soprano with the usual ⌢ signs.

The writing is extremely fluent and vigorous, with fat cross strokes quite detached from the stems of the notes. The direction in bar 2 of the double bass part is *Arco*, that in the vocal part *Lento*.

Vincenzo Bellini (1801-1835)

IL PIRATA (106-107)

Opera ("melodramma") in two acts. Text by Felice Romani.
Act I: 177 leaves; 20 staves to each page. Size: 23.1 x 29.8 cm.
Signed. Undated.
Composed 1827. Published by G. Ricordi & Co., Milan. First performed October 27, 1827, at La Scala, Milan.
Collection: Biblioteca del Conservatorio (Archivio del Real Collegio di Musica) S. Pietro a Majella, Naples.

PLATES 106 and 107 show two successive pages, i.e., the back of leaf 151, and the front of leaf 152, showing a trio sung by *Italbo*, *Gualtiero*, and *Ernesto*.

As the staves are unusually close to each other, Bellini is at times compelled to write notes with several ledger lines so far down that they overlap the upper staff lines. Thus the note is indicated by the number of ledger lines rather than by its relation to the staff lines.

Observe the accent on the second syllable of "Corsari" before the ⌒ on plate 106; and the long instrumental crescendo and decrescendo sign which underlines the recitative.

The crossed-out section shows a change of key which does not occur in the final version.

Felix Mendelssohn-Bartholdy (1809-1847)

ANDANTE MAESTOSO FOR PIANOFORTE (108)

No. 3 of the Fifth Book of the *Lieder ohne Worte*, Op. 62 (so-called *Funeral March*).
One folded sheet, with two written pages of music on the inside, of which the left contains the *Andante Maestoso*, the right the *Allegro con fuoco* (12/8 in B major) which in the Fifth Book of the *Lieder ohne Worte* precedes the *Andante Maestoso*.
16 staves to each page. Size: 30.2 x 22.8 cm.
Autograph heading: on the front page of the sheet: "Zwei Lieder ohne Worte"; and at the right lower corner: "an Mme Clara Schumann/ den 13.ten September 1843/ mit den herzlichsten Glückwünschen/ F M B."
Composed 1843.
The first editions of the Fifth Book of the *Lieder ohne Worte* were published by Novello & Co., and Breitkopf und Härtel.
Collected Works, Series II, vol. 4, Heft 5.
Collection: Rudolf F. Kallir, New York.

The present variant differs somewhat from that in the customary printed editions of the *Lieder ohne Worte*: the fanfares which appear in bars 1-4, 29-31 and 46-48 of the plate reproduced all have upbeats in triplets in the final version; and the introductory and closing fanfares are longer there.

Notice the accurate pedal marks, for instance, the two *Ped* in bars 2 and 4.

The dynamic marks cover a wide range of delicate shadings. The writing and spacing are extremely neat; characteristic are the *ff* signs with the two letters fused into one capricious pattern, and the strangely simplified G clefs.

Frédéric François Chopin (1810-1849)

ALLEGRO DE CONCERT POUR LE PIANOFORTE, OP. 46 (109, 110)

Title page and 11 written pages. Fourteen staves to each page. Score written in five double staves. Size: 21 x 27.5 cm.

Autograph title page: "Allegro de Concert / pour le Pianoforte / dédié / à Mlle F. Müller (de Vienne)./ par F. Chopin. / Oev. 46. / Leipsic Breitkopf et Haertel."

Undated.

Composed in 1841. Published in 1841, by Breitkopf & Härtel, Leipzig.

Collected Works, vol. x, No. 6.

Collection: The Heinemann Foundation for research, educational, charitable & scientific purposes, Inc., New York.

According to Chopin's letters, the piece was originally written as part of a concerto.

PLATE 109 shows the first, plate 110 the fifth page of the manuscript.

The manuscript contains abundant directions for the performer and especially a great number of dynamic marks indicating the minutest gradations of volume. As Chopin often employs crescendos which are built up throughout several bars, the simple < would not do: thus he uses *cresc* followed by long lines of dots, and employs < and > only for smaller dynamic changes. Also characteristic are the extremely long phrasing slurs. The pedal marks are of admirable accuracy: the figure A, which turns up in bar 23, is repeated in the following three bars, but the pedal—in line with the harmony—is at times held over into the fourth chord (i.e., first chord of bars 24 and 26), and at times lifted before the fourth chord (i.e., first chord of bars 25 and 27). A ♩♩♩ B ♫♫♫

Of ingenious simplicity is the method of condensed part-writing employed in the first four bars (B) of plate 110 and frequently found in Chopin's scores. Notice also the length of the cross strokes which either run through the whole bar or almost the whole bar.

Frédéric François Chopin (1810-1849)

POLONAISE IN A FLAT MAJOR, FOR PIANO, OP. 53 (111)

Six pages, 14 staves to each page (five double staves with single blank staves in between). Size: 22 x 28 cm.

Heading in the composer's hand: "Polonaise, pour le piano, dediée à Monsieur Auguste Leo, par F. Chopin./ Op. 53./ Leipsic Breitkopf et Haertel. Paris Schlésinger. Londres Wessel et Stapleton."

Composed in 1840. Published in 1843 by M. Schlesinger, Paris. First performed in 1844 by Clara Schumann.

Collected Works, vol. V, No. 6.

Collection: The Heinemann Foundation for Research, Educational, Charitable and Scientific Purposes, Inc., New York.

The manuscript contains several corrections, cancellations, additions, and some pencil marks apparently added by the printer.

PLATE 111 shows the first page of the manuscript. Note the very accurate, almost pedantic, pedal marks, especially towards the end of the page. In the fifth bar of the last double stave there are no fewer than six pedal marks, one for each eighth-note. Some modern editions deviate unnecessarily from the pedal marks in the Complete Edition which follows closely the autograph.[1]

For crescendos Chopin employs two signs: *cresc* (in bars 10, 15, and the last but one) and crescendo wedges. *Cresc* is always combined with a string of dots to show the length of the swelling. Note that the crescendo leading from bar 10 by a string of dots to the *f* in bar 13 is further shaded by additional $\diagdown$ $\diagup$ $\diagdown$.

Bar 14 of the manuscript has a decrescendo wedge on the third beat which prepares for the following long crescendo.[2]

Note the painstaking corrections, such as the prolongation of a short phrasing slur into a longer one at the turn of bar 21 to bar 22 and the shortening of the decrescendo in bar 22.

[1] For instance, the manuscript, in bars 21 and 22, leaves the pedal on through the fifth eighth-note in the bass. Peters Edition (Hermann Scholtz) has it lifted after the third eighth-note; this, however, appears to be an improvement—at least for a performance on the modern pianoforte with its greater sustaining power—since it brings out the consistent phrasing of the bass line.

In studying Chopin's pedal marks one should bear in mind that his Pleyel pianoforte was not yet cross strung and therefore had comparatively little resonance.

[2] This sign is omitted in the Collected Works and in the edition by Schirmer (Library of Musical Classics, vol. 29, ed. by Carl Mikuli) and replaced in the Peters Edition (Hermann Scholtz) by a $>$ which in Chopin's manuscripts denotes an accent and is frequently used side by side with dynamic marks (see, for instance, bar 25 of the present page).

Robert Alexander Schumann (1810-1856)

FIRST SYMPHONY, B FLAT MAJOR, OP. 38, THE "SPRING" SYMPHONY (112-113)

212 pages bound in half linen, 16 staves a page. Size: 29.5 x 22 cm.

Composed 1841.

Collected Works, Series 1, No. 1.

On the title page is written in Schumann's hand:

> "1) Frühlingsbeginn
> 2) Abend
> 3) Frohe Gespielen
> 4) Voller(?) Frühling"

On a preliminary leaf the performances of the symphony between 1841 and 1852 are noted, also in Schumann's hand, with dates, places, and conductors. On a second preliminary leaf is a presentation autograph from Clara Schumann to the conductor Hermann Levi. The next sixteen pages contain a pencil draft of the whole work in piano score. On page 23 the full orchestra score begins with the heading: "27. Januar 1841. Frühlingssymphonie." Each of the four movements is separately dated.

The autograph is the first complete holograph of the score and was used for the first performance. Frequent alterations and improvements of the instrumentation are visible. Nevertheless the score was thoroughly revised before the first printing.

Collection: The Library of Congress, Washington, D.C. (Acquired in 1927 from the Heyer Museum, Cologne.) Formerly owned by Clara Schumann and Hermann Levi.

The joint diary of Robert and Clara Schumann contains the following statement: "January 25th: Today, Monday, Robert has about finished this symphony; it has been composed mostly at night—my poor Robert has spent some sleepless nights over it. He calls it 'Spring Symphony' . . . On Tuesday Robert finished his symphony; so, begun and ended in four days." . . . Robert adds: "Sketched January 23-26, 1841."

To E. F. Wenzel Schumann wrote in January 1841: "During the last few days I have finished a work (or, at least, the outlines of it), over which I was perfectly blissful, but it has quite exhausted me. Just fancy, a whole symphony, and a spring symphony, too. I can hardly believe myself that it is finished. The score is, however, not written out yet. So you may imagine all that there is to be done, and pray help your

Schumann."[1]

PLATE 112 shows page 36 of the fourth movement. The orchestra is divided into three groups: 1) horns in F and B flat; 2) the woodwinds; 3) the body of strings. The bar lines are rapidly drawn freehand. The writing here is rapid and irregular. In bar 5 of the viola part the last note has been entirely omitted. Often the rests could be mistaken for notes. The notes themselves are drawn in a highly disconnected manner: their stems in most cases do not reach the beams, and in bar 6 of the first violin part a stem is missing. Compare the *p*'s in bars 2 and 6. On the other hand, the flats indicating the key at the beginning of the staves are fused into one single zigzag line.

PLATE 113 shows the last page of the score, terminating in a forcefully drawn last chord and signed: "Beendigt am 20sten/ Februar 1841./ Leipzig / Dr. [?] Robert Schumann."

[1] "Ich hab' in den vorigen Tagen eine Arbeit vollendet (wenigstens in den Umrissen), über die ich ganz selig gewesen, die mich aber auch ganz erschöpft. Denken Sie, eine ganze Symphonie— und obendrein eine Frühlingssymphonie (B dur). Ich kann kaum selber es glauben, dass sie fertig ist. Doch fehlt noch die Ausführung der Partitur. Also denken Sie was es da zu thun gibt, und helfen Ihrem Schumann."
From *Robert Schumann's Briefe*, neue Folge, edited by F. Gustav Jansen, 2nd edition, Leipzig, 1904.

Robert Alexander Schumann (1810-1856)
STRING QUARTET IN F MAJOR, OP. 41, NO. 2 (114)

In a volume containing the holograph scores of all three of the string quartets in op. 41. Quartet

I: 33 pages; quartet II: 29; quartet III: 39. Four quadruple staves to each page. Size: 30.5 x 23 cm. Each quartet is paged separately.

On the flyleaf of the volume: "Meiner lieben Klara dargebracht / am 13ten September 1842."

Title page of the volume: "III. Quartette / für / 2 Violinen, Viola und Violoncell / componirt /von / Robert Schumann / Juni und Juli 1842." At the bottom of the same page: "Herrn Raimund Härtel / zur Erinnerung / R. SCH. / Leipzig / den 19 November 1846."

Each quartet has a separate title page with the composer's signature. At the end of the first quartet: "Den 24sten Juni 1842 / am Geburtstag in Leipzig beendet / Robert Schumann."; of the second: "5 Juli 1842 Lzg / Rob. Schumann"; of the third: "Leipzig den 22sten Juli 1842 / Robert Schumann." The single movements of the quartets are also dated.

Collected Works, Series IV, No. 19.

Collection: Rudolf F. Kallir, New York.

PLATE 114 shows the first page of the second quartet.

Very revealing of Schumann's working method are the numerous corrections: 1) A majestic *andante* introduction of four bars is crossed out; 2) The viola part shows many changes (see bars 17 ff. of the *All° vivace*), and in the violin part the melody has been altered in bars 20 and 21, and correspondingly in bar 24; 3) A $>$ in the part of the first violin, bar 23, is crossed out and the phrasing slurs in bars 27, 28, are replaced by shorter ones; 4) In bars 19 and 20 $<$ and $>$ signs are added in pencil.[1]

The handwriting of the thirty-two-year-old composer is already clearly defined. Even now we find a marked disconnectedness. The stems of the notes frequently do not reach the cross strokes and sometimes are not even connected with the heads. The design of the single letters is also broken: see, for instance, the *f* signs, which are drawn in three separate strokes, and the four *stringendo* marks in the introduction, in all of which the *g* in the middle is detached from the other letters. All these characteristics become more emphasized in Schumann's later works.

Note the simplified clefs. The bar lines, as a rule, are drawn in two separate strokes, one evidently drawn first for the first violin, the other for the three other parts. The present page, like the beginnings of the other movements, shows a metronome mark.

[1] They do not appear in the *Collected Works*.

Robert Alexander Schumann (1810-1856)

DREI PHANTASIESTÜCKE FÜR DAS PIANOFORTE, OP. 111 (115)

Three pages, eight double staves to each page. Size: 26.6 x 34 cm.

No heading. Undated. Signed: "Handschrift von Robert Schumann. Clara Schumann."

Composed and published in 1851.

Collected Works, Series VII, vol. 6, no. 34.

Collection: The Newberry Library, Chicago, Ill.

The first page of the manuscript contains in staves 1-10 a cancelled sketch of the piece in A flat major (*Ziemlich langsam*, no. 2 of Op. 111), and in staves 11-16 the first 16 bars of no. 3 (*Etwas bewegter*), which continues on pages 2 and 3 of the manuscript. The fourth page contains sketches for no. 2.

PLATE 115 shows the first page of the manuscript. The crossed-out section (the first five double staves) differs in many respects from the final version; but theme, key and general contour have already been established. The version of the *Collected Works* counts 25 bars and is in 3/4 time rather than the 3/2 time of the draft. The *Etwas bewegter* coincides with the *Collected Works*, except for a few minor details: the *Collected Works* omit the > in bar 2, and repeat the < of bars 10 and 11 in the bars 12-14.

The *Collected Works* in the last bars of the present page fill in those chords which Schumann indicated only by number (6,6) in his draft; and shift the accents which in the draft appear between the two staves to positions above and beneath the double stave.

In bar 9 Schumann clarified illegible notes by adding the letters *e* and *c*.

The writing, broken into minute, thin, disconnected elements, is typical of the later works of Schumann. Many features are simplified or only hinted in a sort of shorthand: clefs and accidentals, for instance, are condensed to the extreme, stems of notes are indicated only by short juts, often not much larger than the heads of the notes, and sometimes they are entirely omitted. Notes, stems and cross strokes are detached from each other to such degree that the whole script acquires a pointillistic appearance. Schumann's hand had changed considerably since the *Frühlingssymphonie* (Plates 112, 113). Three years after the completion of Op. 111 his mind failed. In the year 1854 Brahms writes to Breitkopf & Härtel from Düsseldorf: "The news about Mr. Schumann is almost always the same. He is very quiet, eats and sleeps well, takes many walks also outside of the institution; he also writes much but the doctor cannot read his writing...."[1]

[1] "Die Nachrichten von Hrn. Schumann sind fast immer dieselben. Er ist sehr ruhig, isst u. schläft gut, geht viel spazieren auch ausserhalb der Anstalt, auch schreibt Er viel, der Hr. Arzt kann jedoch die Handschrift nicht lesen...."

Franz Liszt (1811-1886)

SOIRÉES DE VIENNE (116)

Piano solo. 1 preliminary leaf, 55 pages, verso of page 55 and end fly-leaf blank; 5 or 6 double staves to each page. Size: 28 x 35 cm.

Autograph heading in pencil on title-page: "Soirées d[e] Vienne. Valses-Caprices d'après F. Schubert—dédiées à son ami S. Löwy par F. Liszt. en neuf livraisons...."

Undated. Composed 1852; possibly sketched earlier.

Not in Collected Works. First published: Livraisons 1-5 in 1852; Livraisons 6-9 in 1853, all by C. A. Spina in Vienna.

Collection: The Library of Congress, Washington, D.C.

PLATE 116 shows a section from the *Valse-Caprice* of Livraison (cahier) No. 3, including bars 278-339 (not counting the crossed-out bars). The dynamic marks and nearly all of the numerous tempo indications are added in pencil, likewise the fingering indications which are of particular interest. Liszt who departed radically from the Clementi-Hummel technique, marked the fingering in nearly all of his compositions for the piano. Notice particularly the change of finger for the repetition of the same tone (bar 11 of the third double staff etc.). The script for all its easy flow reveals great energy; all horizontals, that is the cross strokes and ledger lines, are started with broad quill and evident pressure. Some symbols are simplified in the extreme: the 8va signs which consist of one unbroken loop and line (see the two double staves at the bottom) and the trill signs which consist of simple *t*'s followed by straight lines. The bar lines are still, as in Beethoven's script, confined to single staves. There are no pedal marks.

The Spina edition breaks up the long cross strokes in the right hand of the last two double staves; it also adds *a tempo* to bar 1 at the top of the page and omits the *smorzando* in bar 11.

Franz Liszt (1811-1886)

HUNGARIAN MARCH FOR ORCHESTRA (117)

Written for the coronation of Francis Joseph I, Emperor of Austria, as king of Hungary at Budapest, on June 8, 1867.[1]
12 pages, 32 staves to each page. Size: 35 x 27 cm.
Unsigned. Undated.
Composed apparently in 1867.[2]
Collected Works, Series 1, part 3.
Collection: The Library of Congress, Washington, D.C.

PLATE 117 shows the first page of the composition. The page has no tempo indication. The *Collected Works* give *Allegro pomposo*.

Curiously enough there are no dynamic marks except for the two crescendo signs in the kettledrums section, bars 1 and 3.

The handwriting is hurried but clear. While the single eighth-notes show connected writing —the flags being mostly drawn right from the stems—the lettering is very disconnected. The scoring is given in German, as are some directions for the performance; others, such as *con basso*, are in Italian. Note the pointed and extremely simplified G clefs. The *Collected Works* differ in several details: for example, staccato dots are used and the *solo* in bar 9 of the trumpet part is omitted.

[1] Title according to *Collected Works*.
[2] Peter Raabe, *Franz Liszt*, p. 438, claims that the march was not composed until 1870, in contradiction to the title appearing in the *Collected Works*.

Giacomo Meyerbeer (1791-1864)

L'ETOILE DU NORD (118)

Opera in three acts. Text by A. E. Scribe.
The present manuscript consists of 100 pages containing changes which were evidently made for a performance of the opera at the Covent Garden Theatre in London. Most of it was written by a copyist but it includes numerous corrections and directions in Meyerbeer's hand. A number of printed pages, a *Polonaise* (21 pages) for Act I and an *Arioso* (13 pages) for Act III contain, according to their headings, insertions composed for the famous tenor Tichatschek on the occasion of his performance in Dresden. The remaining 10 pages, measuring 27.2 x 37.5 cm., with 20 staves to each page, are entirely in Meyerbeer's hand and comprise the scene with Peter the Great, Danilowitz and Gritzenko.

The opera was originally composed in 1844 under the title *Ein Feldlager in Schlesien* for the Berlin Opera, and later was adapted to the French text by Scribe and in this form first performed on February 16, 1854 at the Opéra Comique in Paris.

Collection: Rudolf F. Kallir, New York.

PLATE 118 shows page 4 of the 10-page autograph mentioned above. The various sections of the large orchestra are listed in an unusual order: first the woodwinds and horns, then the violins and violas, then the trombones and kettledrums, then the vocal parts, and finally the violoncelli and doublebasses. In bar 6 of staff 6 a *corno a piston in C* enters, one of the earliest uses of the valve horn in opera after Halévy had introduced it in *La Juive* (1835) and Richard Wagner employed it in *Rienzi* (1842). There are numerous expression marks and instrumental effects that meticulously follow the dramatic action, such as the *cresc: poco a poco* in bar 2 leading to the simplified *ffm*[o] at the beginning of bar 4; the tremolos with numbers added to indicate their speed (see bar 2); and the trill in the string basses (last bar) that drastically illustrates Gritzenko's fearful trembling, "vor Angst zitternd."

The writing is vigorous and determined, in a very connected hand with the stems always directly drawn out of the note-heads or the ledger lines. In eighth-notes with the stems down the flags are also drawn right out of the stems in one uninterrupted motion of the pen.

Hector Berlioz (1803-1869)

SYMPHONIE FANTASTIQUE (EN 5 PARTIES), OP. 14.
PART I "RÊVERIE" (119)

63 pages; 24 staves to each page. Size: 34¼ x 25½ cm.
Autograph heading: "Rêverie/ No. 1."
Unsigned. Undated.
Composed 1830-31. Published by Berlioz as the first part of *Episode de la Vie d'un Artiste*.
First performed at the Conservatoire, Paris, along with its sequel, the "monodrame lyrique" *Lélio ou Le retour à la vie*, in 1832.
Collected Works, Series 1, No. 1.
Collection: Bibliothèque du Conservatoire National de Musique, Paris.

PLATE 119 shows the first page of the *Rêverie*. The great romantic raconteur of the programmatic symphony (after Beethoven's *Pastorale* and before Richard Strauss' tone poems) was fanatic in his precision. The layout of this score, like his others, is extremely neat[1] and studded with marks indicating the most delicate dynamic shadings. Notice the transition from the initial *pp* to *ppp* in bar 3, or the little $<>$ in the last bar of the page. The l° in the winds in bar 1 indicates that only one of the pairs had to play.

While the notes are written in a fairly connected fashion, with the stems, as a rule, drawn directly out of the heads, the lettering is oddly disconnected; cf. *Violoncello* or *con sordini*. The elegant *Vlni* (violins) reveals calligraphic grace.

[1] Berlioz wrote to his friend Morelon, June 26, 1854: "Je rêve une édition allemande soignée, à Leipzig, de l'ensemble de mes ouvrages. Cela coûterait 20.000 francs! Si jamais je réalise ce projet, alors je pourrai empoisonner les bibliothèques amies sans me gêner, et la vôtre la première victime." Preface to *Collected Works*, vol. 1, p. ix.

Giuseppe Verdi (1813-1901)

I LOMBARDI ALLA PRIMA CROCIATA (120, 121)

Opera in four acts. Text by T. Solera, after the poem of Tommaso Grassi.

Complete score: 313 leaves. Act I, 92 leaves; Act II, 97; Act III, 70; Act IV, 54. Leaf 314, blank; leaves 69, 223, 279, 286, 313, written only on front. Size: 32.5 x 24 cm.; the leaves 315 to 323, size 24 x 31 cm., contain an apparently later variant of the cavatina of *Oronte* in Act II.

Signed by the composer on the first page of Act II.

Composed 1842. Published 1843, Milan. First performed February 11, 1843 at La Scala, Milan.

Collection: G. Ricordi & Co., Milan.

I Lombardi is the most famous of Verdi's early operas.

The plates show the back of leaf 280 and the front of leaf 281 (Act IV, Scene 3), with the beginning part of the famous chorus (*Coro di crociati e pellegrini*) "O Signore, dal tetto natio." Careful accentuation by > marks. The crescendi-decrescendi are not paralleled by similar dynamic marks in the orchestra. The original part for the double bass beneath the chorus has been crossed out, evidently to let the chorus carry itself.

A♪ B♪

Verdi uses A and B interchangeably. The stage direction preceding the beginning of the chorus: "Cielo infuocatissimo in sul tramonto." Text: "O Signore, dal tetto natìo, ci chiamasti con santa promessa. . . ."

Giuseppe Verdi (1813-1901)

ATTILA (122)

Opera ("dramma lirico"), in three acts and a prologue. Text by T. Solera.

246 folios, 24 staves to each page. Size: 32 x 23 cm.

Signed on folio 2 "G. Verdi." Undated.

Composed 1846. First performance March 17, 1846, at the Teatro La Fenice, Venice.

Collection: British Museum, London.

PLATE 122 reproduces the last page of Act I (folio 146 verso).

The five vocal solo parts above the chorus are those of *Odabella*, soprano; *Foresto*, tenor; *Uldino*, tenor; *Attila*, baritone; *Leone*, bass. Note the fine dynamic shading suggested by >>, *sotto voce* and *morendo* in the part of the protagonist, *Attila*, to the text: ". . . dinnanzi ai Numi prostrasi il Rè!" and the differentiation between *ff* and *fff* in various parts in bars 3 and 4.

Verdi, evidently on second thought, crossed out the repetition of bar 4 before he had written it in all the staves.

Giuseppe Verdi (1813-1901)

RIGOLETTO (123)

Opera in three acts. Text by F. M. Piave, based on Victor Hugo's *Le roi s'amuse*.

281 folios, 20 staves to each page. Size: 35 x 27 cm. Backs of folios 58 and 162 are blank. The opera score terminates on folio 279; the following two folios are not written in Verdi's hand.

Unsigned. Undated.

Composed 1850-1851. First published 1851. First performed on March 11, 1851 at the Teatro La Fenice, Venice.

Collection: G. Ricordi & Co., Milan.

PLATE 123 shows the back of folio 224, bar 26-29 of the andante in D flat major, soon after the beginning of Act III. The solo parts are:

Gilda: "Infelice cor tradito. . . ."

Maddalena: "Ah! Ah! rido ben di core, che tai baje costan poco, quanto valga il vostro gioco mel credete, so apprezzar. . . ."

Duca: "Bella figlia dell'amore, schiavo son de' vezzi tuoi. . . ."

Rigoletto: "ch'ei mentiva, ch'ei mentiva. . . ."

Different from Plate 122, the rapid notes in the vocal parts are written singly while in the corresponding instrumental passages they are connected by cross strokes. The writing is extremely rapid, fluent and clear with a marked backward slant. The *solo* in staff 7 and 9 is not carried over into the printed score (Ricordi).

Giuseppe Verdi (1813-1901)

AÏDA (124)

Opera in four acts. Text by A. Ghislanzoni, with the cooperation of the composer.

384 pages; Act I, 108; II, 118; III, 84; IV, 74. Size: 37 x 27 cm.

Signed by the composer at the beginning of each act.

Composed in 1870 for the celebration of the opening of the Suez Canal. Published by G. Ricordi & Co., Milan, 1872. First performed at the Opera in Cairo, December 24, 1871.[1]

Collection: G. Ricordi & Co., Milan.

PLATE 124 shows one of the musical climaxes of Act II: the juxtaposition of the march against Aïda's outcry, "Ah, qual speme omai più restami. . . ." It was perhaps this grandiose spectacle of military pomp, composed shortly after the outbreak of the Franco-Prussian war, to which Verdi referred when he spoke of a "whiff of the Marseillaise" in the second act of *Aïda*.[2]

The entry of the march in the stage brass band (staves 16 and 17) is marked *Banda*. The vocal parts beneath are those of: *Aïda, Amneris, Radames* and *Amonasro, Ramfis, il Rè, Prigioneri, Sacerdoti* (two staves), *Popolo* (three staves).

[1] Christmas Eve may seem a strange date for the premiere of Aïda. The performance was originally scheduled for the 20th of December and then postponed.

[2] Letter to Antonio Ghislanzoni, August 22, 1870.

Marked on top and bottom before the double line: "*allar[gando]: le tre ultime note/ rimettendo[?] il*; at the double line: *Più sostenuto di prima*. The distribution of accents is carefully indicated: cf. the part of *Ramfis* with a > on each beat in bar 3; the > on the fourth beat of the heavy brass in the same bar; the > on the second beat of bar 4 in the parts of *Aïda* and of *il popolo*.

Verdi's writing is more relaxed than in his earlier scores. The stems of the black notes now spring more frequently right out of the middle of the heads.

Giuseppe Verdi (1813-1901)

OTELLO (125)

Opera in four acts. Text by Arrigo Boito (after Shakespeare).
368 folios. Act I, 113; Act II, 96; Act III, 113; Act IV, 66. 24 staves to each page. Size: 35 x 27 cm.
The backs of folios 209 and 388, blank. Written in black ink, now faded brown; folios 332, 333, 334 and 336, in purple ink. Many erasures; occasional corrections in ink. Five leaves with changes pasted over the score. Some corrections in purple ink.
Signed at the beginning of each act.
Composed 1884-1886. Published 1887. First performed February 5, 1887, at La Scala, Milan.
Collection: G. Ricordi & Co., Milan.

PLATE 125 shows leaf 386 verso, three pages before the end of the opera. Score: 1) first violin; 2) second violin; 3) viola; 4) flute I and II; 5) flute III; 6) oboes; 7) clarinets; 8 and 9) horns; 10 and 11) blank; 12 and 13) bassoons; 14-17) blank; 18) vocal part (*Otello*); 19-22) blank; 23) violoncello; 24) bass. This orchestra, large as it is, forms only the *piano* background for the vocal part. The strong influence of Wagner on the orchestration of *Otello* has often been pointed out. Wagner, however, would hardly have resisted the temptation to organize so large an orchestra into a web of several distinct contrapuntal threads, whereas Verdi still adheres to a predominantly homophonic style.

The writing is of unsurpassed clarity. From its energy, one would not guess that Verdi was seventy-two at the time.

The printed score shows the crescendo-decrescendo repeated in all instrumental parts; moreover, it adds *mf* to the third flute (bar 1, staff 5).

Richard Wagner (1813-1883)

TRISTAN UND ISOLDE (126, 127)

Opera in three acts. Text by the composer.
354 pages. Act I, 116 pages; Act II, 138 pages; Act III, 100 pages. Thirty staves to each page. Size: 35.5 x 26 cm.
Autograph heading: "Tristan und Isolde." Signed and dated at the end of Act II: "R W./ Venedig/ 18 März 59," and at the end of Act III: "R W/ Luzern. 6 August 1859."

Composed 1857-1859. Published 1860. First performed June 10, 1865, Munich.
Collection: Haus Wahnfried, Bayreuth.

PLATE 126 shows page 289, with the famous reappearance of the "traurige Weise (mournful tune)" (English horn, staff 7), in the middle of Act III, and its interweaving through the rich polyphonic texture. When the "traurige Weise" is taken up by the powerful unison of the flutes, oboes, clarinets, and bass clarinets, the horns, in counterpoint, introduce the passionate theme from the beginning of Act II, all this over the chromatic bass line carried by the double-bass and the third bassoon. Special directions guarantee different shadings for these three main threads: *sehr gehalten* for the "traurige Weise"; *gut gehalten* for the bass; the *sehr gehalten* for the horn theme is—characteristically—crossed out again.

The page contains some corrections: Upper system: stave 9 was originally reserved for the violoncello, staff 10, for the double bass; but the violoncellos, which began in unison, soon divide as they continue; this evidently necessitated a rearrangement: the assignment of staves 9 and 10 to the violoncello and the addition of an eleventh stave for the double bass (*Cb*) (see corrections in the orchestration marks at the beginning of the staves). Lower system: 1) The bass tuba is added at the bottom of the system by an insertion mark, indicating the insertion of this part beneath that of the bass clarinet. 2) Both double bars are cancelled by the direction: (X *keine Doppelstriche!*) *R W*. Wagner found it necessary to guarantee the authenticity of this correction by adding his initials. Apparently, on second thought, he did not consider the change of key here a sufficient reason for a double bar line. 3) As mentioned above, the *sehr gehalten* in the horns, bar 1, is crossed out; likewise the decrescendo-crescendo in the third and fourth horn (bar 6) while it is retained in—or perhaps transferred to—the trumpet part.

PLATE 127 shows a later section of Act III. This whole section, reflecting Tristan's ecstasy, repeatedly changes meter. In the page reproduced, we see the first bar in 3/4 time, four bars in 5/4 time, and the following bar in 4/4 time. Notice the subdivision, by dotted lines, of the bars in 5/4 time, into 3/4 plus 2/4.

The first trumpet has been shifted from staff 6 to staff 11; for several bars, the double bass (*CB*) is directed to double the violoncello. One bar in the bassoons, immediately after the reinstatement of 4/4 time, has been crossed out, apparently so as not to interfere with the sudden *p* in the main motive given to the English horn and the first violins.

Richard Wagner (1813-1883)

DIE MEISTERSINGER VON NÜRNBERG (128-130)

Opera in three acts. Text by the composer. 459 written pages. Prelude and Act I, 147 pages; Act II, 113; Act III, 199. 30 staves to each page. Size: 35.5 x 26.9 cm.
Autograph heading: "Die Meistersinger." At the end of Act I: "Genf. 23. März 1866/RW." At the beginning of Act II: "Triebschen, 22. März 1867." At the end of Act II: "22.Juni 1867." At the beginning of Act III: "Triebschen, 26. Juni 1867." At the end of Act III: "Ende der Meistersinger/ Triebschen. Donnerstag, 24. Okt. 1867/ Abends 8 Uhr. RW."
Composed 1862-1867.

Libretto published 1863. Score published 1868. First performed June 21, 1868, in Munich. Collection: Haus Wahnfried, Bayreuth.

PLATE 128 shows page 233, containing a section from *Beckmesser's Serenade* in Act II. Each of the first four five-staff systems shows on its second staff *Beckmesser's* part and on its third staff his lute accompaniment. In staff 4 *Hans Sachs'* critical comment *mit dem Hammer* (see bar 1) is given. The violas (top staff) and violoncellos (bottom staff) furnish the noise that so annoyingly interrupts the pedantic serenade of the anxious and increasingly angry suitor. In the bottom system the background noise has increased, bringing the staves to seven.

The critical hammer strokes in the part of *Hans Sachs* are indicated first by $\wedge_{(Schlägt)}$; later, when they pile up, by $\wedge_{(Schl.)}$ and finally by $\widehat{(\not{\cdot})}$

A series of several hammer strokes is indicated by $\sim\!\!\sim\!\!\sim\!\!\sim$

The delicate synchronization of *Beckmesser's* tune with the chords in the lute, the hammer strokes, and the background noise, are laid out in the score with painstaking accuracy, though with no attempt at calligraphic beauty.

PLATE 129 shows page 249, with a short section from the nocturnal riot caused by the angry aesthetic controversy between the suitor and his critic. The double fugue in the chorus is in full swing. *Beckmesser's* tune is taken up by the *Meister* (staff 20), and doubled by the horns, bassoons, violoncellos, and double basses while the vivacious glow-worm motive twinkles through all the other parts, vocal and instrumental. In striking contrast to the preceding plate this page is almost print-like in its clarity and neatness, with each choral group beautifully bracketed and the bar lines drawn by ruler.

PLATE 130 reproduces page 367 showing the bars preceding the quintet and five bars of the latter. With *sehr ruhig* an ascending triplet motive appears in the first violin which is gradually transformed—by Wagner's inimitable protean technique—into the gently flowing main motive of the quintet. These slight and almost imperceptible shifts in melody, metre and rhythm, up to the *langsam, doch leicht fliessend* are admirably mirrored in the graphic picture of this transition.

Note the wide crescendo-decrescendo signs in the woodwinds which furnish the soft and magic gleam to the "Morgentraum-Deutweise."

Richard Wagner (1813-1883)

SKETCHES OF DIE WALKÜRE AND GÖTTERDÄMMERUNG (131)

One sheet written on one side; 28 hand-drawn staves, some of them irregular. Size: 35 x 25 cm. Unsigned. Undated.

Wagner worked on *Die Walküre* from 1854-1856; on the *Götterdämmerung* from 1870-1874. Collection: The Gertrude Clarke Whittall Foundation Collection, The Library of Congress, Washington, D.C.

The autograph contains in its 28 staves several different sketches for *Die Walküre* and *Götterdämmerung*.

PLATE 131 shows only the lower part, i.e. 18 staves of the manuscript. The upper part (10 staves), not reproduced here, contains a draft of: "Einen Wurm zeugten die Riesen . . . Siegfried hat ihn erschlagen." This section of the manuscript contains two different drafts: I) in staves 2-11 sketches for the *Walkürenritt*; II) in staves 13-18 a fragmentary sketch for the duet of *Siegfried* and *Brünnhilde* in the prelude of *Götterdämmerung*.

I) This fragment consists of three parts, all evidently intended for the opening of the third act of *Die Walküre*: a) the first two staves show, in pencil, the motive of the *Walkürenritt*, in B minor, 9/8 time, with the words "nach Süden wir ziehen." These words do not appear in the opera; the motif, however, is found—in the same key—in bars 13 ff. of Act III, Scene 1, where it appears in *f marcato*, in unison between the sixth and eighth horn together with the bass trumpet in D. b) The next two double staves show, in ink, a variant of the same motif, again in B minor, 9/8 time, but in slightly different rhythm, evidently to fit the text; and with a different harmonic progression. The words of this text do not occur in the final score. It may be that Wagner originally planned a chorus of the Valkyries with this motif and later abandoned the idea. The first bar of the upper staff adds the dotted galloping-figure that links itself with the "Valkyries-ride-motive" in just the same manner as in the final version of the opera. c) Beneath are two double staves in ink which transpose the motif into B major, with a few chords in the upper staff suggesting the harmony. This section of the sketch coincides with bars 59ff. of Act III, scene 1, which sets the scene for the appearance of Rossweisse and Grimgerde.

II) The last three double staves of the manuscript contain a pencil draft of the "Vorspiel" (prelude) to *Götterdämmerung*, 80 bars after *Sonnenaufgang, voller Tag*. The words of the text are:

Siegfried:	Ein Wissen doch wahr' ich wohl;
	dass mir Brünnhilde lebt!
	Eine Lehre lernt' ich leicht.
	Brünnhilde's zu gedenken!
Brünnhilde:	Willst du mir Minne schenken,
	gedenke deiner nur,
	gedenke deiner Thaten!
	gedenke des wilden Feuers,
	das furchtlos du durchschrittest,
	da den Felsen es rings umbrann.
Siegfried:	Brünnhilde zu gewinnen!

On the second staff, Wagner adds to this vocal part some suggestions for the harmony. Note the frequent indications of tremolo.

The sketches are good examples of Wagner's neat and vigorous hand and the extraordinarily clear spatial organization of his script. Everything essential is set down definitely and concisely, without a single correction.

Friedrich von Flotow (1812-1883)

NAIDA (132)

Opera in three acts. Libretto by H. de St. Georges and Léon Halévy.
One volume bound in cardboard, 621 written pages, 24 staves to each page. Size: 32 x 25 cm.

Autograph title page: "Naida (auf französisch Le Vannier)/ Oper in drei Akten/ Text/ von H. de St. Georges und Leon Halévy./ deutsch von Franz Dingelstedt./ Musik/ von/ Friedrich von Flotow/ deutsche original partitur/ von mir selbst geschrieben/ beendet im Jahre 1864 in Wien/ Fr. von Flotow."

Composed in 1864. Unpublished. First performed in St. Petersburg at the National Theater, December 11, 1865, in Russian. First performed in Italian at the Teatro Manzoni, Milan, 1873-1874.[1] Since that time the opera has been forgotten.

Collection: The Library of Congress, Washington, D.C.

The manuscript shows numerous erasures, cancellations, and alterations of expression marks.

PLATE 132 shows the beginning of the ballet (*dance furieuse*).

Notice the corrections in the vocal parts and the direction *avec toute la force possible* at the turn to 6/8 time. The German text is written above the vocal part in purple ink: "Der ganze harem soll sich rühren"; beneath is the Italian text in black ink: "Tutto l'harem si muova."

[1] Rosa Rosine von Flotow: *Friedrich von Flotows Leben, von seiner Witwe*, Leipzig 1892.

Bedřich Smetana (1824-1884)

POLKA FOR THE PIANOFORTE (133)

Four pages. 5 double staves to each page. Size: 25 x 34.5 cm.

Autograph heading: "Polka N.2. I.Heft. Op.12/ Fr.Smetana."

Composed in 1861.

First published in 1863 in *Souvenirs de Bohème en forme de Polkas*, op. 12, Cahier I by Universal Edition, Vienna.

Collection: Rudolf F. Kallir, New York.

The manuscript is written in ink, with print-like neatness and clarity and contains exact indications of phrasing and numerous expression marks.

The plate shows page 2 of this manuscript.

The third, fourth and fifth double staves are written over a continuous pencil sketch still faintly visible.

The page is quite characteristic of the great Czech composer and shows at once two equally important aspects of his genius, deeply rooted in folk music, yet reaching full mastery of symphonic structure. The main theme of the present work is a typical Czech polka: from bar 12 of the page a widely arching cantabile melody in the treble is added as a counterpoint to the polka tune, and then both melodies together achieve a symphonic climax, a technique quite reminiscent of many passages in Smetana's operas. The counterpoint marked *espress.* runs consistently in legato—contrasted with the staccato polka tune—and is delicately shaded by dynamic marks, accents, the *dolce*, etc. From bar 32 on, the cantabile counterpoint is reinforced by two lower octaves, their entry being marked by ∧.

Stephen Collins Foster (1826-1864)

FOR THEE, LOVE, FOR THEE (134)

Song with piano accompaniment. Words by William Henry McCarthy.
One leaf, twelve staves. Size: 25 x 20 cm.
Signed. Undated.
Composed in 1859. Published 1859, by Firth, Pond & Co., New York.[1]
Collection: Foster Hall Collection, University of Pittsburgh, Pittsburgh, Pa.

PLATE 134 shows the front page of the leaf. The opening ritornello is written out in full. Usually Foster does this only if the tune of the ritornello differs from that of the vocal part. The heavy-handed writing betrays the self-taught musician. Virtually all note-heads are on the "wrong" side of the stem, i.e. to the left if the stem runs down, and to the right if the stem runs up. The clefs are pedantic but clumsy, the cross strokes and ledger lines erratic.

[1] See John Tasker Howard, *Stephen Foster: America's Troubadour*, New York, 1934, pp. 292 and 303.

Charles François Gounod (1818-1893)

JÉSUS DE NAZARETH (135)

For baritone, chorus and orchestra. Words by A. Porte.
12 leaves (music on leaves 2-12), 26 staves to each page. Size: 35 x 26 cm.
Autograph heading: "Jésus de Nazareth/ Chant Evangélique pour Baryton Solo et Choeurs."
Unsigned. Undated.
There are several versions of this work. The present and last one, for large orchestra, dates from 1864.
Collection: The Library of Congress, Washington, D.C.

No corrections appear in the manuscript, except for a few expression marks in blue pencil by another hand.

The plate shows the first page of the manuscript. Note the large array of instruments, including the recently invented *pistons*, cymbals, large drum, and harps.

The writing is extremely neat, the bar lines drawn freehand. There are many accurate expression marks. Gounod employs several time-saving devices; for example, when notes are crossed by a ledger line, he, instead of making a separate dot for the head of the note, merely thickens the ledger line: see, for instance, the E at the beginning of each bar in the violoncello part.

Charles François Gounod (1818-1893)

CAVATINA FOR THE OPERA FAUST, ACT II (136)

One sheet of 4 pages; 20 staves to each page. Size: 35.9 x 26.3 cm.

Signed on first page.

Autograph heading: "Cavatine (ajoutée au Rôle de Valentin dans le 2ᵈ acte de Faust)." On the last page is the remark: "Ch. Gounod./ pour Mʳ Stanley (sic!), avec mes félicitations./ Paris (Janvier 1864)." The manuscript of the cavatina is bound together with some auto-biographical material of the baritone Mr. Charles Santley. Opera composed in 1852-1858; libretto by J. Barbier and M. Carré (based on Goethe's "Faust").

First performance on March 19, 1859, at the Théâtre Lyrique, Paris; first performance in London, June 11, 1863, with Italian text; first performance with English text, translated by Mr. H. F. Chorley, London, January 23, 1864. The cavatina was composed for this performance and especially for Mr. Charles Santley. English text of cavatina by H. F. Chorley; French text by O. Pradère.

Collection: The New York Public Library, New York.

The text in English is added only to the first page of the cavatina up to the *un peu plus animé*, after the word *battleground*.

The page is a characteristic example of the interpolations composed so frequently for some special performance, written to measure for a special singer.

On the second page of the manuscript, not reproduced here, four bars of the vocal part are carefully crossed out. They are entirely different from the final printed version, and one may assume on this evidence alone that the autograph was written before the orchestral score.

Of particular interest are Gounod's "P.S." instructions at the bottom of the third page (plate 136) to Mr. Chorley, the writer of the English text. The composer modestly suggests that he would be very pleased if Mr. Chorley could preserve the four equal notes in bars 1 and 4 of the vocal part ("P.S. Si Mr. Chorley pouvait conserver, dans la 1ᵉʳᵉ et la 3ᵐᵉ mesure du chant, les 4 notes égales . . . cela me serait très agréable"). It may seem strange that he left a matter as important as the rhythmical articulation of this striking melody to the librettist. The melody of the *Cavatina* is borrowed from the introduction of the opera where it appeared in four equal notes, and certainly Gounod would have preferred not to change its rhythm. The difficulty becomes clear from the way in which the first bars of the *Cavatina* are written on the first page of the manuscript. There they appear with the English text and in dotted rhythm:

Evidently it was the English which had Gounod worried; he was not quite certain of the liberties he could take with the length and weight of English syllables and therefore, most conscientiously, left the final decision to the Englishman. Mr. Chorley was agreeable: the final version has the four equal notes throughout.

César Franck (1822-1890)

PANIS ANGELICUS (137)

For tenor voice with harp, violoncello and organ accompaniment.

3½ pages, 22 staves to each page. Size: 35.3 x 26.8 cm.

At the top of first page: "César Franck," not in the composer's hand. At the end of the score: "À Mademoiselle Chauvot/ Souvenir de l'Auteur/ César Franck."

Composed in 1872. Published in 1872, by Le Bailly, Paris, as part of the *Messe Solenelle* (*en La*) *à 3 Voix S.T.B. avec V^elle, C. Basse, Harpe et Orgue,* op. 12. First performance in Paris, 1879.

Collection: The Library of Congress, Washington, D.C.

The plate shows the first page of the manuscript. Text: "Panis angelicus Fit panis hominum Dat panis coelicus Figuris terminum. . . ."

Franck, as an organist and harmonium player, was very familiar with the recently invented devices for "expression" in these instruments, and requires of the organ the crescendo-decrescendo corresponding to those in the violoncello cantilena (see bars 6, 7 and 9, 10).

Georges Bizet (1838-1875)

LA FUITE (138)

Duet for soprano and tenor voices with piano accompaniment; words by Théophile Gautier.

Title page and 5 written pages. 5 quadruple staves to each page. Size 34.7 x 27 cm.

Autograph heading: "La Fuite—/Duo./Poésie de Théophile Gautier/musique de Georges Bizet." In upper right corner of the first page of music: "Poésies complètes de Théophile Gautier, Charpentier 1845."

Composed in 1870, during the siege of Paris.

Published by Choudens, Paris, 1872.

Collection: the Library of Congress, Washington, D.C.

Besides *La Fuite* Bizet set to music several other oriental subjects: *La Guzla de l'Emir*, 1860 (not preserved); *Les Pêcheurs de Perles*, 1863; *Djamileh*, 1872.

The plate shows the first page of the duet. Bizet's hand, like his music, is fluent and neat. He frequently employs abbreviations customary in his time : repeated notes, for instance, are indicated by the stem only. Characteristic are the wedge-shaped cross strokes, and the double braces joining the two staves of the piano part.

Note the different kinds of lettering: a stately upright calligraphic hand in the title and in *Kadidja* and *Ahmed*; the rapid writing, in right slant, of the text; finally, the even more rapid *crescendo* and *dim*[*inuendo*].

Gabriel Fauré (1845-1924)

QUINTET FOR 2 VIOLINS, VIOLA, VIOLONCELLO AND PIANOFORTE, IN C MINOR, OP. 115 (139)

127 written pages, 18 staves to each page, with one blank stave between the strings and the piano part, and two blank staves between the two systems. Size: 34 x 26 cm.

Each of the four movements has its own autograph title page and is paged separately. The title pages are marked: "3ème Quintette" "I," "II," "III," "IV" respectively. The title page of the fourth movement bears the signature "Gabriel Fauré."

Composed in 1921. Published in 1921 by A. Durand et Fils, Paris, with a dedication to Paul Dukas.

Collection: The Harvard College Library, Cambridge, Mass.

The manuscript is evidently an engraver's copy. There are only a few corrections and erasures by the composer, but numerous pencil annotations in another hand.

PLATE 139 shows the last page of Movement I beginning with the sixth bar after the sign ⊡ 19 in the Durand edition.

Fauré was a skilled draftsman and fond of drawing caricatures. Well known are the ones he made of Saint Saëns, Vincent d'Indy, and of himself. The playful lattice patterns he used for deleting are of varied designs. The accents ($>$) begin one bar earlier in the printed edition, namely, in the chords of the third bar before the end.

Léo Delibes (1836-1891)

LAKMÉ (140)

Opera in three acts. Text by E. Gondinet and P. Gille. 3 portfolios (1 for each act). Size: 35 x 26.5 cm.

Signed and dated: "5 X^bre 82" (end of Act I); "7 janvier 83" (end of Act II); "Léo Delibes/ 21 février 83./ (2^h du matin.)" (end of Act III).

Composed 1881-1883. First performed April 14, 1883, Paris, Opéra Comique.

Collection: The Library of Congress, Washington, D.C.

The plate shows the opening bars of the famous *Bell Song* from Act II, Scene 10. There are many corrections in the directions for scoring. The *Jeu de Timbres* was indicated by a scale and then crossed out. Preceding Lakmé's melismatic exclamations *Sans Mesure* is indicated. The lettering as well as the score-writing is of extreme neatness and print-like clarity.

Johann Strauss, son (1825-1899)

BEI UNS Z'HAUS (141)

Waltz for orchestra, Op. 361.

Twenty-four pages, eighteen staves to each page. Size: 25.8 x 33 cm.

Full score, paged, unsigned, and undated.

Heading (in another hand): "Bei uns z'Haus Walzer/ von Johann Strauss (Sohn)." On the flyleaf: "Bei uns z'Haus Walzer/ v. Joh. Strauss/ Original Partitur/ complet."

There are many erasures and corrections in red and blue pencil. Some corrections are made by pasting fresh pieces of score paper on the script with sealing wax.

Composed in 1873, originally for chorus and orchestra.

First published in 1873 by F. Schreiber, Vienna. First performed in 1873 at the Vienna World's Fair.

Collection: The Library of Congress, Washington, D.C.

The plate shows page 9 of the manuscript. The instruments are: flutes, including piccoli; oboe; two clarinets; bassoon; four horns; two trumpets, indicated only by *1* and *2*; three trombones; kettledrums; and the usual body of strings. Clefs are added only in the string parts.

The writing is rapid and irregular. The bar lines are crooked, the page abounds in erasures. Extremely characteristic of the Viennese waltz is the sliding from the accentuated upbeat to the first beat of the next bar (see sign in bars 12 ff. of the page, in the woodwinds and violins):

Anton Bruckner (1824-1896)

SYMPHONY NO. 5 IN B FLAT, ORIGINAL VERSION (142)

133 leaves. Sixteen staves to each page. Size: 24.2 x 32.5 cm.

Composed 1875-1876. The part for the bass tuba added in 1877.

First published in 1896, by Ludwig Doblinger, Vienna.

First performance April 8, 1894, Vienna.

Autograph heading: "Sinfonie No. 5 in B/3. März 1875/19. Mai 1877."

Collected Works: Vol. v.

Collection: Österreichische Nationalbibliothek, Vienna.

PLATE 142 shows the entrance of the big brass chorale that forms the end of the gigantic fugue which is the fourth movement. The scoring reads as follows: *Fl[auti]*; *O[boi]*; *Cl[arinetti]*; *Fag[otti]*; *C[orni]*; *Tr[ombe]*; *Tymp[ani]*; *Tr[omboni] alt[i] Ten[ori] Bass[i]*; *Bass Tuba*; *I, II, III [violins and violas]*; *C[elli]*; *B[asso]*. The words *Bass Tuba* are a later[1] insertion, and the whole part for the bass tuba was added in darker ink.[2]

---

[1] In 1877. See *Vorlagenbericht* in the *Kritische Gesamtausgabe A. Bruckners sämtl. Werke, herausgegeben von Robert Haas (unter Mitwirkung von Alfred Orel), Musikwissenschaftlicher Verlag der Internationalen Brucknergesellschaft*, Vienna, p. 1.

[2] The 6th and following symphonies incorporate the bass tuba from the start, marked *BT*.

There are numerous erasures and corrections in the wind parts. Above the second bar which is crossed out, is marked: *gilt nicht* (invalid). The beginning of the last choral strophe is marked: *fff* and *Choral bis zum Ende fff*, and *Choral fff bis zum Ende*. The two main themes that form the basic material of the double fugue are carefully distinguished by different accents: the first subject, or rather its simplified version, by > marks in the basses; the second subject (chorale theme) which appears here in augmentation in the brass choir, by heavy ∧ and ∨ marks.

As always in Bruckner's scores, the single bars are numbered underneath. The words are written in rather pedantic calligraphy, some in Latin, others in a German hand, such as was taught at the time in the elementary schools of the German sections of Austria. Bruckner, like Schubert, had begun his career as a school teacher.

Johannes Brahms (1833-1897)

VARIATIONS AND FUGUE ON A THEME BY HANDEL, OP. 24 (143)

For piano, generally known as the "Händel-Variations."

One preliminary leaf, 20 pages; five double staves, separated by single blank staves. Size: 26.5 x 34.5 cm.

Autograph heading: "Variationen/ für eine liebe Freundin/ Johannes Brahms Sept. 61."

Composed 1861 in Hanau, near Hamburg.

Published in 1862 by Breitkopf & Härtel, Leipzig. First performed by Clara Schumann in Hamburg, December 7, 1861.

Collected Works, Vol. XIII, p. 25.

Collection: The Gertrude Clarke Whittall Foundation in The Library of Congress, Washington, D.C. Another autograph of the Variations was preserved in the archive of Breitkopf & Härtel, Leipzig.

The manuscript shows many fingering marks in pencil and numerous pencil additions and corrections of expression marks, slurs, etc.

PLATE 143 reproduces page 3 of the manuscript, showing the second half of variation IV, variation V in full, and the first half of the canon which forms variation VI.

The many alterations show how eager Brahms was to polish up the almost perfected jewel. Individual notes are eliminated from chords either to maintain the consistency of the melodic line (second bar of the page) or to avoid the doubling of notes (variation V, bar 4).[1] Some details of notation may seem inconspicuous enough if regarded separately. But a careful scrutiny of their correlation throughout the single variations reveals the hand of the greatest variation writer since Beethoven. One may examine the accents (>) in variation V and their relation to the *sf* marks in variation IV. Brahms made pertinent changes here even later: in variation IV,

---

[1] One may perhaps recall one of the many wise remarks of Brahms: "Composing is not difficult, but it is fabulously difficult to let the superfluous notes fall under the table." (Es ist nicht schwer zu komponieren, aber es ist fabelhaft schwer die überflüssigen Noten unter den Tisch fallen zu lassen). Max Kalbeck, *Johannes Brahms*, Berlin, 1921, II/2, p. 440.

bar 1, after ||, the *Collected Works* have *sf* marks on the fourth and twelfth sixteenth-note but not on the eighth. Brahms thought very highly of this work, and told his friends so, abandoning his customary reserve concerning his compositions.

Likewise it is not pedantry or mere writing for the eye but the highest artistic responsibility in principal musical matters that causes a correction like that in variation V in the upper stave of bar 1: by crossing out the stem which led up from G to E Brahms separated the melody from the chords in the middle.

Variation V is studded with signs (A) that are crescendos culminating each time in accents, not decrescendos: ᴬ ⎯⎯⎯ > . Only the last bar has a decrescendo, neatly designed. The *Collected Works* place a crescendo before the > in bars 5 and 6 as well.

There are several other alterations in the *Collected Works*: the two *sf* signs in the last bar of variation IV are replaced by *F*'s. The *espress.*in variation V, bar 1, and *sempre* in variation VI, bar 1, which are added in pencil, are respected in the *Collected Works*.

The writing is of great lucidity in spite of the obvious haste revealed in the uneven slant (see the strong right slant in the last beat of variation IV and in the fourth bar of variation VI) and the pressure evident in many wedge-shaped cross strokes. Typical of Brahms' hand is the merging of the G and bass clefs into one single simplified sign.

Johannes Brahms (1833-1897)

WALTZES FOR PIANO, OP. 39 (144)

Originally for four hands.
Eleven pages, five double staves to each page. Size: 24.5 x 32.5 cm.
Autograph heading: "Walzer. J. B. Op. 39."
Collected Works, Series XIV, No. 3.
The sixteen waltzes of Op. 39 were written about 1865 and published 1866, for piano, four hands. The present manuscript is Brahms' version for two hands, published 1867.
Collection: The Gertrude Clarke Whittall Foundation Collection, Library of Congress, Washington, D.C.

PLATE 144 shows the first page of the manuscript, with the first and second waltzes.

In the first waltz, staccato dots are added neatly to both hands. There are several corrections, some in ink, others (bars 7, 8, and 16) in pencil. The *cresc* in bar 14 is continued by a crescendo wedge, obviously for lack of space between the staves, below the lower staff of bar 15. The *Collected Works* add to the following bar (16) a > sign to match the one in bar 12.

In bar 7 of the second waltz, Brahms crossed out the B in the four-note chord E, G-sharp, B, E in the right hand. Arpeggio marks are added in pencil in bars 1-4 and bar 7, third beat; the *Collected Works* continue the arpeggio marks consistently in bars 5 and 6 and the first beat of bar 7.

Both waltzes occasionally have fingering: the first in bars 11 and 12, the second in bars 1 and 2. In the first (bars 11 and 12) Brahms, in order to facilitate a legato melody, wants the performer to lift the thumb from the F-sharp in bar 11 to use it for the upper E, and then change fingers before the grace notes. The same procedure is evidently required for bars 15 and 16 (see the rest in bar 15 on the third beat). Consequently Brahms crossed out the original dots after the half notes in bars 11 and 15. In the second waltz the fingering is marked in bars 1 and 2 to facilitate the leap from the bass chords, sustained by pedal, to the middle voices.

The numbers in the last blank bars refer to those under bars 2, 3, 4, and 5 of the waltz.

The *tempo giusto* indication leaves the tempo to the judgment of the performer, recalling Brahms' remark that he would favor for most pieces the direction "con discrezione."[1]

[1] From a letter to Henschel. See Kalbeck, *Johannes Brahms*, Vienna, 1907, Vol. III, p. 240.

Johannes Brahms (1833-1897)
SCHICKSALSLIED FOR MIXED CHORUS AND ORCHESTRA, OP. 54 (145)

Words by Friedrich Hölderlin.

36 pages, most of them numbered in pencil; 18 staves to each page. Size: 24.3 x 33 cm.
Autograph heading: "Schicksalslied. J. Brahms." At the end: "Mai 18   71."
Composed in 1868-1871. First published in 1871 by N. Simrock, Berlin.
First performed October 18, 1871, in Karlsruhe, the composer conducting from manuscript.[1]
Collected Works, Series XIX, No. 2.
Collection: The Library of Congress, Washington, D.C.[2]

The famous musical depiction of water hurled from cliff to cliff—to Hölderlin's powerful words ". . [es fallen die leidenden Menschen blindlings von einer Stunde zur an]dern, wie Wasser von Klippe zu Klippe geworfen, jahr[lang ins Ungewisse hinab]"—from page 16 of the manuscript, is reproduced in this plate. Here Brahms employs a cross rhythm in which the swelling breakers (in triple time) pound against the cliffs (in duple time). Perhaps it was the grandiose spectacle of the ocean itself that provided the inspiration; for Brahms began the composition of the *Song of Destiny* while visiting Wilhelmshafen on the North Sea.[3] How very concerned Brahms was over this passage is shown by two different kinds of additions: crescendo-decrescendo wedges are added throughout to the "breakers" in pencil, and many of the original staccato dots in the wind parts representing the "cliffs" are turned into heavier

[1] Alfred von Ehrmann, *Johannes Brahms: thematisches Verzeichnis seiner Werke; Ergänzung zu Johannes Brahms: Weg, Werk und Welt*, Leipzig, 1933.

[2] A description of the manuscript, its origin, and a brief account of the work is given by Edward N. Waters in "A Brahms Manuscript: the Schicksalslied," in *The Library of Congress Quarterly Journal*, Vol. 3, No. 3, 1946, pp. 14ff.

[3] ". . . Brahms came again in the summer in order to make some excursion in the neighbourhood with us and the Reinthalers. One morning we went together to Wilhelmshafen, as Brahms wished to see the great naval port.

"On the way thither our friend, who was usually so lively, was quiet and serious. He told us that early that morning (he always rose betimes) he had found Hölderlin's *Poems* in the bookcase, and been most deeply moved by the *Song of Destiny*. When later in the day, after having wandered about and seen everything of interest, we sat down by the sea to rest, we discovered Brahms at a great distance, sitting alone on the beach and writing.

"These were the first sketches for the *Song of Destiny* which soon appeared. A trip to the woods was given up; Brahms hurried back to Hamburg to devote himself entirely to work."

(Quoted from Albert Dietrich and J. V. Widmann, *Erinnerungen an Brahms*, in English translation by Dora E. Hecht, London 1899, p. 71ff.)

accents (wedges). It would seem that Brahms, after starting to change the dots into wedges in the wind parts, abandoned this tedious procedure and added wedges beneath the wind section, with the explanation *Strichpunkt* for the printer. According to this direction, in the printed version, all the winds (woodwinds and horns), kettledrums and double bass have wedges, the strings have dots; the vocal parts have no staccato marks.

The writing, like Mozart's, is rapid yet neat and resolute, the bar lines hand-drawn for single staves or groups. The *GP* (general pause) preceding the *ff* is omitted in the *Collected Works*.

Johannes Brahms (1833-1897)

SYMPHONY NO. 1 IN C MINOR, OP. 68 (146, 147)

Movements II, III, and IV.

91 pages (including several blanks). 14-16 staves to a page. Movement II, 16 pages; movement III, 15 pages; movement IV, 58 pages. Each movement is paged separately and written on paper of different sizes: movement II, 26 x 32.8 cm.; movement III, 24.6 x 31 cm.; movement IV, 25.5 x 30.5 cm.

Signed and dated at the end of movement IV: "J. Brahms/Lichtenthal Sept. 76."

At the end of movement II a piece of paper with five measures has been pasted on the page with the direction to use this instead of the one originally written. An extra page "Beilage" is inserted between pages 14 and 15 of movement III adding 28 measures. Numerous corrections in red and blue pencil.

Composed 1854-1876. Published 1877 by N. Simrock, Berlin. First performed November 4, 1876 in Karlsruhe.

Collected Works, Series 1, No. 1.

Collection: Private collector, U.S.A.

PLATES 146 and 147 show pages 4 and 5 of movement IV, i.e. the bars immediately preceding the famous horn entry at *Più Andante* and two bars of the latter. The first one and a half bars of page 4 contain the climax of the introduction and its diminishment; they are followed by an exact repetition of this whole passage one half tone lower. The little three-note figures that form the descending line in the first and second violin parts are written with scrupulously neat spacing to emphasize their overlapping. But when the two violin parts proceed in unison at the beginning of bar 2 and in the middle of bar 3, Brahms saves work and simply marks *col 1* for the second violin. Although these many thirty-second notes are squeezed together, they press forward further than they should; the bar lines of the lower parts have to yield and the violin parts have to be extended into the margin.

The first bar in the first and second violin parts shows an interesting correction: Brahms connected the second and third notes in the first violin part with a slur and apparently planned to continue with short slurs over each of the little three-note figures, evidently to emphasize their overlapping, but then he crossed them out and they do not reappear in the middle of bar 3.

On page 5, plate 147, the drum roll diminishes from *ff* over groups of twelve notes into *pp* sextolets. *Dim* signs inserted in large wedges enforce the rapid decrescendo in all parts. The entry of the first horn, marked *solo* (the *solo* is not retained in the printed version) bears the direction *f sempre e passionato* (sic!). One bar later the second horn joins the first on the same note—almost imperceptibly—and performs for the full length of the bar $<$ $>$ Meanwhile the first horn is granted a quarter-rest's respite to catch its breath for its reentry in the following bar. In the printed version the $<$ $>$ is further strengthened into $<f>$.

In the first two bars of the *più andante*, in the first trombone part, Brahms crossed out the erroneous slur between E and C and connected G with C. Later in the printed version he even abandoned this slur and retained only the ties connecting the two G's with the two E's.

As often in Brahms' manuscripts, symbols or groups of symbols are simplified by writing them in one single stroke without lifting the pen; see, for instance, the *pp*'s in bar 4 which appear to be connected, and the ♮ signs which are transformed into zigzag lines.

Johannes Brahms (1833-1897)

TRAGISCHE OUVERTURE, OP. 81 (148, 149)

For orchestra.

56 pages, sixteen staves to each page. Size: 27¼ x 35 cm.

Heading: "Tragische Ouverture." In the right upper corner the signature of the composer. Undated.

Composed 1880. First published by Simrock, Berlin, 1881. First performed in Vienna, December 26, 1880, Hans Richter conducting.

Collected Works, Series III, No. 2.

Collection: The Memorial Library of Music, Stanford University, California.

The manuscript shows numerous corrections and additions, some of them in pencil. The first word of the title has apparently been rewritten over an erasure. The traces of the erased initial look vaguely like an H. Was the word "Hamlet"? There exist references to a planned "Hamlet Overture." Kalbeck, however, thinks that the *Tragic Overture* as well as the two middle movements of the *Third Symphony* were originally planned as music to accompany Goethe's *Faust*.[1] At any rate, Brahms' correspondence tells us that he had a hard time finding an appropriate title.[2]

PLATE 148 shows the first seven bars of the work. The instruments, marked in German, are: piccolo, two flutes, two oboes, two clarinets in B flat, two bassoons, two horns in D, two horns in F, two trumpets in D, three trombones and bass tuba (all four noted on two staves), kettledrums, first violin, second violin, viola, violoncello, double bass.

Notice the trill in the kettledrums subsiding from *fp* to *pp* in bars 1 and 2, and the consistent decrescendos at the end of the *sotto voce* phrases in the violins, bars 4 and 6. The accents ($>$) in bar 7 are added in pencil, apparently on second thought.

Page 14 of the score shown in Plate 149 is a good example of the extremely sensitive dynamics employed by this great master of orchestral writing: —————— ——————
A

In the first six bars A marks a soft crescendo and decrescendo of the whole orchestra, against

---

[1] Kalbeck, *Johannes Brahms*, Vienna, 1907, III, 1., p. 256.

[2] Letter of Brahms to Bernhard Scholz, September 17, 1880.

which background the horn part stands out with individual shorter crescendos. A similar effect is the contrast between the lyric theme in the violins and the $<$ $>$ in the woodwinds (bars 7 ff.).

The unison of the two clarinets (bars 7 and 8, fourth stave from top) is indicated by the time-saving B instead of by C.

Johannes Brahms (1833-1897)

VERGEBLICHES STÄNDCHEN (150)

Song with pianoforte accompaniment.
Four pages, three triple staves to each page. Size: 25.5 x 32.7 cm.
Autograph heading: "Vergebliches Ständchen. (Niederrheinisches Volkslied.)"
Undated. Unsigned.
Composed in 1882. Published by N. Simrock, Berlin, 1882, and in Collected Works, Vol. 25, page 92, as no. 4 of the group "Romanzen und Lieder für eine oder zwei Stimmen, Op. 84"[1]
Collection: The Newberry Library, Chicago, Ill.

PLATE 150 shows the first page of the manuscript. In the left upper corner is written: *Lebhaft u. gut gelaunt.*

There are several corrections; Brahms evidently planned to write this song as a strophic song, intending simply to fit the text of "Er" and "Sie" to the same vocal part, but since this, it seems, did not work out, he decided to "through-compose" the song and consequently canceled the words sung by "Sie" in the first staff.

At first he had adapted the first two notes of the vocal part to both the upper and the lower text: to the upper text (two syllables: "Gu-ten") by means of two separate eighth-notes, and to the lower text (one syllable: "Mein") by means of a crossbar connecting the two notes; but after deciding to "durchkomponieren" the song, he did not take the trouble to obliterate the crossbar.

This page, as well as the rest of the manuscript, shows unusually swift writing with a marked slant to the right which affects even the slurs and the crescendo and decrescendo signs; the rests, accidentals and braces are sometimes simplified in the extreme. But this haste does not prevent Brahms from indicating phrasing, dynamics, and legato and staccato with his usual precision. After the first triple staff Brahms does not repeat the clefs and key signatures.

The phrasing slurs in the right hand of the piano part are not repeated in the vocal part. The *Collected Works* add these and other phrasing slurs to the vocal part.

[1] When Hanslick congratulated Brahms on this song, Brahms replied: ". . . For this one song I would gladly give all the others . . ." (". . . Für das eine Lied gebe ich die andern alle. . . .") See Max Kalbeck, *Johannes Brahms*, Vienna 1907, Vol. III, p. 337.

Johannes Brahms (1833-1897)

TWO INTERMEZZI FOR PIANO: OP. 118, NO. 1, IN A MINOR, AND OP. 119, NO. 1 IN B MINOR (151)

4 and 5 pages; three double staves to each page.

Size: 12 x 20 cm.

Unsigned. Undated.

The leaves of the manuscript seem to have been torn out of a notebook. The two compositions contained in the autograph belong to two different sets of *Intermezzi*. Both sets were composed in 1892 and first published by N. Simrock, Berlin, in 1893.

Collected Works, Series XIV, Nos. 9-10.

Collection: The Library of Congress, Washington, D.C.

The upper illustration shows the opening of Op. 118, No. 1. There are elaborate dynamic and pedal marks. It is puzzling that some of the $<>$ wedges are clearly added to the long sustained chords in the right or left hand and not to the ascending passages of eighth-notes (see bars, 1, 2, 3, 4, 6). While these directions are impracticable on the piano, they are quite revealing of Brahms' intentions. In the *Collected Works* the long decrescendo beneath the lower staff in bars 2 and 4 appears shrunk to $>$ exactly beneath the chords in the left hand.

The tempo indication *Nicht schnell aber sehr leidenschaftlich* is translated in the *Collected Works* into "Allegro non assai, ma molto appassionato."

Note that the cross strokes, together with the phrasing slurs, repeatedly intersect the bar lines, thus connecting 12 eighth-notes into one unbroken line.

The lower illustration shows the opening of Op. 119, No. 1. Again cross strokes intersect the bar lines (bars 7 and 8). It is not without interest that the successive piling up of the tones into chords finds a different graphic expression in the first 3 bars and in bars 9-11. The first method is employed in bars 1-2-3, the other in bars 9-10-11 and later in the manuscript. The *Collected Works*, supervised by Brahms, consistently employ the second method.

While this, however, is strictly a question of notation and has no bearing on the music itself, we find in another instance a minor change which does affect the music. In bars 4 and 6 the chords formed by the middle parts are written out in dotted sixteenth-notes separated by thirty-second rests, producing somewhat the effect of broken chords. From the twelfth bar on, the same chords appear in the form of undotted sixteenth-notes, the rests are sixteenth rests, and the effect produced is that of a more even flow. Here again the *Collected Works* use the second notation throughout.

These marks in bars 12 and 13 after *dol*[*ce*], which emphasize the little pseudo-canon, are not employed in bars 4 and 6 where this canon first appears.

Modest Petrovitch Moussorgsky (1839-1881)

KINDER-SCHERZ FOR PIANO, OP. 15 (152)

Entitled "Une plaisanterie (ein Kinderscherz)" in the edition of W. Bessel et Cie., St. Petersburg, authorized by Belaieff.

Four pages, eighteen staves to each page. Size: 26.3 x 38 cm.

The autograph title page is written in Russian, with the exception of the title proper "Kinder-Scherz." Many marks show that the manuscript has been thoroughly revised for publication.

Composed in 1860. Published in 1873 by A. Belaieff, Moscow.

Collected Works: Vol. VIII, p. 37.

Collection: The Library of Congress, Washington, D.C.

PLATE 152 shows the last page of the manuscript with the composer's signature in Russian at the end: "Fine./ Selo Toshkovo, Maia 28vo 1860 g./ Modest Musorskij."

The handwriting is fluent and precise, with ledger lines almost as thick as the cross strokes. There are pedal marks and meticulous dynamic indications of the finest gradation. In the *Edition complète* by W. Bessel & Cie., St. Petersburg, Moscow, these marks are frequently reversed; for instance, the long crescendo over the last three bars in the next to the last double staff is replaced by decrescendo.

Notice the beautiful handwriting in the date and signature and the playful calligraphy of the conclusion sign.

Peter Ilich Tchaikovsky (1840-1893)

AVEUX PASSIONNÉ [SIC], FOR PIANO (153)

2 leaves; verso of leaf 2 blank; 7 double staves with 1 blank staff between the systems. Size: 30.5 x 22.5 cm.

Autograph heading on first page: "Aveux passionné/ P. Tschaikovsky."

Undated.

Probably unpublished.

Collection: The Library of Congress, Washington, D.C.

The plate shows page 1 of the manuscript. Characteristic is the profusion of expression marks and other directions for the performer, many of them added in pencil (for instance, *dolce espressivo* and *poco animando*). Great attention to detail is given already in the opening instructions: *Moderato mosso, molto rubato / p cantabile ed apassionato* [sic].

Typical of Tchaikovsky's hand are the signs that separate the systems at the left margin and the braces that tie the two staves together; the latter begin with a horizontal dash and terminate in a little hook. The pseudo-orchestral structure of the piano score is consistently maintained, with the numerous dynamic marks always added to the leading melody, that is, for the first fourteen bars to the lower staff and from there on to the upper one. There are neither pedal nor fingering marks.

Antonin Dvořák (1841-1904)

SKETCH TO SYMPHONY IN E MINOR, OP. 95 (154)

("From the New World.") Heading: "Sinfonie E moll/ Předehra k Sinfonii E moll/ New York 18 ¹⁹⁄₄ 93."

Data concerning size and condition of the manuscript and its present owner could not be obtained from Czechoslovakia.

At the end of bar 4 Dvořák writes ⸫ ; in the final version he inserts one bar with a horn tone rapidly decreasing from *sf* to *pp*. Above bars 4 and 5 is written: *Fl[utes]*, beneath bar 11: *Es ml* (Es moll). The bars 12 (crossed out), 13, and 15 refer to bars 15 and 17 of the final version and are simpler in rhythm. Dvořák, however, notes beneath bar 12: *O půl tonu níže* (half a tone lower), and beneath bar 13: *Synkopy* (syncopes). In bars 14 and 16 of the draft the famous syncopated horn motive makes its first appearance shaded dynamically at its climax by crescendo-decrescendo wedges, and its second by a crescendo wedge. Basses are frequently indicated by letters of the alphabet. Bar 20 is marked *fff* (in the printed version only *sf*); the drumroll immediately preceding the Allegro is indicated by *tymp:* and marked by a decrescendo wedge above it. The opening of the Allegro (in the final version "Allegro molto") presents the horn motive (*corni*) in its new form in *p* (in the final version in *mf*). Above the horn motive violin tremolos are indicated.

Antonin Dvořák (1841-1904)

SYMPHONY IN E MINOR, OP. 95 (155)

"Z nového svĕta" ("From the New World").

118 pages. 20 staves to each page. Size: 26 x 35.5 cm.

Title page: "Z nového svĕta"/"From the New-world"/Sinfonie/E-moll/, číslo 8./opus 95/ pro orkestr/složil/Antonín Dvořák./ Složil a Instrumentaci začal v New-Yorku dne 9. února 1893."

Heading of first page: "Sinfonie (E-moll) New-York 18 ⁹⁄₂ 93."

Dated February 9, 1893.

Pencil remarks in the middle of the page: "První provozavání v New-Yorku/"Philharmonie Society" 15.a 16./prosince/Seidl 1893." (First performed in New York by the Philharmonic Society/ December 15 and 16 / Seidl/ 1893). At the bottom of page pencil remarks: "Provozováno v Bostonu 29.30. ho prosince Paur a v Brooklyne 12.ledna 1894/Seidl." (Performed in Boston December 29 and 30, Paur, and in Brooklyn January 12, 1894, Seidl.)" At the end of movement IV to the right of page 118: "Fine/Chvála Bohu/Dokončeno/dne 24.kvetna/ 1893/ráno v 9 hodin/Antonín Dvořák." (End/ Glory be to God/ Finished the 24 of May 1893/ early morning at 9 o'clock/ Antonín Dvořák). On the last page of the score Dvořák wrote: "Dĕti přijeli do Southampton/ 1.33. odp.telegram přišel." (The children arrived in Southampton. A telegram arrived at 1:33 in the afternoon)."[1]

[1] Dvořák expected his family to visit him in New York.

Composed 1893 while Dvořák was residing in New York as the director of the National Conservatory of Music.

Published 1894 by Simrock under the title "Fifth Symphony."

Collection: Dr. Otokar Dvořák, Prague.

PLATE 155 shows the first page of the manuscript with the opening of the *Adagio* introduction to the first movement. The metronome mark on top of the string section does not seem to be in the composer's hand. The third trombone has—by mistake—6/8 as time signature. The expression marks are scrupulously exact though not always easily legible; see, for instance, *a 2. fz > pp* in bars 4 and 5 of the *Corni in C*.

Edvard Hagerup Grieg (1843-1907)

I LIDEN HÖJT DEROPPE, SONG WITH PIANO
ACCOMPANIMENT, OP. 39, NO. 3 (156)

Text by Jonas Lie.

1 leaf, written on both sides; 16 staves to each page. Size: 34.5 x 26 cm.

Autograph heading: "I Liden höjt deroppe—Edvard Grieg / (Jonas Lie)."

Undated.

This song is included in the edition published by Wilhelm Hansen, Kopenhagen and Leipzig, No. 1311, as the third of six songs which form Op. 39. In G. Grove, Dictionary of Music and Musicians, 12 songs are mentioned as Op. 39; the *Verzeichnis der Werke Griegs*, C. F. Peters, 1910, lists 5 songs under Op. 39.

Collection: The Library of Congress, Washington, D.C.

PLATE 156 shows the front page of the manuscript. It differs in several respects from the *Wilhelm Hansen* Edition; the latter a) has a two bar prelude consisting of the first two bars of the piano accompaniment in the manuscript, transposed one octave higher, b) replaces the duplets in bar 14 by a new time signature: 2/4; c) omits the crescendo-decrescendo wedges over "Granernes" in bar 15 and moves the *tempo 1* back there from bar 16.

The writing, score as well as lettering, is fluent and shows a high degree of connectedness which gives to some chords a strange pattern: the note-heads of a chord, instead of being threaded to one single stem, each has its own little stems which pass directly into the next lower note-head, thus forming a saw-shaped zigzag line (see especially bars 8-11, lower piano staff, and bars 12-14, upper piano staff).

Sir Edward Elgar (1857-1934)

PIANO ARRANGEMENT OF THE VARIATIONS FOR
ORCHESTRA, OP. 36 (157)

Known as "Enigma Variations."

Thirty-four leaves: one title page, forty-six pages score, twenty-one pages blank. Four double staves to each page. Size: 31 x 24 cm.

Autograph heading: "Variations for orchestra, op. 36. Pianoforte arrangement."
Signed by the composer on the title page. Undated.
Date of composition 1899 or shortly before.
First published by Novello & Co., London, 1899.
Collection: The Memorial Library of Music, Stanford University, California.

The printed version contains the remark "dedicated to my friends pictured within," and beneath the number of each variation are initials, nicknames or other signs hinting at the person meant.[1]

The thirteenth variation, reproduced in the plate, has three stars and, in the printed version, the title *Romanza*. In the orchestral version this variation begins with a clarinet solo supported by passages of the second violin and the violoncello. Elgar transferred the dynamic marks from the orchestral score to the piano arrangement with great accuracy. He adds, moreover, occasional accents ∧ as for instance at the beginning of bar 4, and pedal marks.

[1] It has been said that the friend to whom this variation was dedicated was Lady Mary Lygon who was en route to Australia when this piece was written. Clues to the meaning of this piece are the quotation from Mendelssohn's *Meeresstille und Glückliche Fahrt* and a dull drum tremolo in the orchestral score which perhaps depicts the rhythm of the liner's engines.

Edward Alexander MacDowell (1861-1908)

FIRST SUITE FOR ORCHESTRA, OP. 42 (158)

Full holograph score, eighty-four pages, eighteen staves. Size: 35 x 27 cm.
Autograph heading: "E. A. Mac Dowell op. 42." Above this, in center of page, the title of the first part: "In einem verwünschten Walde."[1] Paged, undated.
Composed in 1882. First published in 1891 by Arthur P. Schmidt, Boston & Leipzig, as "Suite für grosses Orchester / componirt von E. A. Mac Dowell," with the exception of the third part which was published in 1893.
First performed September, 1891, at the Music Festival in Worcester, Mass.
Collection: The Library of Congress, Washington, D.C. (Presented by the publisher in 1914.)

The manuscript of the Suite in five movements represents the American composer's first important orchestral work.

PLATE 158 shows the last climax in the first movement (*Largamente, Misterioso*). The *fff* at the beginning of the page gains even more force in the last bar of the page; then on the next page a diminuendo sets in leading to a *pppp* in the last pizzicato chords of the movement. The instruments are, from top to bottom: 1) piccolo; 2) two flutes; 3) two oboes; 4) four clarinets in B flat; 5) two bassoons; 6 and 7) valve horns in F; 8) two valve trumpets in F; 9) two trombones; 10) third trombone and tuba; 11) two kettledrums in A and E; 12) cymbals and large drum; 13) first violin; 14) second violin; 15) viola; 16) violoncello; 17) double bass.

The writing is of printlike precision and neatness. The tempo and other indications are a mixture of Italian and German.

[1] In a haunted forest.

Victor Herbert (1859-1924)

IF I WERE ON THE STAGE (159)

Scene 4 from the comic opera *Mlle. Modiste*, text by Henry Blossom. Soprano solo, piano accompaniment.

One preliminary leaf, 10 pages with music. 12 staves to each page. Size: 34.5 x 27.5 cm.

Autograph heading: "If I Were on the Stage /(Fifi)/(Henry Blossom)/Victor Herbert." Undated.

Composed 1905, probably in New York.

First performed December 25, 1905 in New York at the Knickerbocker Theater.

The vocal score of *Mlle. Modiste* first published 1905 by M. Witmark & Sons, New York.

Collection: The Library of Congress, Washington, D.C.

Scene 4 of the opera consists of an Allegro in 2/4, "If I were asked to play the part"; a Polonaise, "Ah you will agree"; a Valse Lente, "Sweet summer breeze" culminating in the phrase, "Kiss me again," the beginning of which is shown in Plate 159.

The first edition omits the $>$ in bar 15 and replaces the $>>$ in bars 7 and 8 by $<>$. One wonders whether this correction is justified.

The writing indicates the speed and fluency of a routine hand, and also, in places, unusual verve as exemplified especially by the large and vigorous interlaced clefs and braces.

Charles Martin Loeffler (1861-1935)

CANTICUM FRATRIS SOLIS (160)

Setting for solo voice and chamber orchestra of the hymn by St. Francis of Assisi in a modern Italian version by Gino Perera. Full score.

1 preliminary leaf, 64 pages; 22 staves to each page. Size: 35.5 x 31 cm. (including cloth binding).

Autograph heading: "To Mrs. Elizabeth Sprague Coolidge/ in profound admiration/'The Canticle of the Sun'/(words by St. Francis of Assisi)/ for/ Voice and Chamber-orchestra:/ 8 Violins, 3 Violas, 3 V'cellos, 1 Double Bass,/ 3 Flutes, English Horn, Horn in F, Celesta, Piano and 2 Harps / Composed/by/Ch. M. Loeffler."

Composed in 1925.

Published in 1929 by the Library of Congress, Elizabeth Sprague Coolidge Foundation. First performed at the first Coolidge Foundation Chamber Music Festival in the Library of Congress, Washington, D.C. (October 28, 1925), by Povla Frijsh, Frederick A. Stock conducting.

Collection: The Elizabeth Sprague Coolidge Foundation Collection, The Library of Congress, Washington, D.C.

The manuscript is a clear and extremely neat copy, with careful phrasing and expression signs.

PLATE 160 shows page 1 of the manuscript, with the beginning of the *Andante con moto* in 5/4 time.

The tremolo in the double bass is indicated only in the beginning, likewise the pedal point in the organ part. The organ is not mentioned in the list of instruments in the autograph heading, since it is not used after this point.

Notice the curious G clefs. The empty heads of notes are usually designed in two half circles, with the stem drawn out from one of them.

Hugo Wolf (1860-1903)

SEEMANNS ABSCHIED (161)

No. 20 of the *Eichendorff Lieder* (*Gedichte von Eichendorff für eine Singstimme und Klavier componirt von Hugo Wolf*); No. 17 in the printed version.
Two leaves written on all four sides in ink. Size: 34.3 x 26.3 cm.
Composed September 21, 1887 (1888?)[1] in Unterach, Upper Austria.
Composer's signature in pencil in the upper right corner.
Published by Lacom, Vienna, 1889.
Collection: The Library of Congress, Washington, D.C.

PLATE 161 shows the first page. Many expression marks have been added with red pencil, as well as *Sehr flott* in the upper left corner and (*geheimnisvoll*) over bars 13 and 14. Some accidentals were added in blue pencil. The first edition supervised by Wolf and published by L. Lacom, Vienna, as "property of the composer," changed the *Sehr flott* into *Stürmisch bewegt* and added a *ff* in the third bar.

Characteristic of the subtlety of Wolf's dynamic shadings are the marks in bars 9 to 13; leading from *p* (*pp* in the piano part) through a crescendo wedge to *pp*.

The page shown is a good example of Hugo Wolf's thin and rapid writing; eighth rests, for instance, become simple dashes of various curvature. The G clefs are extremely simplified. In bar 3 of the piano part, right hand, the tails of three notes, instead of starting from the heads, are drawn directly out of the ledger line.

Hugo Wolf, like Handel and Schubert, composed with incredible speed: in his irregular periods of feverish production he frequently composed one and occasionally two or three songs a day. Between 1888 and 1890, in almost uninterrupted flow, Wolf wrote 53 "Mörike Songs," 51 "Goethe Songs," 44 "Spanish Songs," 17 "Eichendorff Songs," 10 "Keller Songs," and some of the "Italian Songs," that is, about 200 songs altogether.

The script shows a high degree of disconnectedness: heads, stems, flags, and strokes are jotted down in single separate sweeps of the pen. The same haste and disconnectedness are shown in the letters of the text; only three or four words are in connected writing. There are letters of Wolf in which nearly every character stands by itself.

The introductory chord (bars 1 and 2) created a sensation: Bruckner, to whom Wolf showed this song, cried: "The devil! From where did you get this chord?"[2]

[1] Ernest Newman: *Hugo Wolf*, Leipzig 1910, gives two different dates: 1887 on page 55, 1888 on page 245. Frank Walker, *Hugo Wolf*, London 1951, page 485, dates the song 1888.

[2] Max Auer: *Anton Bruckner*, Vienna 1922, page 274.

Hugo Wolf (1860-1903)

EIN STÄNDCHEN EUCH ZU BRINGEN (162)

No. 22 of the first volume of the "Italienisches Liederbuch nach Paul Heyse für eine Singstimme und Klavier von Hugo Wolf."

Two leaves, written in ink, page 4 blank. Size: 34.3 x 26.3 cm.

Composed December 10, 1891, in Döbling, a suburb of Vienna.

Composer's signature in the upper right hand corner of first page.

First published by B. Schott's Söhne, Mainz, 1892.[1]

Collection: The Library of Congress, Washington, D.C.

PLATE 162 shows the first page. There are numerous blue and black pencil marks. On page 2, for instance, *Sehr zurückhaltend* is changed to *Immer zurückhaltend*. Wolf's writing is here even more abbreviated than in the preceding plate. Compare, for instance, the even sketchier G clefs.

The first edition, published by K. Ferd. Heckel, Mannheim, and supervised by the composer, adds at the beginning of the piano part: (*mit Verschiebung, ohne Pedal*) evidently to guarantee a guitar-like timbre. The imitation of the voice in the piano part is carefully suggested by > marks.

The numerous numbers written in pencil around the heading show the composer's concern about the definite sequence of the single songs within the *Liederbuch*, a crucial problem for any writer of song cycles; 16, 14, and 16 have all been crossed out, and the piece was finally numbered 22.

[1] Frank Walker, *Hugo Wolf*, gives 1891, which is hardly possible considering the date of composition.

Gustav Mahler (1860-1911)

DER SCHILDWACHE NACHTLIED (163)

Song with piano accompaniment. Words from "Des Knaben Wunderhorn." (Also arranged by the composer for voice and orchestra.)

Three pages, 18 staves to each page, written in triple staves, one stave for the vocal part, two for the piano accompaniment. Size: 26 x 34.5 cm.

Composed circa 1890. First published by Josef Weinberger, Vienna, 1900, as no. 1 of the song cycle *Des Knaben Wunderhorn*.

Collection: The Library of Congress, Washington, D.C.

The manuscript of which the first page is shown in Plate 163 is a sketch, with numerous changes and incisive corrections. It differs in many respects from the printed version in *Universaledition* no. 1691a; for example, in the vocal part. The printed version begins in 4/4 time and remains so for several bars. The present draft changes time in each of the first three bars, and the composer was still undecided: in bar 1, vocal part and upper stave of the piano part, the original 3/4 time is changed to 4/4, while the bottom stave remains in 3/4 time.

This evidently led to the correction of the F major chord at the end of bar 1 from ♩ to ♩. A comparison of the numerous marks and time signatures shows how hesitant the composer was about a definite solution: over bar 1: *Gemächliches Marschtempo*; over bar 13: *Merklich Langsamer*. After bar 15, the 4/4 time changes to 6/4. Over bar 16, with the quarter notes in two triplets: *Immer langsamer* is crossed out; over bar 18, the *Noch Langsamer* is crossed out and replaced by the 3/4 sign and the indication, ♪ ♪ ♪ = ♪ ♪ ♪

The following bars are alternately in 4/4 and 3/4 time. Bar 22 reinstates *Tempo I*, and continues the measure by measure alternation of time. It is evidently in connection with this, that the double line between bars 16 and 17 has been moved to *Tempo I* between bars 21 and 22.

Note the consistent drum-roll imitation in the pianoforte part of the first triple stave with the imitation of trumpet calls in the right hand.

Several bars in the bottom stave are incomplete. The last bars of the page, with the text "voll Helleparten! Bin ich gestellt!" differ entirely from the printed version: the fanfare-like major triads in the vocal part were softened down to minor.

The extremely nervous and irregular hand, in the score as well as in the text, reflects Mahler's hesitating, ever-changing process of creation.

Richard Strauss (1864-1949)

TILL EULENSPIEGEL (164)

Tone poem, for orchestra.
55 pages, 28 staves to each page. Size: 35 x 26.7 cm.
Autograph heading: "Till Eulenspiegels lustige Streiche/ nach alter Schelmenweise in Rondeauform für grosses Orchester gesetzt von Richard Strauss."
Dated by composer on last page: "6 Mai 1895/München."
Composed 1895. First performed 1895 in Frankfurt a. M.
Collection: Maria and Rudolph Floersheim, Wildegg, Switzerland.

The manuscript is a clean copy, with orchestration marks always on the left margin.

PLATE 164 shows the upper and lower half of the next-to-the-last page of the manuscript with the beginning of the epilogue.

Strauss writes at times *po*, at times only *p*. Note the characteristic G clefs with no spiral in the center. Great care is given to the phrasing slurs (see, for instance, the different phrasing slurs in the first and second violin, bars 10 and 11 of the epilogue).

The writing is of needle-sharp clarity, the spacing of utmost precision.

It is interesting to see how elements of score writing also appear in the regular script. Many capital letters (upper case) such as *B* in *Basscl[arinette]* and *Br[atsche]*, *F* in *Fl[öte]*, *D* in *Doppelt so langsam*, are given with little horizontal pennants just like the flags of notes.

Richard Strauss (1864-1949)

KLING! (165)

Song for tenor with piano accompaniment, Op. 48. Words by Karl Henckell.

Three pages of music, three triple staves to each page. Size: 32 x 25.7 cm.

Autograph heading: "Kling! . . . (Karl Henckell)/ (für Tenor)/ Richard Strauss Op. 48. No. III." At the end: "Charlottenburg, 30. September 1900./ Tief in G dur." On page 4 a copy of the text in the composer's hand. Composed in 1900. Published as the third of *Fünf Lieder* by Adolf Fürstner in Berlin, 1901.

Collection: The Library of Congress, Washington, D.C.

PLATE 165 shows the first page of the manuscript. There are precise pedal marks, *forte* is abbreviated as *fo*. Typical of Richard Strauss' hand are the G clefs with the spiral omitted. The writing is thin, fluent and lucid, with strictly vertical stems and bar lines and an emphasis on the vertical even in the textwriting.

Richard Strauss (1864-1949)

SKETCHES FOR DIE ÄGYPTISCHE HELENA (166-168)

Opera in two acts. Text by Hugo von Hofmannsthal.

One of the small, inexpensive notebooks which Strauss used to carry in his pocket.

64 pages, most of them written in pencil, some in ink, some in both; six staves to each page. Size: 8 x 12.9 cm.

On the first page: "Meinem lieben Freund Gustav Brecher. Richard Strauss, Garmisch, 24. Juni 1927."

Opera composed 1927-1928. Published in 1928, by Adolf Fürstner, Berlin.

First performed June 6, 1928 at Dresden.

Collection: The Heinemann Foundation for Research, Educational, Charitable and Scientific Purposes, Inc., New York.

PLATE 166 shows the top half of page 19 (see no. 120ff. of the printed orchestral score and p. 255ff. of the piano score) with a sketch of motives for the backstage music that accompanies the banquet given by Altair for Helena. The page is headed "Tanzrytmen für die Fantasia. . . ." The orchestration is indicated; see *Oboen, tb* [*tambourin*].

PLATE 167 shows the top half of page 50 of the notebook. The sketch is in the form of a piano score written partly in ink, partly in pencil. It contains only a skeleton—melodic contour with basic harmony. The whole iridescent texture, characteristic of Strauss's orchestral scores, with its multitude of nervous contrapuntal threads, is still missing.

PLATE 168 shows page 51. The part of *Princess Aithra* (soprano), with the repeated outcry "Bereite dich" is written beneath the part of *Menelaos* (baritone), both on the same staff. In the last two bars the part of *Menelaos* is written in ink in the middle staff, although one can see from the penciled text words on top of the first staff that Strauss had intended to continue at that point.

The time indications are added only occasionally, and evidently later (see bars 8 and 10). The 2/4 time which prevails for five bars, beginning in bar 3, in the final version of the opera, is not indicated at all in the sketch.

Ruggiero Leoncavallo (1858-1919)

I PAGLIACCI (169, 170)

Musical drama in one act and a prologue. Libretto by the composer.

179 leaves (358 pages), twenty-four staves to each page. Size: 37.5 x 25 cm.

The manuscript bears five signatures of the composer; each single sheet is imprinted with "Proprietà del R. Stabilimento Musicale Tito di Gio. Riccordi—Milano." Mounted on the cover, the label of the publisher: "Stabilimento dell'Editore, Edoardo Sonzogno in Milano/ Pagliacci/ Musica del Maestro R. Leoncavallo/ Grande Partitura/ Autografo." Autograph title page: "Pagliacci/ Dramma in un atto/ parole e musica di/ R. Leoncavallo/ Prologo/ Partitura." At the end: "Fine dell'Opera/ R. Leoncavallo." The *Intermezzo*, inserted after page 206, and consisting of nine unnumbered pages (but six leaves), is entitled: " 'Pagliacci'/ Intermezzo/ R. Leoncavallo/ Partitura."

First performed on May 21, 1892, at the Teatro dal Verme, Milan.

Collection: The Library of Congress, Washington, D.C. (A memorial to Florence Hinkle Witherspoon, obtained in 1939 through the bequest of Herbert Witherspoon.)

The ink on every page has a peculiar, smeared appearance, evidently from having been put in a letter press for purposes of duplication.

While this opera is usually produced in two acts, the manuscript is written as one act to be performed without interruption. *Pagliacci* was written for the Sonzogno prize competition for an opera in one act.

PLATES 169, 170 show pages 196 and 197 of the manuscript near the end of the first act, immediately before *Canio's* famous aria, "Vesti la giubba." They contain the recitative which introduces this aria, except for the first words: "Recitar! Mentre preso dal delirio non so più. . . ." Note the two very different manners of lettering: in the words of the text, thin upright and disconnected; in the indications of the instruments and the directions for the performers, *con tristezza; affrett:*[*ando*], *col canto*, a vigorous hand with a decided forward slant. Characteristic are the fine shadings that support the dramatic expression, such as the accents > and the use of different dynamic marks for various instruments at the same point of the score. Canio's outburst "Bah! . . . Sei tu forse un uom! . . . ah! ah! ah! ah! ah! Tu sei Pagliaccio! . . ." is accompanied by a whole sequence of directions for the singer: *string*: *un poco (con ira) sghignazzando con dolore rit-*°-. His violent laugh is indicated by five "pitchless" notes represented only by their stems.

Giacomo Puccini (1858-1924)

LA BOHÈME (171, 172)

Opera in four acts. Text by G. Giocosa and L. Illica, based on the novel by H. Murger.

263 folios. Act I, 90; II, 53; III, 55; IV, 65. Back of folios 144 and 198 blank; back of folios 12, 52, 76 and 252 crossed out; on the back of folio 216 pencil notes. Size: mostly 48 x 33 cm., some smaller. Signed and dated: beginning of act I: "21—1—95"; end of act I: "8—6—95 ore 2 di notte Milano"; end of act II: "19—7—95 Pescia (Castellaccio)"; end of act III: "18—7bre 95 Pescia"; end of act IV: "10 dicembre 95 ore 12 di notte Torre del Lago."

The manuscript is the first version of the opera. It does not contain the quartet of act II and has an earlier version of the second finale.

First published 1896, Milan. First performed February 1, 1896, at the Teatro Regio, Turin.

Many cancellations and corrections in ink and many marginal remarks.

Collection: G. Ricordi & Co., Milan.

PLATE 171 shows page 192 verso which contains bars 26-29 after No. 30 of the third act, with the words of *Mimi*: "[Mentre a prima]vera c'è compagno il sol." The other vocal parts are those of *Rodolfo, Musetta*, and *Marcello*. As can be seen from the hand-drawn bar lines the vocal parts were written first. Changes in tempo, *affret.—Rallentando* ⁓ *a tempo*, are marked on top and bottom of the page and in addition occasionally within the single parts. In line with the old usage,[1] expression marks such as the crescendo-decrescendo and the *espressivo* in the first violin part are not imposed upon the corresponding vocal part. The stage direction *rumore di piatti e bicchieri che si rompono* is crossed out and replaced by *fracasso di piatti e bicchieri rotti*.

The writing is extremely hasty, even to the point of hampering legibility: see, for instance, the accent > in *Musetta's* part which could be mistaken for an x.

PLATE 172 shows page 295 recto with a section beginning two bars before No. 29 from the fourth act which culminates in *Mimi's* death. An earlier tempo direction is scratched out and replaced by: *Andante lento e sostenuto*. In the space of the long pause (*lunga*) is written: *Rodolfo si allontana cautamente a Mimi facendo segno agli amici di far piano e si avvicina a Marcello.* The two-line staff for the cymbals bears the direction: *piatto solo pppp con la mazzuola* (one disk only, touched on the rim). The > in the violin part before the ⌒ is not retained in the printed version.

Note the different styles of handwriting employed by Puccini, for instance *Musetta* or *Madonna* in heavy, upright characters with a marked backhand slant; and *senza sordini* in a thin hand, slanting forward.

Puccini was an accomplished and witty caricaturist and a doodler. His feelings about Mimi's impending departure find a somewhat macabre expression in the doodle at the left margin. Or might it have been directed at the performer?

---

[1] See plates 67-74 and plates 101, 102.

Claude Achille Debussy (1862-1918)
PELLÉAS ET MÉLISANDE (173, 174)

Opera ("drame lyrique") in five acts. Text after Maurice Maeterlinck's play, with some changes.

Volume of 135 pages, written on one side of the leaves only. Thirty to thirty-six staves to each page. Size: 39.7 x 29.7 cm.

Each act is paged separately and has its own autograph title page. Complete holograph of an elaborate draft of the whole opera written in systems of from 3 to 5 staves with numerous marks indicating the orchestration.

Unsigned. Dated at the end of Acts I, II, and IV, as follows: I.: "Dec. 93/ Janv.-Febr. 94"; II: "Paris / 17. Aout, 95."; IV: "Sept. Oct. 93 / Mai 95 / Janvier 1900 / Sept. 1901."

Composed 1892-1902.

Published in 1902 by Eugène Fromont, Paris. First performed April 30, 1902 at the Opéra Comique, Paris.

Collection: The New England Conservatory of Music, Boston, Mass. (presented by Mr. Eben D. Jordan).

PLATE 173 shows page 12 of Act III. The whole page is studded with minute orchestration marks in ink and pencil in various colors, such as *Fl. H 1* (flute, first horn); *vs* (violins I and II); *C Ang* (cor anglais); *Vc* (violoncello). Frequently, notes in different staves which belong together vertically are connected by lines (see, for instance, the two bars after the sectional number 29). Likewise the melodic lines leading from one chord to the next are traced by connecting strokes and marked with different numbers (see, for instance, bars 8 and 9 after 28).

PLATE 174 shows page 19 of Act IV. There are many cancellations. The crossing out is done so neatly and with such a variety of lattice work that it would seem that Debussy had to make a special effort to reduce his own ideas to nothingness. Observe the time saving device ⊢————(which amounts to a shorthand for repetition (bars 7-8, 11-12, 17-20). These signs are sometimes equipped with numbers referring to those preceding bars which have to be repeated.

Claude Achille Debussy (1862-1918)
APPARITION (175)

Song with pianoforte accompaniment. Text by Stéphane Mallarmé.

Title page and three pages. Five triple staves to each page. Size: 35 x 27 cm.

Autograph title page written in red ink with minute letters and beautifully rounded ornamental initials.

Composed in 1884. The fourth of *Quatre Mélodies* which were composed in 1882-1884 and first published in 1926 as a supplement to *La revue musicale*, Paris.

Collection: The Library of Congress, Washington, D.C.

The plate shows page 2 of the manuscript. Many expression marks and slurs added in red ink, see, for instance,

FF ⤢ ⌒ in the first staff,

P >< ⌒ in the second,

PP - - - - in the third, etc.

The last two triple staves are corrected in black pencil, moving the vocal part one bar back of the original ink notation.

The writing is of refined elegance, the layout meticulously planned. The note heads are small round or oval dots, all of them written with a left to right motion of the pen. All horizontals are fat, verticals thin; not only in the score, but also in the lettering. (Cf. the *PP* over bar 9 with the *P* in the text beneath). Frequently certain letters are distinguished by their size or by a fuller ornamental swing. It is interesting to observe that this usually happens where the beginning of a musical phrase coincides with that of a sentence, revealing that most intimate and sensitive relationship between music and text, which is so important in Debussy's work.

Maurice Ravel (1875-1937)

CHANSONS MADÉCASSES (176)

For voice, with flute (alternating with piccolo), violoncello, and pianoforte. Text by Evariste Parny. I. Nahandove. II. Aoua! III. Il est doux. . . .

9 leaves, the score written in quintuple staves. Size: 35 x 27 cm.

Composed 1925-1926. First published 1926, by A. Durand et fils, Paris. First performed in October, 1925, in Paris, with the composer at the piano.

This work is one of the last compositions completed by Ravel.

Collection: The Elizabeth Sprague Coolidge Foundation Collection, The Library of Congress, Washington, D.C. The work is dedicated to Mrs. Elizabeth Sprague Coolidge, and was presented by her to The Library of Congress in 1926.

PLATE 176 shows page 2 of *Nahandove*, the first of the three *Chansons*. From Evariste Parny's French translation of a group of Madagascar poems Ravel chose the fifth, eighth and twelfth poems.

The writing resembles Debussy's in many respects: the cross strokes are drawn straight, with precisely even width; the G clefs end in a point at the top. The bar lines are drawn separately for each part.

The vocal part shows careful phrasing. See pencil marks: *rit poco a poco* and *A tempo*, and pencil corrections in the lower stave of the piano part, bar 2.

With its intricate rhythms, artfully superimposed on the basic 6/8 meter, the composition is the queen, an exotic queen, of all berceuses. With what admirable precision and space-sensitivity this complex web of four and even five rhythmical strata is organized on paper!

Sergei Rachmaninoff (1873-1943)

CONCERTO NO. 4 FOR PIANO AND ORCHESTRA, IN G MINOR, OP. 40 (177)

171 pages, 30 staves to each page. Size: 42.5 x 34.2 cm.
Autograph heading: "Concert pour piano (No. 4)./ op. 40./ S. Rachmaninoff."
Dated on last page: "January—August 25
New York—Dresden"
Composed in 1926, and completely revised by the author in 1941.
Published by Edition Tair, Paris, 1927.
First performed on March 18, 1927, in Philadelphia, with the composer at the piano.
Collection: Mrs. Natalie Rachmaninoff, New York.

PLATE 177 shows page 152 of the third movement. Note the phrasing slurs added to the piano part (staves 19 and 20). The two bottom staves represent a piano reduction of the orchestra. The phrasing marks in the woodwinds are precisely repeated in the piano reduction. No pedal marks. The layout and writing are neat in the extreme. The cross strokes are always detached from the stems.

Jean Sibelius (1865-1957)

SVANEHVIT, "SNOW WHITE" (178)

Incidental music to August Strindberg's play of the same name, for small orchestra.
41 pages, twenty-two staves to each page. Size: 35.5 x 28 cm. (including cloth binding).
On the cover, autograph title: "Svanehvit/ Musiken av Jean Sibelius." On the first page:
"Svanehvit/(Aug. Strindberg) Musiken af Jean Sibelius/ En hornsignal i fjarren [I. Sid/17]
Corno   "
Composed in 1908 for the performance of Strindberg's play at the Svenska Teater in Helsingfors. Strindberg intended to write the music for his play himself but abandoned the idea when he learned that Sibelius wanted to do it.[1] One year later Sibelius rearranged the music into a concert suite which was published in 1909 by M. Schlesinger, Berlin, as op. 54.
Collection: The Library of Congress, Washington, D.C.

The present manuscript was evidently used at the first performance of the play. There are many Finnish, Swedish, and German marks and directions in colored pencil. A comparison between the present holograph and the concert suite reveals numerous divergencies. The latter, as it is considerably shorter than the original version, does not include all the numbers; it is set for larger orchestra and shows many small changes.

PLATE 178 shows the beginning of piece no. 8, marked no. 5 in the printed edition. The different, conflicting tempo indications at the beginning are interesting: The original *Andante* is crossed

[1] See Karl Ekman, *Jean Sibelius*, Alan Wilmer, London 1936, p. 177.

out and replaced by *Adagio*; nonetheless there remains an *Andante* in the second violin part, and a *langsamer* after the crossed out *Andante*. The printed version of the suite compromised with *Andante sostenuto*. Likewise the time indication 2/2 is crossed out and replaced by C, which is retained in the suite.

The present page indicates flute, clarinet in B flat, two horns in F, trumpet, and strings, while the corresponding piece in the suite requires, besides the strings, double woodwinds, four horns, and bassoons. The solo theme appears here as a clarinet solo beginning $p <$ *sonore* while in the suite it is given to the first and second violins, f *patetico*, with the woodwinds furnishing the accompanying chords.

Max Reger (1873-1916)

EINSAMKEIT (179)

Song for low voice with piano accompaniment, words by Goethe. No. 18 of "18 Gesänge für eine Singstimme und Klavier, Op. 75."
One leaf written on both sides, four triple staves to each page. Size: 34.7 x 27.4 cm. Many phrase and expression marks in red ink.
Autograph heading: "Einsamkeit./ (Goethe)/ Frau Dr. A. Gimkiewicz zugeeignet./ Max Reger Op 75 No 18./ Für tiefe Stime." At the end, in pencil: "bleibt in der Tonart!" (remains in the key).
Undated.
First published by Lauterbach & Kuhn, Leipzig, 1905.
Collection: The Library of Congress, Washington, D.C.

PLATE 179 shows page 1 of the manuscript. The staff lines are extended to the right edge of the paper by hand.

Characteristic of Reger's chromatic progressions, the page bristles with accidentals and natural signs. The breaking up of the vocal line into short, discontinuous phrases requires a superabundance of expression marks. Reger is one of the first masters who do not take any chances with the performer. His anxiety to prevent any possible misinterpretation is surpassed only by Mahler and the school of Schoenberg.

Arnold Schoenberg (1874-1951)

STRING QUARTET NO. 4, OP. 37 (180)

Fifty-four pages, three quadruple staves to each page. Size: 24 x 35 cm. (including binding).
Bound in a blue paper cover with a typewritten vignette: "Arnold Schoenberg/ original manuscript of/ IV. String Quartett Opus 37/ (Dedicated to Mrs. E. S. Coolidge.)" Autograph heading on first page: "IV. String-Quartett opus 37./ fulfilling with/ pleasure the/ commission of/ the great/ patroness of/ music/ Mrs. Elizabeth/Sprague-/Coolidge/ Arnold Schoenberg/ April 27, 1936." Each of the four movements is dated at the end: the first, June 12, 1935; the second, June 10, 1935; the third, June 18, 1935; the fourth, July 26, 1935.

Published by G. Schirmer, New York, 1939.

Collection: The Elizabeth Sprague Coolidge Foundation Collection, The Library of Congress, Washington, D.C.

PLATE 180 shows the first page of the quartet. This page is a typical example of the great number and variety of directions to the performer whose freedom of interpretation is narrowed to the extreme. How little is left to chance appears most strikingly in Schoenberg's method of indicating the parts of primary and secondary importance by ⊢ (*Hauptstimme*) and ∏ (*Nebenstimme*).

ᴬ∧ ! > ⁄ • ∪ ᴮ∧ ∧ ⥸

There is a rich array of expression marks and bowing indications, for instance A. Frequently they are used in combinations, as B. There are, furthermore, many meticulously graded dynamic signs (cf. the transition from bar 13 to bar 14, with the dynamic emphasis upon the first violin against the other parts). The strings required are indicated by (*G*), (*D*), etc.

The time is indicated by large figures. The bars are numbered. In the bottom quadruple stave of the page shown, part of bar 16 and the whole of bar 17 are pasted over, and bar 15 shows erasures.

One notices that, although the script was intended to be of printlike clarity and regularity, there is, nevertheless, a good deal of individuality in several expression marks; see, for example, the gracefully intertwined *ff*'s, *fp*'s, and *sf*'s.

Alban Berg (1885-1935)

WOZZECK (181, 182)

Music drama in 3 acts, Op. 7. Text from the unfinished drama "Woyzek" written in 1836 by Georg Büchner. The 25 scenes of the drama have been reduced to 15 in the opera.

Full score in 3 volumes, each paged separately. Volume I: 165 pages; volume II: 187; volume III: 100. 30 staves to each page. Size: 34 x 26.9 cm. Each volume has its own autograph title page. Dedication on the third page of volume I: "Alma Maria Mahler zugeeignet." Page 4, the list of instruments, including, apart from the gigantic main body of the orchestra, a smaller orchestra on the stage and a solo string quintet. Page 5, the cast; page 6, the scenario. Inscription at the end of volume III: "Ende der Oper."

Composed 1914-1921 (?).

First published in 1930 by the Universal Edition, Vienna, as piano score; first performed at the Staatsoper in Berlin, Dec. 14, 1925.

Collection: The Library of Congress, Washington, D.C. (Purchased from the composer in 1934 with the help of funds presented by the "Friends of Music of the Library of Congress").

A gigantic score, full of subtle and original effects, requiring a great variety and number of symbols to direct the performers. The present score is organized with unsurpassable accuracy and lucidity, the layout for the many parts neatly planned for every page. There is a superabundance of directions of all kinds, especially of expression marks. The indications of Hauptstimme by ⊢ and Nebenstimme by ∏ are modeled after those used by Berg's teacher and friend Schoenberg (see above). The score is written in ink and has numerous red and blue pencil marks, some of them evidently warnings for the conductor. There are no key signatures; as is usual in the school of Schoenberg, the brass instruments are noted as non-transposing instruments.

PLATE 181 shows page 29 of vol. I (Act I), with the beginning of the dialogue between the captain, *Hauptmann* (*Hptm* in the score), and *Wozzeck* (*Woyz*). It is written in the form of a gavotte and marked *quasi gavotte*. Berg employed old musical forms to depict by their peculiar emotional flavor corresponding dramatic situations. Beneath *quasi gavotte* is written, in small characters, *mit viel Würde* (with great dignity). The dialogue begins with the sermon delivered by the eccentric *Hauptmann* to the naive *Wozzeck*: "Moral! Moral: das ist, wenn man moralisch ist. (Versteht er? Es ist ein gutes Wort.)"

Notice the extremely meticulous employment of dynamic shadings. The writing itself evidently aims at print-like clarity.

PLATE 182 shows page III of vol. I, the beginning of Act I, Scene 4. Wozzeck visits the study of the fanatical doctor, for whose physiological research he sold himself as guinea pig, and is bitterly reproached for not obeying the doctor's orders. As Wozzeck enters, the doctor approaches him impatiently, addressing him in a *quasi recitativo* marked *mit viel Freiheit des Tempos*: "Was erleb' ich, Wozzeck? Ein Mann, ein Wort! Ei, ei, ei! Ich hab's gesehen, Wozzeck, Er hat wieder gehustet, auf der Strasse gehustet. . . ."

This recitative is organized as a passacaglia (see the mark *Passacaglia-Thema* beneath bar I of the violoncello part). As Berg once explained to the author, the passacaglia, with its obstinate bass, was the ideal form to express the *idée fixe* of the doctor. With great dramatic effect the passacaglia theme is presented in several successive spasms of increasing rhythmic animation: in bar 2 the fast notes have staccato dots; in bar 3, accents (>) and the indication *immer aufgeregter* (more and more excited); in bar 4 they become *marcatissimo*, and swell with a sudden crescendo to *ffp*. Pencil marks 3, 6, 8, explain the time value of the small notes.

There are many red and blue pencil marks. Some of them, such as the dashes in the middle staves clarifying the rhythm, and the subsequent large 4/4, are evidently for the use of the conductor. At the beginning of the violoncello part, a pencil mark, *alle*, indicates that the violoncelli, after having been divided, are to continue together. Notice the meticulous employment of different writing types and sizes; for instance, *Passacaglia-Thema* in print-like lettering, *Sehr langsam* and *Vorhang rasch auf* in a Latin hand, *Studierstube des Doktors* in Gothic writing, etc.

Charles E. Ives (1874-1954)

SECOND PIANOFORTE SONATA (183)

"Concord, Mass., 1840-1860."
The movements are entitled: I "Emerson"; II "Hawthorne"; III "The Alcotts"; IV "Thoreau."
Signed and dated by composer.
Composed 1908-1915. Privately printed in New York, 1919.
Second edition by Arrow Music Press 1947. First complete public performance 1939.
Through the kindness of the composer.

PLATE 183 shows a section near the end of the second movement, *Hawthorne*.

In the directions for performance appended to the second edition (Arrow Music Press), the composer says of *Hawthorne*: "For the most part, this movement is supposed to be played as fast as possible and not too literally. Marks of tempo, expression, etc. are used as little as possible. If the score itself, the preface or an interest in Hawthorne suggest nothing, marks may only make things worse. It is not intended that the relation 2:1 between the 32nd and 16th notes here be held to always literally. The use of the sustaining pedal is almost constantly required."

No bar lines are used in the section reproduced here, and they appear only sporadically in the rest of the sonata. The phrasing is suggested by slurs and accents ($>$). Changes in tempo—the movement begins *very fast*—are minutely indicated. The ones penciled on this page are not retained in the printed version. The use of the left or right hand is carefully indicated by letters, often in combination with dotted lines. A score of such extraordinary complexity and difficulty could not easily be grasped without the extreme clarity of its script and its meticulous spacing.

For the series of chords that starts the page the composer's comment in the printed version is: "As it is very difficult to play this 'Call of the cloud breakers' as fast as it wants to go, the lowest note in the R.H. chords may be omitted (ad lib.)."

Ernest Bloch (1880-1959)

QUINTET FOR PIANO AND STRINGS (184)

107 pages, two score groups of six staves to each page. Size: 34 x 27 cm.

Autograph heading: "Quintet/ Ernest Bloch." Underneath, in pencil: "To Harold Bauer and the Lenox Quartet." At the end: "Cleveland, Ohio/ March 27th 1923/ Ernest Bloch." At the top of the score and each part, in very small writing; "The sign / before a note/ indicates ¼ tone above that note/ the sign \ = ¼ tone below."

Many additional expression marks in blue ink. The manuscript evidently has been used as an engraver's copy.

Composed in 1923. First performed November 11, 1923, at the Concert of the League of Composers, New York, by Harold Bauer and the Lenox Quartet.

First published in 1924 by G. Schirmer, Inc., New York.

Collection: The Library of Congress, Washington, D.C. (Presented in 1936 by G. Schirmer.)

PLATE 184 shows page 58 of the manuscript with a section from the third movement. Great care to insure the correct printing of the score has been taken in spacing and clear writing. The relative importance of the individual instrumental parts is indicated by meticulous dynamic shadings. For instance, in bar 1, the violin and right hand of the piano are marked *f* and the rest is *mf*. In bars 4 and 5 the crescendos start at various points and last for various periods in the first violin, viola and piano, while the second violin has two decrescendo wedges. Bar 6 has *f* in the viola and *mf* in the piano part; bar 10 has *mf* in the right hand of the piano part and *mp* in the other parts.

Igor Stravinsky (1882–   )

CONCERTINO FOR STRING QUARTET (185)

Full score with added condensation (also autograph) for pianoforte, four hands. One preliminary leaf, twenty-three pages, two sextuple staves to each page. Size: 33.5 x 24 cm. including cloth binding.

On title page: "Concertino/composé pour/Le Quattuor de Flonzaley/ Partition d'ensemble/ et/ réduction pour Piano à 4 m." Also on the title page, upper right: "À Monsieur/André de Coppet/hommage de/l'auteur/Garches/ Oct. 1920." Signature on first page: "Igor Strawinsky 1920."

Published by Wilhelm Hansen, Copenhagen, 1923.

Collection: The Library of Congress, Washington, D.C.

The manuscript is written in brownish-black ink with many expression marks added in black. It is a most accurate and neat copy, evidently a printer's copy, and coincides completely with the printed edition. The bar lines are drawn with a ruler and there are metronome marks.

Page 1 of the manuscript, shown in plate 185 is a typical example of modern score-writing, of machine-like precision, with countless directions for the performer. Practically nothing is left to his imagination, virtually every note having an expression mark or bowing indication: *arco, pizzicato, au talon*, ○ ⊓ ❚ ❙ ·

Notice the changes of time, which occur in almost each bar.

Igor Stravinsky (1882–   )

CONCERTO IN E FLAT FOR CHAMBER ORCHESTRA (186)

Score for five wind and ten string instruments. 109 pages, 20 staves to each page. Size: 35.5 x 27 cm.

Autograph heading: "Dumbarton Oaks/ 8-5-38/ Concerto en Mi b / pour orch. de chambre." Also: "Igor Strawinsky/ 1937-38." At the end "I. Strawinsky/ Paris/ 29 mars//38."

Published by Schott & Co., London, 1938. First performed in 1938 at Dumbarton Oaks, Washington, D.C. There exists also an arrangement of this concerto made by the composer for two pianos, four hands.

Collection: The Library of Congress, Washington, D.C., deposited there by Mr. and Mrs. Robert Woods Bliss.

Careful copy for the printer, all in pencil, with ruled bar lines, and meticulously planned spacing.

PLATE 186 shows page 18 of the manuscript. The instruments are, from top to bottom: flute, clarinet in B flat, bassoon, horns in F, 3 violins (two staves), 3 violas (two staves), 2 violoncellos, 2 double basses.

The time signature changes in each bar.

Serge Prokofieff (1891-1953)

QUARTET FOR TWO VIOLINS, VIOLA AND VIOLONCELLO, OP. 50 (187)

Seventeen leaves, 33 pages (verso of page 33 blank), three quadruple staves to each page, with only two staves on the first and last page. Size: 26.8 x 35 cm.

Autograph heading: "Quartet/ Serge Prokofieff, op. 50./ 1930." At the end, the date, in Russian: "Finished:/ sketches 26 July 1930,/ score 14 Dec. 1930./ Paris."

Commissioned by the Elizabeth Sprague Coolidge Foundation, and first performed at the Coolidge Foundation Festival of chamber music, April 25, 1931, in the Library of Congress, Washington, D.C. First published in 1931, by the Edition Russe de Musique, Paris.

Collection: The Elizabeth Sprague Coolidge Foundation Collection, The Library of Congress, Washington, D.C.

The manuscript is a presentation copy written with greatest care and almost printlike regularity. It coincides entirely with the printed edition. Notable are the numerous meticulous bowing indications, such as ∨ > ◯ ⊔

PLATE 187 shows page 6 of the manuscript, a section from the middle of the first movement (*Allegro*), with a highly arched melody of the carefree happiness so characteristic of many themes of Prokofieff.

Dimitry Dimitrevich Shostakovich (1906-   )

FRAGMENT FROM LADY MACBETH OF MZENSK, OR "KATERINA IZMAILOVA" (188)

Opera in four acts, Op. 29. Text by A. Preis and D. Shostakovich after the novel *Katerina Izmailova* written in 1864 by Nikolai S. Leskov.

Four pages numbered with indelible pencil "55-58." The signature at the end of this fragment suggests that the composer himself has torn out these 4 pages from the score. Size: 35.7 x 24.5 cm.

A draft of the orchestral score with one, two or three staves for the vocal parts, and two staves for a condensed orchestration. Written in ink; annotations indicating the planned instrumentation, are marked in pencil on the margins. The bar lines are hand drawn. The words are in Russian, except the scoring indications. Signed at the end in Russian: "Dimitri Shostakovich/ from the 2nd act of the opera / "Lady Macbeth of Mzensk" / (Leningrad) 13.IX. 1935."[1]

The opera was composed in 1930-1932.

First published in 1935, by the Musical State Publishing House, Moscow. First performance in Russia, 1934, at Leningrad. First performance in America in 1935, Cleveland, Ohio.

Collection: The Boston Public Library, Boston, Mass. (Gift of the composer, presented in 1936.)

[1] The notation, "Dimitri Shostakovich, Nov. 5, 1935," at the bottom of the first page was added by the Boston Public Library when the manuscript was acquired.

PLATE 188 shows the first page of the fragment numbered 55. The score-writing—even more than the lettering—is thin and disconnected with tiny note-heads and fine indecisive cross strokes; the bar lines hand drawn with a marked back slant. No expression marks. The orchestration marks penciled in the right margin were evidently tentative, as many have been crossed out.

Béla Bartók (1881-1945)

STRING QUARTET NO. 5 (189, 190)

Fifty leaves of thin, transparent paper written on one side only, 3 to 4 quadruple staves to each page. Size: 33 x 25.8 cm.

On cover, autograph title: "Béla Bartók/ 5. stringquartette/ (Manuscript) Budapest, IX. 1934." At the top of first page, dedication in Hungarian: "Mrs. Elizabeth Sprague Coolidgenak,/ a jelenkori kamarazene lelkes támogatójának/ Budapest, 1934. nov./ 5. vonósnégyes/ Bartók Béla."[1] At the end: "Budapest, 1934. aug. 6.-szept. 6."

The five movements are headed as follows:

1. Allegro
2. Adagio molto
3. Scherzo (Alla bulgarese), with the time signature $\frac{4+2+3}{8}$.
4. Andante
5. Finale (Allegro vivace).

Capital letters in circles marking the sections of the single movements. Bars numbered by tens. Metronomic indications throughout. No key signatures. At the end of each of the five movements: "Durée d'exécution," and figures indicating the time of performance in minutes and seconds.

Commissioned by the Elizabeth Sprague Coolidge Foundation, and first performed at the Coolidge Foundation Festival of Chamber Music, April 8, 1935, in the Library of Congress, Washington, D.C.

Published by Universal Edition, Vienna, 1936.

Collection: The Elizabeth Sprague Coolidge Foundation Collection, The Library of Congress, Washington, D.C.

PLATE 189 reproduces page 49 of the manuscript, that is, the last page but one of the fifth movement (*Allegro vivace*). The writing is neat and the layout careful in the extreme; a closer approximation to print can hardly be imagined. Still, the script as a whole by no means lacks personality; there are many individual features. The clefs are unusually small, and the strokes frequently extend over two bars. The long stepwise ascending or descending melodic lines also help to give the page a peculiar character of its own. The bar lines and braces are hand-drawn.

PLATE 190 shows the last page (page 50) of the quartet. A neat tabulation accounts for the "Durée d'exécution" of the fifth movement by adding the performance time section by section (A-O). This is followed by an addition of the performance time of all five movements in minutes and seconds.

---

[1] "To Mrs. Elizabeth Sprague Coolidge, the enthusiastic sponsor of contemporary chamber music, Budapest, November 1934, 5th string quartet, Béla Bartók."

George Gershwin (1898-1937)

ROLL DEM BONES (191)

A pencil draft of Mingo's popular song "Oh, nobody knows when the Lord is goin' to call..." from the opera "Porgy and Bess." Libretto by Du Bose Heyward, lyrics by Du Bose Heyward and Ira Gershwin.

Four pages, three triple staves to each page. Size: 33.5 x 26.5 cm.

Stapled to the bottom of the first page is the signature "George Gershwin," in ink, cut from a cancelled check.

First performed Sept. 30, 1935.

Collection: The Library of Congress, Washington, D.C. (Presented by Mr. Ira Gershwin.)

PLATE 191 shows 9 bars from Act I (compare with pages 18-21 in printed vocal score) with *Mingo's* "Oh, nobody . . ." continued at the end of the third bar by *Sporting Life*, whose entry is marked in the right upper corner of the page. The edition printed by the Gershwin Publishing Co. in 1935 corresponds to the present draft in general and especially in the course of the harmony. It is, however, written in 2/4 time throughout, and bears at the beginning of the vocal solo parts the mark *freely*. The printed version, moreover, supplies numerous expression marks which are missing in the draft. The *rhythmic* in the third bar of the draft is replaced by *mf ritmato* in the printed version.

To each occurrence of the refrain "Roll Dem Bones" the final version adds a quartet of male voices (in bars 3, 6, 9). This is indicated in the present draft by the word *harmony*, but only in bars 3 and 9.

Heitor Villa-Lobos (1881-1959)

SONATA PHANTASTICA, OP. 35 (192)

For violin and pianoforte.

13 pages; 12 staves to each page. Size: 32.7 x 27 cm.

Autograph heading on title page: "Iª Sonata phantastica/(em um tempo)/ para/ Violino e piano/"Dezesperança"/Rio de Janeiro 1913." Left upper corner: "Ao Leonidas Antuori/ Gratissima recordação do Seu amigo e admiradôr Villa-Lobos/Rio, 5/5/923." Dated on last page: "Rio 8/913."

Published 1929, Max Eschig, Paris.

Collection: The Boston Public Library, Boston, Mass.

PLATE 192 shows page 12 of the manuscript. Many expression marks, some in ink, some in red pencil. After bar 3 a pencil mark: *longa cadencia de violino*. Some additions, such as the accidentals in bars 2 and 8, in black pencil. The layout is neat and well planned.

Paul Hindemith (1895-1963)

SKETCHES FOR SYMPHONY IN B FLAT (193, 194)

For Concert Band.

The volume is one of several sketchbooks. The present one has 33 sheets, last page blank; 8 staves to each page. Written in black pencil with some parts and other indications written in purple pencil on page 6 and 8. Bound in soft cardboard. Size: 8 x 22.5 cm.

On the cover in autograph: "Paul Hindemith / Symphony in B flat for Concert Band / 1951." On the first page autograph: "Paul Hindemith Symphony in B flat for Concert Band / Feb / March 1951." Several erasures and corrections.

Owner: the composer.

The two pages reproduced in PLATES 193, 194 show the climax of the fugue which terminates the symphony. The 20 bars contained in these two pages correspond to the section from *L* on page 51 of the final version to the end of that page.

The sketch is written in four staves, three of which contain three distinct themes. The theme in stave 1 is given in the final version to trumpets and trombones, the one in stave 2 to the first horn, the one in stave 4 to the basses, baritone, sax and bass clarinet. Staff 3 of the sketch contains the harmonic background marching on in dotted rhythm. The sketch contains no indication of the instrumentation, nor any expression marks.

The spacing reflects the time values so clearly that, among other things, the triplets in staff 4 are recognizable as such without the usual ⌐ 3 ¬.

Paul Hindemith (1895-1963)

SYMPHONY IN B FLAT (195, 196)

For Concert Band.

54 pages written in ink; 28 staves to each page. Size: 45.3 x 33.7 cm.

Autograph heading in capitals: "Paul Hindemith / Symphony in B flat / For Concert Band / score." On end of last page: "New Haven, Conn. / March 19, 1951."

Composed 1951.

First performance in Washington, D.C., April 5, 1951, by the United States Army Band conducted by the composer.

Published 1952 by B. Schott's Söhne, Mainz.

Through the kindness of the composer.

A comparison with the sketch (cf. the preceding pages) shows the distribution of the sketch notation among the single instruments, the addition of expression marks and other clarifications such as the 2 | 2 at *M* and the 3 signs for triplets.

INDEX

INDEX